GW00493139

John Donne and religious authority in the reformed English church

John Donne and religious authority in the reformed English church

Mark S. Sweetnam

FOUR COURTS PRESS

Set in 10.5 on 12.5 point Ehrhardt for
FOUR COURTS PRESS LTD
7 Malpas Street, Dublin 8, Ireland
e-mail: info@fourcourtspress.ie
www.fourcourtspress.ie
and in North America for
FOUR COURTS PRESS
c/o ISBS, 920 N.E. 58th Street, Suite 300, Portland, OR 97213.

© Mark Sweetnam and Four Courts Press 2014

A catalogue record for this title
is available from the British Library.

ISBN 978-1-84682-394-7

All rights reserved. No part of this publication may be
reproduced, stored in or introduced into a retrieval system,
or transmitted, in any form or by any means (electronic,
mechanical, photocopying, recording or otherwise), without
the prior written permission of both the copyright owner
and the publisher of this book.

Printed in England
by Antony Rowe, Chippenham, Wilts.

Contents

Preface and acknowledgments

This book has been a long time in the making. It had its inception when, at the age of seventeen, I bought a copy of Logan Pearsall Smith's selection from Donne's sermons. I knew very little about Donne and, apart from Pearsall Smith's introduction, nothing about the sermons. A more mature perspective may have led me to question the basis of his selection, but the effect of the purple passages that he gathered together was undeniable; entranced by their strange music, I determined that some time, somewhere and somehow I was going to spend time studying Donne and his sermons more completely.

That ambition could not have been fulfilled without the assistance of a great number of people and institutions. Special thanks are due to Eiléan Ní Chuilleanáin, who read an earlier draft of this book. Eiléan's erudition is matched only by her kindness, and I could not have wished for a better supervisor. Knowing her, and working with her, as a student, a colleague and a friend has been a tremendous privilege, and I have profited enormously from her generous counsel and encouragement.

I wish also to acknowledge the great debt that I owe to Crawford Gribben. As a teacher, a colleague and especially as a friend he has been an invaluable source of encouragement, advice and ideas, to say nothing of hours of theological debate.

I would also like to thank Peter McCullough for his encouraging and insightful comments on an early draft of this volume.

Special thanks go to Deirdre Sarjeantson for her eagle-eyed proof-reading skills, and a great deal beside, and to Erin Sebo for her encouragement.

I would also like to thank the colleagues with whom I have worked during the completion of this book: Barbara Fennell, Deirdre O'Regan and Nicci MacLeod at Aberdeen and the CULTURA team at Trinity College Dublin (TCD), especially Jane Ohlmeyer, Micheál Ó Siochrú, Shay Lawless, Owen Conlan and Eamon Darcy. I am also grateful to the School of English and the School of Histories and Humanities at TCD, which have both been congenial places to work. Special thanks go to Eve Patten for her kindness and support.

I wish to thank the Irish Research Council for the Humanities and Social Sciences, whose generous financial support funded the research for this volume.

My students have provided a testing ground for some of my ideas, and have borne the intrusion of Donne into all manner of tutorials with a great deal of patience. I would also like to thank the librarians at TCD, especially Isolde

Harpur, who bore with very good grace my convincing impression of one of the horseleech's daughters.

The debts I owe to my teachers and friends are great, but they are insignificant compared to those that I owe to my family. I wish especially to thank my parents and Ernest and Ruth for all their love, help and support.

To Sara I want to express my love and my gratitude. Her love and support, her courage and patience through a difficult time of serious illness, and the warmth of her smile make a liar of every winter. To Josiah, all my love, and the hope that he never stops asking questions.

But above all this, I wish to acknowledge all that I owe to God who spared not his only Son, and who, with Him, has freely given all things. By His grace I am what I am, and it is to His glory that this book is dedicated.

EDITORIAL NOTE

References to Donne's works throughout this thesis are given parenthetically in the text. The following abbreviations are used:

B   *Biathanatos*, ed. Ernest W. Sullivan (Newark, DE: University of Delaware Press, 1984).

D   *Devotions upon emergent occasions*, ed. John Hanbury, Angus Sparrow and Geoffrey Keynes (Cambridge: Cambridge University Press, 1923).

ED   *Essayes in divinity: being several disquisitions interwoven with meditations and prayers*, ed. Anthony Raspa (Montreal: McGill-Queen's University Press, 2001).

I   *Ignatius, his conclave*, ed. Timothy S. Healy SJ (Oxford: Clarendon Press, 1969).

PM   *Pseudo-martyr: wherein out of certaine propositions and gradations, this conclusion is evicted, that those who are of the Romane religion in this kingdome, may and ought to take the Oath of Allegience*, ed. Anthony Raspa (Montreal: McGill-Queen's University Press, 1993).

SP   *Selected prose*, ed. Neil Rhodes (London: Penguin, 1987).

Quotations from Donne's sermons are taken from *The sermons of John Donne*, ed. G.R. Potter and Evelyn Mary Simpson (Berkley: California University Press, 1953–62), and are referenced by (VOLUME, page). Quotations from Donne's poetic works are taken from *The complete English poems of John Donne*, ed. C.A. Patrides (London: Dent, 1985). Unless otherwise indicated, all quotations from scripture are taken from the Authorised (King James) Version.

Introduction

This book examines the work of John Donne. It can hardly be said to be unique in this – the field of Donne studies is not sparsely populated. Notwithsatanding this, this book does make a significant contribution in a number of important ways. Firstly, it addresses an important lacuna by concentrating on Donne's theology. Theology has been a neglected element of the sermons, even in the recent more historicised work of Peter McCullough, Lori Anne Ferrell, Jeanne Shami et al. Their engagements with the sermons have delineated the detail of Donne's political views, his negotiation of contemporary power structures and his spoiling of the Eygptians in making use of the learning and experience of his secular life. They have approached these issues with an unprecedented amount of sensitivity to the importance of theological concerns and have shed a good deal of incidental light on a number of these concerns but, on the whole, they have been so preoccupied with Donne's societal contexts that the theological has been displaced from their study of the sermons. While Jeffrey Johnson's contribution to this topic has somewhat redressed the balance, and has been of immense importance in its highlighting of Donne's status as a theologian in his own right, it can scarcely claim to be exhaustive. Equally problematic is the nature of this inexhaustiveness – Johnson's concentration on issues like images and common prayer assumes the centrality of these issues in Donne's theology. They were both hot issues,[1] although of very different significance in contemporary context and Donne's own thought, and Donne did engage with them, but to allow their currency to shape our critical agenda is to impose a reactive aspect upon Donne's theology, and to throw into sharp relief views that had an important but relatively minor place in his wider theology.

It has been an aim of this study to allow Donne to set the agenda. Therefore, it focuses on issues of theological authority not because they were the most fundamental issues of the Reformation – though it would be difficult to deny their basic importance – nor because it is engaged in a Marxist attempt to read religion as an elaborately encoded discourse of power. Rather, the choice of the

---

[1] For discussions of these issues, see, respectively, Keith Thomas, 'Art and iconoclasm in early modern England' in *Religious politics in post-reformation England: essays in honour of Nicholas Tyacke*, ed. Kenneth Fincham and Peter Lake (Woodbridge, 2006), pp 16–40; Ernest B. Gilman, '"To adore, or scorne an image": Donne and the Iconoclast Controversy', *John Donne Journal* 5 (1986); Judith D. Maltby, *Prayer book and people in Elizabethan and early Stuart England* (Cambridge, 1998).

issues around which this study clusters has been dictated by Donne's consistent and considered engagement with them. They have also the advantage of being crucial issues right from the beginning of the European Reformation, and, thus, our study of their treatment by Donne allows us to locate his work in the longer context of the Reformation. And this is no minor contribution. It has been common to view Donne's theology on the one hand in terms of a reactive paradigm. Biographical theories of Donne as establishment lackey and opportunist have increased this tendency, even when these ideas are being reacted against. On the other hand, the same biographical speculations have lent currency to the idea that Donne's religion was a Catholicism that conformed as much as necessary, but reformed as little as possible. Both of these views are called into serious question by the material discussed in this study. Our investigation of the importance of scripture, the church and the preacher as sources of theological authority uncovers a Donne far more Protestant than has usually been recognised, an eclectic theologian who values highly the fruits of the humanist return *ad fontes*, and who insists on the individual's responsibility to choose wisely the religion worthy of his allegiance. Equally noteworthy is the sort of Protestant that Donne emerges as. In an English church that encompassed a vast range of ecclesiological possibility, Donne's allegiance did not lie, as has often been suggested, with Andrewes, Buckeridge, Laud and the other avant-garde conformists. His churchmanship is ultimately *sui generis* but it finds its model much closer to the conformist mainstream of the English church.

This study breaks some new ground in establishing this position. Scholars of Donne are constantly faced with basic questions about their choice of sources from Donne's extensive and varied *oeuvre*. These questions are not easily answered: a smooth integration of the available sources is not easy to achieve. This study concentrates principally on the sermons. However, it also draws, when appropriate, on Donne's other works of prose, and, less frequently, on the poetry. What emerges from this use of the wider canon is an encouraging confirmation of the appropriateness of the parameters of this study – these issues of authority interested Donne throughout his career and their importance can be traced, oftentimes with remarkable consistency, right through the canon. This study is not the only work to range the canon, but it is unprecedented in the comprehensive and integrated picture that it presents.

The nature of the Donneian canon defines the scope of this enquiry. But of equal importance is the nature of the methodology by which that canon is understood. The approach adopted throughout this book draws on the concepts developed by those scholars who have recently called for a turn to religion in early modern studies. This approach provides a corrective to the enduring tendency of literary critics to read religion as a coded discourse referring to something quite different from its ostensible preoccupation. In addition, this approach self-consciously moves beyond New Historicism's obsession with alterity. Religion, in New Historicist work, is almost always a marginal ideology – the traces of a suppressed Catholicism, for instance, have a fascination that the established mainstream of religion quite lacks. New Historicism's interest in cultural power plays has, as its concomitant, a preoccupation with alterity, with the marginal and displaced. This taste is satiated – often very productively – by the glamour of recusancy and a vestigial 'traditional religion', but is less sure what to make of the commonplace religion of the Protestant conformist majority.[2] Ironically, as Debora Shuger suggests, this tendency results in a weakness of engagement with precisely those power structures that New Historicism is most interested in:

> Conversely, the modern obsession with subversive and revolutionary change has discouraged inquiry into popular beliefs, unless, like witchcraft or presbyterianism, they seem to threaten the established order. But this tendency to resolve Tudor/Stuart religion into the dialectic of popular resistance and government repression renders invisible what it purports to illuminate: the role played by religion in early modern state formation.[3]

Donne's theology is complex and not infrequently challenging to some popular contemporary views, but it would be a stretch to describe it as subversive. He is constantly engaged in a principled negotiation with the 'established order' and approaching his work from a New Historicist perspective therefore distorts the nature of his religious thought. This book, then, makes an incidental but useful contribution to a growing literature on conformist religion in the early modern period because it understands that religion does not have to be subversive or marginal to be both interesting and important.

Equally valuable in terms of this study is an emerging refocusing of religious studies on the communal aspect of religion. This is salutary, even though work of outstanding usefulness has been produced by scholars – especially new Historicists – who have dealt, almost exclusively with subjectivity and the individual. This approach has its place in Donne studies – the Holy Sonnets are the outstanding example of a tortured religious interiority. But in many ways the sonnets are atypical of Donne's work. In the chapters that follow, we will see a different sort of Donne, a religious thinker who is most particularly interested in the communal aspects of religious life, who is most exercised by the need to forge a religious community. All of Donne's interactions with, and discussions of,

2 See, for exemplars of this trend, Stephen Greenblatt and Christine Gallagher, *Practising new historicism* (Chicago, IL, 2000); Stephen Greenblatt, *Hamlet in purgatory* (Princeton, NJ, 2001); Mark S. Sweetnam, '*Hamlet* and the reformation of the eucharist', *Literature and Theology* 21:1 (2007), 11–28. 3 Debora Kuller Shuger, '"Societie supernaturall": the imagined community of Hooker's *Lawes*' in *Richard Hooker and the construction of Christian community*, ed. A.S. McGrade (Tempe, AZ, 1997), p. 325.

authority are informed by his concern about communal Christianity in a reformed church. Again, this may not have the drama of the agonising of a fractured self seeking to integrate the spirit and the flesh. It is, however, one of the most pressing concerns to inform Donne's work and, as such, deserves and will reward our attention.

This book also adopts a highly interdisciplinary approach. The value of an interdisciplinary methodology scarcely needs to be defended – it is abundantly evident in a number of the most successful recent studies of early modern religious literature. This has been true of the work of historians who have drawn on the insights of English studies and of the work of scholars of English litera-ture who have drawn on the insights and models provided by historians. Much of the work carried out on the early modern sermon by McCullough, Shami and Morrissey is eloquent of the benefits of this sort of engagement. Indeed, Mary Morrissey has issued an explicit call for the cross-fertilisation of Literary Studies and History in the study of the sermon.[4] This study attempts to follow this example of historical awareness. Of course, it is not sufficient to claim historical awareness: we must specify what sort of history it is that we mean. Studies carried out by an earlier generation drew on the classical works of Whig historiography and found their background in the stable distinctions and divisions embodied in this history of the grand narrative. More recent work on early modern religion has drawn on revisionist history and has found an engage-ment with the fractured and shifting picture delineated by contemporary ecclesiastical historians to be a very fruitful encounter. A glance at the bibliog-raphy of the present project is indicative of a dependence on this sort of history: Tyacke, Lake, Milton and Fincham loom large as historians whose work has been essential for our understanding of Donne. But this study also grasps beyond the historical. Our investigation of elements of Donne's theology requires a greater focus upon theological issues than has been required by the more politically focused interests of other recent studies. This endeavour has not involved us in systematic theology – Donne, after all, is neither a theological innovator nor the wholesale follower of someone else's system – but a consciousness of the theological questions and debates that drove the project of reformation has been of considerable importance to our consideration of Donne.

It is also fundamental to this study that our understanding of Donne's theology must be based upon a study of the entire Donneian canon. This is especially important in the light of a tendency in Donne studies identified by Jeanne Shami in the important methodological discussion that emerged from her response to Debora Shuger,[5] but that went beyond that immediate discussion to embrace a far wider range of scholarship:

4 Mary Morrissey, 'Interdisciplinarity and the study of early modern sermons', *Historical Journal* 42:4 (1999), 1111–23. 5 Jeanne M. Shami, 'Donne's Sermons and the absolutist politics of quotation' in *John Donne's religious imagination: essays in honor of John T. Shawcross*,

> [R]arely are the sermons seen as issuing from any specific context –
> generic, historical, theological, political or cultural. Too often they
> become a Scripture which any poor devil looking for a publication can
> quote to her own purposes – usually by lifting passages, at will, from
> anywhere, with the aid of the *Index* – and using them to create a
> collage of comments that supposedly represents Donne's 'mature'
> views.[6]

The risks arising from the misuse of Troy Reeves' *Index* – invaluable though it
may be when properly used – pale by comparison with the potential for the
disjointed study of the sermons provided by the electronic, phrase-searchable
archive of the Potter and Simpson sermons now available.[7] It is in the interests
of avoiding this sort of distortion that this study has been based on a careful
reading, not only of the sermons, but of all Donne's prose and poetry, and has
avoided, with all possible care, the temptation first to shape a theory, and then
select quotations to support it. As noted at the outset, I have, as far as possible,
allowed Donne to set the terms of this study, and theory has followed after text.
And the textual context has been, as already stated, wider than the sermons: it
has included Donne's canon in its entirety, with special emphasis on the prose
writings. What will become very apparent in the detail of this study, however, is
that the prose works do not have an equal relevance at all times. So, *Pseudo-
martyr* and the *Essayes* are very relevant to both Donne's view of scripture and
his ecclesiology but they have little to say about his understanding of ministerial
authority, a subject that is dealt with almost exclusively in the sermons.

Lastly, this study is underpinned by an awareness of the sermon as entity and
event, rooted in time and place. We cannot treat the sermons as a homogeneous
body of text: our understanding of their importance is determined as much by
political context, audience and liturgical setting as by their bare textual content.
There is, however, need for a nuanced flexibility in applying this principle. In an
ideal world, no doubt, the discussion of each sermon would be prefaced by a
careful excursus on the details of time, place and audience incidental to its
preaching. This is not practical for two reasons. Firstly, it is an unfortunate but

---

ed. Raymond-Jean Frontain and Frances M. Malpezzi (Conway, AR, 1995) is not an isolated
exercise in constructing a methodology for studying Donne's sermons. Further examples are to
be found in Jeanne Shami, 'Reading Donne's sermons', *John Donne Journal* 11 (1992), 1–20;
Jeanne Shami, '"Trying to walk on logs in water": John Donne, religion, and the critical tradition', *Renaissance and Reformation* 25:4 (2001), 81–99 and Jeanne M. Shami, *John Donne and
conformity in crisis in the late Jacobean pulpit* (Cambridge, 2003), pp 2–12. 6 Shami, *Donne and
conformity*, pp 383–4. This point, and a number of valuable related observations are helpfully
discussed in Peter E. McCullough, 'Donne as preacher' in *The Cambridge companion to John
Donne*, ed. Achsah Guibbory (Cambridge, 2006). 7 However, the fact that these electronic
sermons are also browseable by location, date and occasion should also facilitate the sort of
contextually informed discussion more amenable to the methodology outlined here.

unavoidable reality that we possess these hard facts for only some of Donne's sermons: for others we lack details of date, location and audience. It would, of course, be possible to simply exclude these problematic sermons from consideration, but to do so would be to narrow the available evidence in a very unhelpful way. Using undated sermons requires a consciousness of the limitations they impose upon us: this seems a lesser evil than not using them at all. Secondly, considerations of space mean that there will always be a trade-off between macro and micro approaches to Donne's sermons. Recent scholarship has excelled at the micro level and, while this book attempts to maintain its focus on the specific accidents of the occasion, it is ultimately more concerned with sketching a broad intellectual framework within which more detailed studies of individual sermons or groups of sermons can be located.

These, then, are the methodological assumptions of this book. It will be helpful to say a little about the way in which Donne's works are used. For the purposes of this study, they divide themselves into three main groupings: the sermons, the prose works (*Pseudo-martyr*, *Ignatius*, *Biathanatos*, *Essayes in divinity* and, to a lesser extent, the letters) and the poetry.[8] The nature of all these texts, and their value in informing an understanding of Donne's thought, have been the subject of a good deal of debate. This might seem surprising in the context of the sermons: they apparently present an unproblematic and authentic version of Donne's voice. This view has proved too naïve for a number of critics, including, most prominently, T.S. Eliot and John Carey. For these writers, the sermons echo with the power-seeking and self-serving hypocritical cant of a man who has sought preferment in a church to which he owes no meaningful allegiance. We do not need to subscribe to the excesses of these critics to recognise the truth of their contention that the sermon is a performative genre and that the preacher Donne may only be providing us with the illusion of authentic access to the interiority of Donne, the man. However, it would be unhelpful to allow our caution to become cynicism, and too radically to underestimate the evidentiary usefulness of the sermons. Certainly, the sort of consistency of approach and viewpoint delineated in this study, the nuanced defence of royal policy and the emphasis given, at times, to politically or ecclesiastically unpopular positions give a very different impression. Donne is aware of the power of the pulpit and he is also very conscious of the burden of authority that rests upon a man who is God's ambassador. The very evident sense of the responsibility to God and the congregation as a concomitant of this authority is no less clear.

Claims of self-advertisement have considerably more force in relation to *Pseudo-martyr*, Donne's contribution to the oath of allegiance controversy.[9]

8 Donne's *The courtier's library*, while deserving of greater critical attention than it has yet garnered, does not feature in the present study.   9 In keeping with the general tenor of his defence of Donne, David L. Edwards, *John Donne: man of flesh and spirit* (Grand Rapids, MI,

There can be little doubt that, in this rather impenetrable volume, Donne is demonstrating his abilities, his loyalty to his king and his general suitability for advancement in service to the crown. That notwithstanding, the contours of thought that emerge in the volume are borne out by the tenor of Donne's broader thought. Furthermore, the fact that considerations of expediency required Donne to curtail the original plan of the work indicates that its initial conception was something rather more than a doffing of his cap to prevailing opinion. *Ignatius, his conclave*, the delightfully scurrilous piece of fantasy writing that addressed anti-papal polemic from the same viewpoint as *Pseudo-matryr* is still more resistant to being read purely as advertising – there is a strength in the anti-Jesuitical rhetoric that suggests considerable sincerity.

Biathanatos, that decidedly odd product of the hand of 'Jack Donne', whose ordained alter ego later forbade it the fire and the press, is clearly very different to the *Pseudo-martyr* and *Ignatius*. Meg Lota Brown has compellingly identified it as an accomplished piece of Protestant casuistry and the work is, perhaps, best understood as an exercise in mental dexterity, a private entertainment, shared with a few chosen friends. In its choice of subject, though, its seriousness of engagement and the place that it gives to the informed individual conscience, it is eloquent of some of the most interesting elements of Donne's personality. It is saying too much, however, to identify *Biathanatos* as representative of Donne's supposed lifelong preoccupation with death. The preoccupation is there – though often overstated – but Donne's choice of subject in this treatise has more to do with his desire to crack a tough intellectual nut than it does with a preemptive defence of the option of suicide.

The *Essayes in divinity* come with complexities all of their own. They existed only in manuscript until published by John Donne the younger in 1651, there is scope for doubt as to their purpose. It is common for the *Essayes* to be read as just another performance on Donne's part: as an exercise in displaying his suitability for ecclesiastical office. There are elements of the work that seem to support this thesis but on the whole it reads less as a sample work designed to impress, more as a personal experiment in theology. Donne is pushing the limits of scriptural interpretation and ecclesiological option and if the work does bear a connection to Donne's impending ordination, it seems rather a last experiment in the farther reaches of theology before Donne confined himself to the interpretative and theological norms of the established church.

Finally, it remains to remark on the evidentiary status of the poetry. This has been a hotly contested issue: the considerations of authenticity and performance that dog engagements with the prose texts occur *a fortiori* when the poetry is in question. This study does its best to circumvent the most pressing issues. It considers those poems that deal explicitly with subjects raised in other parts of

2002) finds both *Pseudo-martyr* and *Ignatius* so embarrassing that he is driven to conjecture that Donne wrote both while experiencing a nervous breakdown (pp 77–8).

the canon and interprets them in the light of those other texts. This can be justified because Donne's poetry is not the main focus of this study: it adds texture
and strength to our consideration of Donne's thought but is not central to it.

These, then, are the terms of engagement. The book is structured around the
three central areas of authority in Donne's thought – scripture, the church and
the preacher. Chapter one examines Donne's interaction with contemporary
questions about the uniqueness of scriptural revelation. It also discusses
Donne's high estimation of the possibilities of philological endeavour. The
second chapter discusses the way in which Donne conceptualises the interaction
between scripture and the church. It examines his emphasis on the role of the
church in validating doctrine and in propagating it, once validated. However, it
also stresses Donne's insistence on the importance of the individual Christian's
engagement with scripture and the value he places upon intelligent assent to the
word of God. It notes the increased emphasis on the individual reading of scripture towards the end of Donne's career and argues that this can be understood
in terms of his wider opposition to the avant-garde conformists.

The next two chapters address Donne's ecclesiology. Chapter three begins by
discussing the inadequacy of previous attempts to label Donne's particular
brand of churchmanship. Building on passages where Donne himself juxtaposes
the terms puritan and papist, it argues that he cannot be properly understood in
binary terms. It then surveys the crucial concepts in the reformed understanding
of ecclesiastical authority and concludes with a close reading of Satyre III,
arguing that it reveals the importance of Hooker's influence upon Donne's
ecclesiology. Chapter four builds on this, unravelling Donne's own idiosyncratic
understanding of the authority of the Church of England. In doing so, it takes
its cue from Satyre III and demonstrates how the important issues raised in that
early poem telescope out of that setting and appear throughout Donne's career.
It examines the basis of Donne's appeal to his congregation to remain loyal to
the English church and contends that Donne's approach to ecclesiological
controversy was marked by a 'fundamentalist ecumenism' that adumbrated a
core of Christian belief and that relegated everything else to the realm of
adiaphora. This confirmed by a discussion of Donne's view of the Synod of
Dort and the Council of Trent.

The final two chapters address Donne's conceptualisation of the office of the
preacher. Chapter five draws upon scholarship by Peter Lake, Peter
McCullough, Mary Morrissey and others to demonstrate the change in the
status of preaching implicit in the piety of the avant-garde conformists, from
Hooker, to Andrewes and Buckeridge. It argues that Donne consistently engages
in an implicit defence of preaching against novel stresses on sacramentalism,
liturgy and catechising. It demonstrates this defence at work in sermons
preached at sacramentally or lirurgically significant moments. His negotiation
between the place of preaching and prayer is examined in the context of his

sermon preached at the consecration of the Chapel at Lincoln's Inn. Finally we turn to his sermon preached in defence of James I's *Directions*, examining it as defence of preaching against catechetics, and as a wider manifesto for the continuing importance of preaching in a reformed church. The final chapter discusses Donne's understanding of the office of the minister in the Church of England. It looks, in detail, at sermons that are of particular importance in terms of what they reveal about Donne's relationship with his congregations. Donne's sermon of valediction to his Lincoln's Inn congregation and his introductory sermons to his new cure at St Dunstan's give us unparalleled insight on Donne's understanding of the office that he had come to fill. The chapter closes with a brief discussion of Donne's theory of teaching, his insistence upon the importance of the power of the Holy Spirit in enabling the preacher.

It will be helpful before concluding this introduction to comment briefly on some terminology that will be important throughout this work. Terminological considerations are notoriously problematic in the context of Jacobean and Caroline ecclesiastical history. Terms like 'puritan', 'Godly', 'Arminian' and even 'Protestant' have long proved slippery and difficult to pin down. This study follows the shift in recent historiography away from the depiction of the early Stuart church as a body best understood in terms of a binary opposition between radical puritans and High Church ceremonialists or, in a slightly different formulation, between Calvinists and Arminians. It also adopts the spectrum model that these historians have suggested best represents the make-up of the English church. We identify four categories within that church: not as watertight divisions, but as representing definite contemporary ideological options. By the terms 'puritan' or 'proto-presbyterian' we mean those members of the church characterised by 'demands for ecclesiastical reform and a commitment to an intense word-centred piety'.[10] Because of the extremity of their views, these individuals are relatively easy to spot. Closer to the centre, and thus less distinctive than these radicals, were the group that Kenneth Fincham describes as moderate puritans, a term that we use occasionally, while preferring Patrick Collinson's distinctive term 'Godly'. This group encompassed those who were

> partial conformists. . . . Clergy among them offered a token subscription in return for the opportunity to preach the gospel and supplement parish services with the round of fasts, household prayers, psalm-singing and sermon repetition, all extra legal rather than illegal manifestations of that 'voluntary religion' which Collinson has sensitively evoked.[11]

10 Kenneth Fincham, 'Introduction' in *The early Stuart church, 1603–1642*, ed. Kenneth Fincham (Basingstoke, 1993), p. 6. Fincham uses the term 'radical Puritans' to describe this group. 11 Ibid., p. 7.

Adjoining this group, and frequently shading into it, are those who are often termed moderate conformists. These individuals subscribed to most of the official beliefs of the English church, most of the time. They represent the broad mainstream of that church, and, while less colourful than their compatriots at either end of the ecclesiastical spectrum, were both more numerous and more important than their relative polemical inactivity might lead us to assume. The final group occupies a position on the right wing of the church. Peter Lake, concentrating on a Jacobean context, has designated these as avant-garde conformists.[12] This label draws focuses attention on what Lake considers the essential novelty of this strand within the English church, and his identification of this novelty is worth quoting at some length:

> The conventional defence of the Elizabethan church from its puritan critics was formulated within certain conceptual limits, limits set by what might best be termed the English reformed tradition. ... [T]he central features of that tradition were a doctrine of double predestination, a vision of the Church and its evangelical mission centred on preaching and a view of the world stretched tight between the true church of Christ and the false church of Antichrist. The leading conformist apologists – John Whitgift, John Bridges, Thomas Cooper, Matthew Sutcliffe amongst them – were as committed to that reformed tradition as their puritan opponents. On the basis of this common reformed heritage, Elizabethan conformists erected a defence of the status quo founded on the idea of things indifferent and on the need, in such matters, to obey the commands of the Christian prince. They defined puritans almost exclusively in terms of their attitude to the power of the prince and to the government and ceremonies of the church and not in terms of their doctrinal beliefs or style of piety. Thus, the polemical image of Puritanism current in the 1590s concentrated on disobedience to the prince in matters of ceremony and on the allegedly subversive implications of Presbyterian populism and clericalism.

---

12 Cf. Anthony Milton's comments on the term: 'There is no entirely satisfactory term to describe the new patterns of ceremonialist and sacerdotal conformist thought which began to find expression later in the Elizabethan period ... The term "avant-garde conformity" has been employed by Professor Lake to describe this trend, a term which serves a useful purpose in distinguishing their style of piety from that of other conformists who had not granted the same edifying value to these ceremonies, while avoiding the anachronistic label of "Anglican" ... [The term] helps to capture the dynamic and evolving nature of this style of piety in the early Stuart period, and does not simply collapse it into the ideas and policies of Archbishop Laud': Anthony Milton, *Catholic and reformed: the Roman and protestant churches in English protestant thought, 1600–1640* (Cambridge, 1995), pp 8–9.

However, while this remained the dominant mode of conformist argument, thanks to Richard Hooker, there was another more emotionally compelling and comprehensively religious style of conformity available, in the public domain, by the middle of the 1590s. Whatever Hooker's own position on the issue of predestination (and this clearly shifted over time and arguably never achieved stable coherence) he can be seen almost to have invented the style of piety associated with the rise of English Arminianism and the ecclesiastical policies pursued by Charles I, Laud and their supporters during the personal rule. A broadly based vision of the Christian community, propounded in conscious contrast to the division between the godly and the profane which was taken to be central to puritan piety and Presbyterian ecclesiology; a view of the visible church centres far more on the sacrament and on public worship than on preaching; a justification of the ceremonial arrangements of the English church that transcended the realm of *adiaphora* and instead attributed a positively religious role and significance to the rituals and observances of the church – all these can be found fully developed in Hooker's thought. Moreover, they were developed in deliberate and overt opposition to an image of Puritanism that was not limited to the realms of ceremony and external government but included a whole style of piety – word-centred, predestinarian, concerned with separating the godly off from the ungodly rather than celebrating the mystical union which bound all baptized members of the national church together as members of Christ's body.[13] It is only later, after Laud rose to prominence and pursued the programme of ceremonial reform envisaged by these conformists, that we are justified in using the term Laudian. For the greater part of Donne's career, the term is anachronistic.

It should be noted too that we have not made use of the terms Calvinist and Arminian. This is expressive of caution of making assumptions about the packaging of doctrine and discipline. Nicholas Tyacke's *Anti-Calvinists* identifies the theology of grace as a crucial element of the Laudian programme, and, *pace* the contentions of Peter White, the importance of the Calvinist/Arminian debate is clear. Nonetheless it is unhelpful, if seductive, to extend Tyacke's argument so as to use a particular doctrine of election as a synecdoche for a wider view of ecclesiastical polity and praxis. This is certainly true of Calvinism, which has emerged from the researches of Patrick Collinson and Tyacke as the

---

13 Peter Lake, 'Lancelot Andrewes, John Buckeridge, and avant-garde conformity at the court of James I' in *The mental world of the Jacobean court*, ed. Linda Levy Peck (Cambridge, 1991), pp 113–14. See also Peter Lake, *Anglicans and puritans? Presbyterianism and English conformist thought from Whitgift to Hooker* (London, 1988), ch. 4. There can be little doubt as to Hooker's influence upon Andrewes. We should, however, note Peter McCullough's observation that notes of Andrewes' Cambridge lectures provide us with 'categorical proof that Andrewes was venturing criticisms of mainstream moderate puritansim at least a decade before Hooker's *Laws of ecclesiastical polity*': Peter E. McCullough (ed.), *Lancelot Andrewes: selected sermons and lectures* (Oxford, 2005), p. xvi.

'theological cement' of the English church, 'a common and ameliorating bond uniting conformists and moderate puritans'.[14] As such, a Calvinist view of grace could be found in association with the most *outré* fringes of presbyterianism, as well as with the episcopalian conformity of the main-stream of the English church. Similarly, on the anti-Calvinist side, Peter Lake suggests that 'whether they were Arminians of not, it is difficult to argue that any scholastic development of the doctrine of predestination lay at the center of the Laudian's concerns'.[15] And if this is true of the Laudian shoots, *a fortiori* does it hold for the avant-garde conformist roots. It is an index of the complexity of the relationship between doctrine and discipline that Hooker's own predestinarian position remains a subject of some perplexity and no little debate.[16] The use of a Calvinist or Arminian theology of grace is particularly unhelpful when dealing with Donne, for it is the ceremonial renegotiation of the English church that is at the forefront of his thought, and not the predestinarian debate.

This study of Donne builds on the insights of the revisionist historiography of the early Stuart church. It also draws upon a wide range of previous engagements with Donne, and especially upon the solid body of very useful scholarship that has emerged from the study of the early modern sermon and of Donne's sermons particularly. It shares the principles of this scholarship in its historical contextualised reading of the sermons and its emphasis on the particularity of the sermon. Thus provided with a basis for our investigations we move beyond existing scholarship to examine the broad range of Donne's *oeuvre*. We take seriously the religious and theological concerns that informed Donne's milieu and that interested, concerned and motivated him throughout his adult life.

14 Patrick Collinson, *The religion of protestants: the Church in English society, 1559–1625* (Oxford, 1979), p. 81. 15 Peter Lake, 'The Laudians and the argument from authority' in *Court, country and culture: essays on early modern British history in honor of Perez Zagorin*, ed. Bonnelyn Young Kunze and Dwight D. Brautigam (Rochester, NY, 1992), pp 149–50. 16 The essays by W. David Neelands, Daniel Eppley and Egil Grislis, collected in W.J. Torrance Kirby (ed.), *Richard Hooker and the English reformation* (Dordrecht, 2003), provide very useful discussions of this issue.

The authority of scripture

In an undated sermon preached in St Paul's Cathedral, John Donne addressed one of the chief preoccupations of his preaching career:

> This is one of those places of Scripture, which afford an argument for *that*, which I finde often occasion to say, That there are not so *eloquent* books in the world, as the *Scriptures*. ... The *Holy Ghost* in his instruments (in those whose tongues or pens he makes use of) doth not forbid, nor decline elegant and cheerfull and delightful expression; but as God gave his Children a bread of *Manna*, that tasted to every man like that that he liked best, so hath God given us *Scriptures*, in which the plain and simple man may heare God speaking to him in his own plain and familiar language, and men of larger capacity and more curiosity, may heare God in that Musique that they love best, in a curious, in an harmonious style, unparalleled by any. (X,103) [cf. (VIII, 270) (VIII, 273) (IX, 226)]

This quotation illustrates some of the key features of Donne's understanding of scripture. Scripture is literature of surpassing beauty; the canonical works are 'the eloquentest books in the world' (IX, 226). However, it is more than beautiful literature: its separation from all other literary production is one of kind, as well as of degree. Scripture is the word of God, mediated by human tongues or pens, but ultimately having its origins with the Holy Ghost. This truth gives scripture a vital importance; 'next to Christ' Christianity is most immediately concerned with 'Scripture and the canon thereof' (V, 216). But that concern was not unproblematic, a point underscored by the fact that this discussion takes place in the context of a sermon, where Donne, as the preacher, is 'digesting' the scripture for the benefit of his congregation (X, 104). Scripture must be understood. Therefore, it must be interpreted. Donne's task, like that of any preacher in the Reformation, was to identify, propagate and police the boundaries of acceptable interpretation.

That task was never trivial, but it acquired an unprecedented importance and urgency in the century before Donne's ministry.[1] The effect of the Reformation,

---

1 An outstanding introduction to some of the crucial issues of reading and writing, which go beyond but include the strictly Biblical can be found in Brian Cummings, *The literary culture of the reformation: grammar and grace* (Oxford, 2002), pp 15–53. More specifically concerned with

in all its ramifications, was to place a greater burden of significance upon the text of the Bible than was ever the case before or since. Jaroslav Pelikan has summed up this interplay of scripture and reformation:

> The Bible of the Reformation and the Reformation of the Bible became two sides to one coin, for the Reformation of the sixteenth century – whether Protestant, Roman Catholic or Radical – is unthinkable apart from the Bible; and the Bible – at any rate as we know it in the realms of western culture, literature and faith – is almost equally unthinkable apart from the Reformation.[2]

Jonathan Sheehan, who very capably surveys the interrelationship of reformation and textual scholarship as a preliminary to his discussion of the emergence of Enlightenment criticism, has captured the unique importance of scripture in this context:

> The Reformation made the Protestant Bible the engine of political, religious and imaginative life … Even more than *gratia* and *fides*, the Bible powered the very project of Reformation. Whatever the theological controversies that arose … beneath all these, the Bible lurked. … To say 'scripture alone' was to deny the efficacy and relevance of the Roman Church to divine matters. To say 'scripture alone' was to invest reform and reformers with the very authority of God, before which no human institution – church or state – might stand. To say 'scripture alone' was, in short, to set up a tribunal before which unbelievers would be judged. In the new religious order

Scripture are Jonathan Sheehan, *The Enlightenment Bible* (Princeton, NJ, 2005), pp 1–25; Debora Kuller Shuger, *The Renaissance Bible: scholarship, sacrifice, and subjectivity* (Berkeley, CA, 1994); Jaroslav Pelikan, *The reformation of the Bible: the Bible of the Reformation* (New Haven, CT, 1996); Werner Schwarz, *Principles and problems of Biblical translation* (Cambridge, 1955); G.R. Evans, *The language and logic of the Bible: the road to reformation* (Cambridge, 1985); Jerry H. Bentley, *Humanists and holy writ: New Testament scholarship in the Renaissance* (Princeton, NJ, 1983); Roland H. Bainton, 'The Bible in the reformation' in *The Cambridge history of the Bible*, ed. S.L. Greenslade (Cambridge, 1963), pp 1–37; Basil Hall, 'Biblical scholarship: editions and commentaries' in *Cambridge history of the Bible*, ed. Stephen Greenslade (Cambridge, 1963), pp 38–93; 'Bibles of the Protestant reformation', ch. 9 in Christopher De Hamel, *The Book: a history of the Bible* (London, 2001), pp 216–45; Paul Saenger and Kimberly Van Kampen (eds), *The Bible as book: the first printed editions* (London, 1999); Orlaith O'Sullivan (ed.), *The Bible as book: the reformation* (London, 2000). A terse introduction is provided by Alister E. McGrath, *Reformation thought: an introduction* (Oxford, 1999), pp 145–68. Discussions of the translation of the King James Version, and of the wider context of the work are provided in Gordon Campbell, *Bible: the story of the King James version, 1611–2011* (Oxford, 2010); Alister E. McGrath, *In the beginning: the story of the King James Bible and how it changed a nation, a language and a culture* (London, 2002); Adam Nicholson, *Power and glory: Jacobean England and the making of the King James Bible* (London, 2003). **2** Pelikan, *Reformation of the Bible*, 1.

emerging in sixteenth-century Europe, only scripture would, in the words of St Paul, be needed for teaching, reproof, correction and training.[3]

The demolition of the authority of the church by the reformers was the chief engine of this emphasis on the supreme authority of the written word of God. However, also implicit in projects like the *Novum Instrumentum* of Erasmus, was the belief that scriptures purged of the accreted errors of centuries would provide the best basis for a similar cleansing of the church.

Donne, then, ministered in a context in which scripture was both vitally important and hotly contested. The authority of scripture was, in many ways, the central issue for reformation divines. Certainly, it was a central issue for Donne. The scale of his dependence on and saturation in scripture, obvious even to the casual reader of the sermons, is quantified and emphasised by the statistical surveys provided by Potter and Simpson. They extrapolated from a survey of one representative volume, and suggested that the sermons, in their entirety, contain over 7,000 references to, or citations of, Biblical passages. Based on these rather crude metrics, then, scripture has a place right at the centre of Donne's theology and of his pastoral mission.

And its importance goes beyond the quantitative, for textual authority is a preoccupation of Donne's thought. In view of his constant immersion in texts, as law student, as poet and as controversialist, such a concentration on the importance of the text is hardly unexpected. At times Donne seems to exult in the polyvalence of the texts in which he deals. On other occasions it is the perversion of the text that concerns him, the possibility that texts may be transformed and deformed to the damnation of their readers. While such a perversion is reprehensible in relation to any text, when scripture is the text, the stakes become far higher. Charles Coffin has captured this aspect of Donne's scholarship, contending that his engagement with texts was characterised by

> ... first, insistence on the accuracy of any text used and the obligation of the scholar to make accurate use of this text as well as his obligation to consider the meaning of any part in its relations to the larger context and not to be contented with the meaning of isolated passages; second, the necessity of subordinating authors cited to the purpose of the writer; third, the importance of comparison, contrast and correlation of opinions, in order to make a just evaluation of their worth; and fourth, recognition of the relativity of all human knowledge and its dependence upon its historical environment.[4]

3 Sheehan, *Enlightenment Bible*, 1. For a further important statement of the importance of scripture to the reformation, see Alister E. McGrath, *The intellectual origins of the European reformation* (2nd ed., Oxford, 2004), esp. pp 152–74. 4 Charles Monroe Coffin, *John Donne and*

Coffin somewhat underplays the scale of Donne's polemical intention, but his overall account of Donne's scholarship is accurate.

In this context, the often-quoted description of Donne's own conversion serves as an exemplar of careful, painstaking textual engagement:

> I used no inordinate hast, nor precipitation in binding my conscience to any local religion. I had a longer worke to doe then many other men; for I was first to blot out, certaine impressions of the Romane religion, and to wrestle both against the examples and against the reasons, by which some hold was taken; and some anticipations early layde upon my conscience ... [I] surveyed and digested the whole body of Divinity controverted betweene ours and the Romane Church. (_PM_, 13)

In the context of Donne's project in _Pseudo-martyr_, he presents himself as an example to his Catholic readers because of his care in the interpretation of this controverted doctrine. He is not, of course, speaking about scripture here – rather he engages his Catholic readership on the grounds of dogma. He lays great stress on his refusal to adopt the reading impressed upon him by 'Persons who by nature had a power and superiority over [his] will, and others who by their learning and good life, seem'd to me justly to claime an interest for the guiding, and rectifying of [his] understanding in these matters'. The contrast with the blind obedience of Franciscans and Jesuits excoriated by Donne in _Pseudo-martyr_ could scarcely be greater (_PM_, 115). Donne insists on the importance of his intellectual independence and the freedom to arrive at his own reading of church tradition and doctrine.[5] These principles transfer to his treatment of scripture and he seeks to inculcate something very like them in his hearers. To be sure, the requirements of Donne's pastoral mission do qualify the fine independence of _Pseudo-martyr_. As a preacher and a pastor, it was his duty to guide his own flock to a proper understanding of the scriptures that must provide a basis for their life and religion. Furthermore, that understanding had to fall within the range of interpretation endorsed by the church that enfolded both Donne and his flock. Notwithstanding this, Donne's statement of his own interpretative independence should alert us to the importance that he attached

---

the new philosophy (London, 1937), pp 232–3.   5 Donne's paradigmatic engagement with the issue of the correct choice of religion is found in Satire III. For valuable discussions of this issue, see Richard Strier, 'Radical Donne: "Satire III"', _ELH_ 60:2 (1993), 283–332; Richard Strier, _Resistant structures: particularity, radicalism, and Renaissance texts_ (Berkley, CA, 1995), pp 118–64; Joshua Scodel, 'John Donne and the religious politics of the mean' in _John Donne's religious imagination: essays in honor of John T. Shawcross_, ed. Raymond-Jean Frontain and Frances M. Malpezzi (Conway, AR, 1995), pp 45–80. See especially Scodel's discussions of the sermons, pp 60–70. Satyre III is central to our study of the Church's authority in Donne's thought: see below, ch. 2.

to intelligent engagement with scriptures, an importance that we will come to recognise as a recurring motif fundamental to his pastoral approach.

In the third of a series of sermons on John 1:8, preached in St Paul's in October 1622, Donne summarised the crucial points of the debate about the status of scripture in a way that highlights the three issues that I discuss in this section. He contended:

> ... first that there are *certaine Scriptures*, that are the revealed will of God. Secondly, that these books which we call *Canonicall*, are those Scriptures. And lastly, that this and this is the true sense and meaning of such and such a place of Scripture. (IV, 216)

Thus it is that a key issue for Donne is the accurate identification of the canon; he must ensure that the status and authority deserved only by scripture be ascribed only to true scriptures. He must save his auditors from the fate of Gratian, who *'never stood upon Authoritie of Bookes, but tooke all, as if they had beene written with the finger of God, as certainly as Moses Table'* (*PM*, 192). It was an unavoidable consequence of the Reformation that this question should be reopened:

> But if the Scripture were the authority, what then was the Scripture? That question might seem long ago to have been settled because the canon, both of the Old Testament, and the New, had been fixed since the days of the early church. But if, as the Reformers said, the Gospel was prior to the canon and only those books should be received which proclaimed the Gospel, might not the canon be re-examined?[6]

In the absence of ecclesiastical decree, it became necessary to develop other criteria by which the canon could be determined. This very considerable problem exercised the reformers a good deal: Luther's qualms about the status of Revelation and James are simply the best known of the canonical dilemmas that had to be addressed.[7] The denial of the church's authority made discussions about the canon feasible; it was another doctrine that gave them polemical and controversial edge. Purgatory was 'the one of the most contested doctrines of the Reformation,' and a factor in the controversy over the canon was the lack of support for the teaching in those books that the reformers were prepared to accept as canonical.[8] Attempts to lend the doctrine credibility by appeal to the

6 Bainton, 'The Bible in the reformation', p. 6. See also Pelikan, *Reformation of the Bible*, pp 20–1. 7 On Luther's views on the canonicity of Revelation, see Irena Backus, *reformation readings of the Apocalypse: Geneva, Zurich and Wittenberg* (Oxford, 2000), pp 6–11. 8 Greenblatt, *Hamlet*, p. 13. On the wider canon debate, see Hans von Campenhausen, *The formation of the Christian Bible*, trans., John Austin Baker (London, 1972), and the very compre-

writings of the Biblical Apocrypha inevitably focused attention on the status and utility of these books. This Biblical Apocrypha comprised books included in the Septuagint – the Greek translation of the Old Testament carried out in Alexandria between in the third century before Christ, and widely used by Hellenistic Jews, and later by Greek-speaking Christians – and in the Vulgate, but not found in the Hebrew Old Testament. By the time of Donne's ministry, the identity and utility of the Apocrypha had been codified in the Thirty-Nine Articles:

> Holy Scripture containeth all things necessary to salvation: so that whatsoever is not read therein, nor may be proved thereby, is not to be required of any man, that it should be believed as an article of the Faith, or be thought requisite or necessary to salvation. In the name of the holy Scripture, we do understand those Canonical books of the Old and New Testament, of whose authority was never any doubt in the Church. ... And the other Books (as *Hierome* saith) the Church doth read for example of life and instruction of manners; but yet doth it not apply them to establish any doctrine. ...
>
> All the Books of the New Testament, as they are commonly received, we do receive, and account them Canonical.[9]

This understanding of the Apocrypha was given a physical expression by their retention in the King James translation of 1611, as a separate section between the Old and New Testaments, useful to read but marked off from scripture proper.

Among Donne's writings, the *Essayes in divinity* provide a key discussion of the identification of scripture. This work is more complicated in its genre, content and audience than any other in Donne's *oeuvre*. In it, Donne exercises a greater degree of hermeneutical freedom than he ever subsequently allowed himself. However, his meditations on the uniqueness of scripture make explicit those assumptions that underlie his later engagement with scripture. His definition is, broadly, a negative one – he emphasises what the scriptures are not.

The first broad category of books that are not scripture are the 'two other

hensive collection of essays in Lee Martin McDonald and James A. Sanders (eds), *The canon debate* (Peabody, MA, 2002), esp. Eugene Ulrich, 'The notion and definition of canon', pp 21–35; Albert C. Sundberg Jr, 'The Septuagint: the Bible of Hellenistic Judaism', pp 68–90; Daniel J. Harrington SJ, 'The Old Testament apocrypha in the early church and today', pp 196–210. For an interesting perspective on the interaction between reformation and canon from a Roman Catholic theologian, see Oswald Loretz, *The truth of the Bible*, trans., David J. Bourke (London, 1968), pp 96–113. Lee Martin McDonald, 'Canon' in *The Oxford handbook of Biblical studies*, ed. J.W. Rogerson and Judith M. Lieu (Oxford, 2006) provides a convenient and illuminating overview of the subject.   9 Thirty-Nine Articles, VI.

books (within our knowledge) by which great Nations or Troops are govern'd in matter of Religion; The *Alcoran*, and *Talmud* (*ED*, 10). The Alcoran, the Qur'an, is esteemed only where the scriptures are not read. It provides the basis for just another 'weak, and suspicious, and crasie religion' and is 'so obnoxious, and self-accusing, that, to confute it, all Christian churches have ever thought it the readiest and presentest way to divulge it' (*ED*, 11). In contrast to the scriptures, which not only withstand, but demand, searching (III, 367), the Qur'an is egregiously inadequate. The Talmud is equally defective. Galatinus' efforts to deduce all Christianity from this undermine, rather than support, the case for the Talmud's credibility – 'this flexibility and appliablenesse to a contrary religion, shews perfectly, how leaden a rule these lawes are' (*ED*, 11). Once again, close and careful engagement with this text is sufficient to dismiss this volume as alternative scriptures, to rob it of any glamour. Publication is damnation: 'without doubt, their books would have been received with much more hunger then they are, if the Emperour *Maximilian*, by *Reuchlyns* counsel, had not allowed them free and open passage'. Donne's dismissal of these counterfeit scriptures combines with his concern for the seriousness of the issues of faith involved: 'If there were not some compassion belong'd to them who are seduced by them; I should professe, that I never read merrier books than these two'. For Donne, then, both of these putative scriptures can be dismissed, almost out of hand, and the conclusion is obvious: 'Ours therefore, begun, not only in the first stone, but in the intire foundation, by Gods own finger, and pursued by his Spirit, is the only legible book of life; and is without doubt devolv'd from those to our times' (*ED*, 11–2).

Donne then addresses a second category of texts, 'the books of Philosophers' (*ED*, 10). These books 'only instruct this life'. Donne, at this stage, does not deny them some use, but he does limit their scope and power. 'As then this life compared to blessed eternity, is but a death, so the books of philosophers ... have but such a proportion to this book'. In the sermons, Donne dilutes this toleration, and becomes increasingly dismissive of secular writers, and increasingly impatient with the efforts of the Roman church to 'bring other authors into the ranke, and nature, and dignity of being Scripture' (VII, 120). So, preaching in 1622, he emphasised the dichotomy between the profane and the divine in terms of ability, as much as of spiritual value:

> *Saint Paul* is a more powerful orator, then *Cicero*, ... *Moses* is an
> ancienter *Philosopher*, then *Trismegistus*; and his picture of God, is the
> Creation of the world. *David* is a better *Poet* then *Virgil*; ... The
> power of *oratory*, in the force of perswasion, the strength of conclu-
> sions, in the pressing of *Philosophy*, the harmony of *Poetry*, in the
> sweetnesse of composition, never met in any man, as fully as in the
> Prophet *Esay*. (IV, 167)

Within the broad category of 'prophane' literature, Donne especially reacts against the use of classical writings.[10] He emphatically endorses Tertullian's impatience with those who, in his view, pass over useful moral lessons and fasten on imagined impeachments of Christian doctrine:

> If, sayes [Tertullian], we for our Religion produce your own Authors against youhe speaks to naturall men, secular Philosophers) and shew you out of them, what Passions, what Vices even they impute to those whom you have made your gods, then you say, ... Those authors were but vaine, and frivolous poets: but when those authors speake any thing which sound against our religion, then they are philosophers, and reverend and classique authors. (V, 68)

Therefore, the utility of these writers is circumscribed for 'they have this perverse, this left-handed happinesse, to be believed when they lye, better then when they say true' (VI, 42). In this regard, Donne is clearly at odds with the intention and scope of projects like that of Philippe de Mornay (1549–1623). De Mornay was a French Huguenot and member of the Monarchomachs. In his volume *De la verité de la religion chrétienne contre les athées, épicuriens, payens, juifs, mahométans et autres infidèles* (1581), translated as *A work concerning the trunesse of Christian religion against atheists, epicures, paynims, Jewes, Mahumetists and other infidels*, De Mornay set about the correction of an impressive range of opponents. He attempted this by constructing a spectrum of revelation that began at nature, and progressed, by way of heathen philosophers, to scripture. Or, as phrased by the translator of the 1587 edition,

> The Author ... hath conveyed into this work what soever he found eyther in the common reason of all nations, or in the peculiar principles of the chiefe philosophers, or in the misticall doctrine of the Jewish Rabbines, or in the writings of historiographers and poets; that might conveniently make to the manifestation of that trueth, which he taketh in hand to prove.[11]

---

10 Donne's dislike of classical literature echoes the views of Augustine. Often, Christian use of classical material drew upon a tradition, extending back to the writings of the Greek Fathers, of retaining a place for classical literature by reading it as Christian allegory. See, on the allegorization of classical sources, E.K Rand, *Ovid and his influence* (New York, 1963), esp. pp 131–41; Domenico Comparetti, *Vergil in the middle ages* (Princeton, NJ, 1997); Rudoph Schevill, *Ovid and the renascence in Spain* (Berkeley, CA, 1913), esp. pp 13–14; and, for an excellent overview of the topic, Lester K. Born, 'Ovid and allegory', *Speculum* 9:4 (1934), 362–79.   11 Lord of Plessie Marlie Mornay, Philip, *A woorke concerning the trewnesse of Christian religion, written in French, against atheists, epicures, paynims, Jewes, Mahumetists and other infidels*, trans., Sir Philip Sidney and Arthur Golding (London, 1587), sig. *3. See, for Mornay's biography, Charlotte Mornay, *A Huguenot family in the XVI century: the memoirs of Philippe de Mornay, Sieur du Plessis Marly*,

De Mornay's views are interesting because of his impeccably Protestant credentials: his work is, at least partially, an attempt to delineate the Protestant form of the religion revealed in nature. The Protestant agenda of the work is confirmed by its translation into English by Sir Philip Sidney and Arthur Golding.[12] Donne stands opposed to the cultural omnivorousness of this approach, and to the textual distortion that it inevitably entailed.

Donne is equally forceful in his dismissal of efforts to prove Purgatory from the works of the pagan authors, opining that, in this matter, 'Virgil is a perfect, a downright Catholic', for, he pithily notes 'an upright Catholic in point of Purgatory were hard to find' (VII, 176–7). Donne's impatience with the misapplied veneration of classical writers extends beyond the machinations of Rome. He also condemns those who, identifying divine judgment in mythology, give it more importance than the scriptural record. He despairs that they

> beleeve it in their fables, and would not beleeve it in the Scriptures, They would beleeve it in the Nine Muses and would not believe it in the Twelve Apostles; they would believe it by Apollo, and they would not believe it by the Holy Ghost; They would be saved poetically, and fantastically, and would not reasonably and spiritually; by copies, and not by originals; by counterfeit things at first deduced by their authors, out of our Scriptures, and yet not by the word of God himself. (VII, 234)

Likewise, Donne was gravely concerned by the possibility that divines would go beyond scriptures, using classical authorities in their effort to 'compass unrevealed mysteries'. It is, therefore, 'an offence' in churchmen to 'be over-vehemently transported with poetry, or other secular learning' (IV, 143). Ultimately, the over-valuing of classical authors and the concomitant under-valuation of scripture is indicative of a truly diabolical hubris:

> ... to think we can believe out of *Plato*, where we may find a god, but without a christ, or come to be good men out of *Plutarch* or *Seneca*, without a church and sacraments, to pursue the truth it selfe by any other way then he hath laid open to us, this is pride, and the pride of the angels. (IX, 379)

To a large degree, it is a simple matter for Donne to dismiss these other texts. They are the productions of human endeavour. For Donne, however, God is 'the

trans., Lucy Cramp (London, n.d.).   12 See John Considine, 'Golding, Arthur (1535/6–1606)', *Oxford dictionary of national biography* (2004). www.oxforddnb.com/view/article/10908 (accessed 24 May 2013); H.R. Woudhuysen, 'Sidney, Sir Philip (1554–1586)', *Oxford dictionary of national biography* (2004; online ed., May 2005). www.oxforddnb.com/view/article/25522 (accessed 24 May 2013).

author of nature, her voice is but his instrument'.[13] Scripture, begun by the finger of God, and pursued by the operation of his spirit, occupies, by virtue of the radical ontological otherness of its author, a hermeneutical space all of its own. Its superiority over secular texts is one of kind, as well as of degree.

There remains, however, a more complex source of revelation, the 'book of creatures'. The book of creatures has the same author as scripture and its relationship to scripture was central to the ongoing debate about natural theology. The status of God's revelation in nature was a source of some contention, and that contention had a long history. In the first instance, it was deduced from scripture, especially from Psalm 19 ('the heavens declare the glory of God ...'), and Paul's teaching of the responsibility to respond to the creatorial revelation of God as seen in the opening chapters of the Epistle to the Romans, in particular 1:19–25:

> For the wrath of God is revealed from heaven against all ungodliness and unrighteousness of men, who hold the truth in unrighteousness; because that which may be known of God is manifest in them; for God hath shewed *it* unto them. For the invisible things of him from the creation of the world are clearly seen, being understood by the things that are made, *even* his eternal power and Godhead; so that they are without excuse: because that, when they knew God, they glorified *him* not as God, neither were thankful; but became vain in their imaginations, and their foolish heart was darkened.
>
> Professing themselves to be wise, they became fools, and changed the glory of the uncorruptible God into an image made like to corruptible man, and to birds, and fourfooted beasts, and creeping things. Wherefore God also gave them up to uncleanness through the lusts of their own hearts, to dishonour their own bodies between themselves: who changed the truth of God into a lie, and worshipped and served the creature more than the Creator, who is blessed for ever. Amen.[14]

The utility of natural revelation was fundamental to the *Summa contra gentiles* (1265) of Thomas Aquinas. This methodology was the result of the fact that Aquinas' work was aimed at non-Christian readers:

> because some of them, like the Mohammedans and pagans, do not agree with us as to the authority of any Scripture whereby they may

13 Richard Hooker, *The Folger Library edition of the works of Richard Hooker, 1: of the laws of ecclesiastical polity*, ed. Georges Edelen (Cambridge, MA, 1977), I, p. 84. 14 Rom. 1:19–25 (KJV). See Michel de Montaigne, *An apology for Raymond Sebond*, ed. M.A. Screech (London, 1987), pp viii–xx.

be convinced, in the same way as we are able to dispute with the Jews by means of the Old Testament, and with heretics by means of the New: whereas the former accept neither. Wherefore it is necessary to have recourse to natural reason, to which all are compelled to assent.[15]

Aquinas' magnum opus, the *Summa theologiae*, was written for those who assented to the authority of scripture, and this has obvious implications for his method. However, 'he remains careful to distinguish between truths discoverable by reason and truths available only through revelation'.[16] Thomistic philosophy continued to be influential throughout the medieval period, and its importance was in no way lessened by the Reformation or the Renaissance. Indeed, a number of the important concerns of the early modern period had given a new currency to Aquinas' ideas. As the exploration of new lands led to the encounter of new peoples, the fate of those who spent their entire lives without hearing the gospel preached became more than an academic concern. The discovery of those who had not lived within the sound of church or chapel bell prompted a re-evaluation of the saving efficacy of natural revelation. The high regard in which classical writers were held made the question still more relevant. Could the virtuous pagan have responded to a natural revelation and, if so, did that response ensure the value of his writings for seventeenth century Christians?

These concerns were raised most controversially by Raymond of Sebond (d. 1432). Sebond's *Theologia naturalis* (written 1434–6) argued, as Anthony Raspa summarises it in his introduction to Donne's *Essayes in divinity*, 'that God had created the universe to give man knowledge of his divine being and that, in the divine mind, this book of the created universe pre-existed the Bible as a source of revelation for humanity, and so in that sense was a surer volume of information than the Scriptures' (*ED*, 112).[17] This was a considerable extension of Aquinas' ideas, and proved a step too far for the Catholic Church, who condemned Raymond as a heretic. Sebond's ideas had a particular currency at the end of the sixteenth century, because of their influence on Michel de Montaigne.[18] Montaigne published a translation of Sebond's *Theologia* in 1569

15 Thomas Aquinas, *The summa contra Gentiles*, trans., The English Dominican Fathers, I (London, 1924), p. 4. 16 Anthony Kenney, *Medieval philosophy* (Oxford, 2005), p. 70. 17 Screech, in Montaigne, *Apology*, pp xiii–xiv points out that it was only Sebond's prologue that was placed on the Tridentine Index of Forbidden Books (1564), and that the orthodoxy of Montaigne's translation, published with a revised prologue, was never called into question. Sebond's version described the doctrine he propounded as 'necessary', while Montaigne merely states that it is useful. Likewise, Sebond claimed, without qualification, that his understanding of nature was capable of teaching truth. Montaine argued that it taught the truth 'insofar as it is possible for human reason'. Sebond's heresy was, therefore, more the result of a demarcation dispute than a radical challenge to orthodox Christianity or Catholicism. 18 The issue of Montaigne's influence on Donne is a difficult one, because we have no direct proof that Donne had read, or was influenced by Montaigne. Louis I. Bredvold, 'The naturalism of Donne in relation to some renaissance traditions', *Journal of English and Germanic Philology* 22 (1923),

and his *Apology for Raymond Sebond* in 1576. This was published as the twelfth chapter of the second part of Montaigne's *Essays* in 1580. Montaigne's translation of Sebond recovered the orthodoxy of his teaching, and his defence of Sebond is an important and influential exercise in the Christian scepticism that touched Donne.

Similarly Thomistic ideas were expressed in an English context by Richard Hooker.[19] The precise extent of Hooker's dependence on natural reason has been hotly debated in recent scholarship.[20] Most critics agree, however, that Hooker's valorisation of the possibilities of natural reason was a direct response to the extreme scripturalism of his Puritan opponents, who contended that scripture alone was the guide for all actions. Hooker responded by adumbrating a hierarchy of laws – natural law, the celestial law (binding for angels) and the law of reason, obeyed by men as reasonable creatures, and tending to direct them in the imitation of God. This law, Hooker contends, can be seen at work shaping the actions of pious pagans like Plato (inevitably) and Mercurius Trismegistus, who proceeded in the 'knowledge of truth' and grew in 'the exercise of virtue'.[21] In further proof of this, Hooker appeals to the force of custom, and to the *locus classicus* of Romans 2:

417–502, supports his argument that Montaigne was Donne's 'master' on the basis of the similarity of ideas in their works, concentrating, in Donne's case, upon the earlier, 'libertine' poetry. Richard Ornstein, 'Donne, Montaigne, and natural law' in *Essential articles for the study of John Donne's poetry*, ed. John R. Roberts (Hassocks, 1975), p. 130, contends, against Brevold, that 'Donne and Montaigne criticized natural law independently from the Libertine tradition and from each other'. **19** Hooker's indebtedness to Aquinas has been debated. W.D.J. Cargill Thompson, 'The philosopher of the "politic society"' in *Studies in Richard Hooker: essays preliminary to an edition of his works*, ed. William Speed Hill (Cleveland, OH, 1972); Robert K. Faulkner, 'Reason and revelation in Hooker's Ethics', *American Political Science Review* 59:3 (1965), 3–76 , 680–90; Robert K. Faulkner, *Richard Hooker and the politics of a christian England* (Berkeley, CA, 1981) contend for an Aristotelian Hooker. Hooker's debt to Aristotle cannot be denied: it was, indeed, a chief objection of the authors of *A Christian letter* that Hooker was happy to depend on a pagan philosopher [see 'A Christian Letter' in Richard Hooker, *The Folger Library edition of the works of Richard Hooker, 4: lawes: attack and response*, ed. John E. Booty (Cambridge, MA, 1982), pp 65–7]. This does not, however, eliminate the importance of Thomism in Hooker's epistemology, a dependence tellingly discussed by A.P. d'Entrèves, *The medieval contribution to political thought: Thomas Aquinas, Marsilius of Padua, Richard Hooker* (Oxford, 1939), A.P. d'Entrèves, *Natural law: an introduction to legal philosophy* (2nd (rev.) ed., London, 1970); Peter Munz, *The place of Hooker in the history of thought* (London, 1952); John Sedberry Marshall, *Hooker and the Anglican tradition: an historical and theological study of Hooker's Ecclesiastical polity* (London, 1964); Damien Grace, 'Natural law in Hooker's *Of the laws of ecclesiastical polity*', *Journal of Religious History* 21:1 (1997), 10–22; John K. Stafford, 'Richard Hooker's doctrine of the Holy Spirit' (PhD, U Manitoba, 2005). **20** See Nigel Atkinson, *Richard Hooker and the authority of scripture, tradition and reason* (Carlisle, 1997) and Stafford, 'Richard Hooker's doctrine', for the primacy of Scripture in Hooker's theology, and Nigel Voak, *Richard Hooker and reformed theology: a study of reason, will and grace* (Oxford, 2003) for an opposing view. **21** Hooker, *Works*, I, p. 74.

The generall and perpetuall voice of men is as the sentence of God him selfe. For that which all men have at all times learned, nature her selfe must needes have taught; and God being the author of nature, her voice is but his instrument. By her from him we receive whatsoever in such sort we learn. Infinite duties there are, the goodness wherof is by this rule sufficiently manifested, although we had no other warrant besides to approve them. Thapostle S. Paul having speech concerning the Heathen saith of them, *They are a law unto themselves.* His meaning is, that by force of the light of reason, wherewith God illuminated every one which commeth into the world, men being inabled to know truth from falsehood, and good from evill, do thereby learne in many things what the will of God is; which will himselfe not revealing by any extraordinary meanes unto them, but they by naturall discourse attaining the knowledge therof, seeme the makers of those lawes which are indeed his, and they but only the finders of them out.[22]

Hooker is very clearly envisaging a process of revelation: nature is God's instrument, and what she reveals we receive by her from Him.

Hooker's claims for the utility of reason are considerable, if contested. It is clear that he did not simply replace the Puritan emphasis on the omnicompetence of scripture with a similarly far-reaching view of reason. So, for example, he was careful to stress that it was important not 'so far to extend the law of reason, so as to conteine in it all maner lawes whereunto reasonable creatures are bound, but ... we restraine it to those only duties, which all men by force of naturall wit either do or might understand to be such duties as concerne all men'.[23] Hooker goes on to argue for the necessity of scripture. He does so by appeal to human potential. Man's sensual and intellectual desires are natural, and therefore able to be satiated by natural means. Humanity's spiritual desires are supernatural, and thus, by definition, require something beyond the natural to satisfy them. Scripture provides this supernatural resource, and is therefore a far greater revelation than the natural:

The light of nature is never able to finde out any way of obtaining the reward of blisse, but by performing exactly the duties and workes of righteousness. For salvation therefore and life all flesh being excluded this way, behold how the wisdom of God hath revealed a way mysticall and supernaturall, a way directing unto the same ende of life by a course which groundeth it selfe upon the guiltiness of sinne, and through sinne desert of condemnation and death. For in this waye the

22 Ibid., pp 83–4. 23 Ibid., p. 91.

first thing is the tender compassion of God respecting us drowned
and swallowed up in myserie; the next is redemption out of the same
by the pretious death and merit of a mightie Saviour, which hath
witnessed of himself saying *I am the way*, the way that leadeth us
from miserie into blisse.[24]

Hooker's understanding of natural revelation maintained a vital place for God's
revelation in scripture.

Donne's discussion of natural revelation is informed by the wider context of
this debate, most explicitly by the work of Raymond of Sebond. Throughout his
writings, he parallels very closely the process of divine creation and divine
revelation:

> The Holy Ghost hovered on the waters, and so God wrought. The
> Holy Ghost hovered upon Moses and so he wrought. (IX, 48)

In an undated sermon, Donne appeared to toy with a very broad definition of
the word of God, along the lines followed by de Mornay. Ultimately, however,
he identifies a dichotomy between all human production and that which originates with God:

> The word of God is either the co-eternall and co-essentiall Sonne, our
> Saviour, which tooke flesh ... or it is the spirit of his mouth, by which
> we live, and *not bread onely*. And so, in a large acceptation, every truth
> is the word of God; for truth is uniforme, and irrepugnant, and
> indivisible, as God. ... More strictly the word of God, is that which
> God hath uttered, either in writing, as twice in the Tables to *Moses*; or
> by the ministry of Angels, or Prophets, in words; or by the unborne,
> in action, as in *John Baptists* exultation within his mother; or by the
> new-borne, from the mouths of babes and sucklings; or by things
> unreasonable, as in *Balaams* Asse; or insensible, as in the whole booke
> of such creatures, *The heavens declare the glory of God &c*. But
> nothing is more properly the word of God to us, then that which God
> himself speakes in those organs and instruments, which himself hath
> assumed for his chiefest worke, our redemption. (V, 231)

Donne's use of the Book of Creatures never strays close to Sebondian heresy
or Herbertian deism.[25] Indeed, his reluctance to ascribe too much to natural

---

24 Ibid., p. 118.   25 A number of scholars have discussed the nature of Herbert's influence
upon Deism, suggesting in general that his ideas were rather later appropriations than fundamental in their importance. See R.W. Serjeantson, 'Herbert of Cherbury before deism: the early
reception of the *De Veritate*', *Seventeenth Century* 16:2 (2001), 217–38; David A. Pailin, 'Should

revelation was stated clearly very early on in his career, in Paradox IV, 'That nature is our worst guide'. In approaching Donne's *Problems and paradoxes*, we are faced by the difficulties of dating and by the questions of intent implicit in the nature of these exercises in witty casuistry. However, the tone of this paradox is less flippant than is elsewhere the case, and there is a clear continuity between the views expressed by the young Donne and his later circumspection when dealing with nature as revelation:

> Shall she be *guide* to all *Creatures*, which is her selfe one? . . .The affections of *lust* and *anger*, yea euen to *erre* is *Naturall*; shall we follow these? Can she be a good *guide* to us, which hath corrupted not us but only herselfe? Was not the *first man* by the desire of *knowledge* corrupted even in the *whitest integrity* of *Nature*? And did not *Nature* (if *Nature* did any thing) infuse into him this desire of *knowledge*, & so this *Corruption* in him, into us? If by *Nature* we shall understand our *essence*, our *definition*, or *reason*, *noblenesse*, then this being alike common to all (the *Idiot* and the *wizard* being equally *reasonable*) why should not all men having equally all one *nature*, follow one course? Or if wee shall understand our *inclinations*; alas! how unable a guide is that which followes the *temperature* of our slimie *bodies*? (*SP*, 40)

Later, in *Pseudo-martyr*, Donne stated more clearly his belief that natural revelation was an insufficient basis for true religion, as he theorised about a race of savages coming to faith. He claimed that any such group of people would first establish a hierarchical order: 'for magistracie and superioritie is so naturall and so immediate from God, that *Adam* was created a magistrate' (*PM*, 79). Having thus arranged themselves into a 'commonwealth', the company moves towards enlightenment 'through understanding the law written in all hearts, and in the booke of creatures'. Even the careful reading of these sources is insufficient, however; 'further light' and 'the relation of some instructors' is required before the company can 'arrive at a saving knowledge, and faith in our blessed Saviours Passion'.[26]

In the *Essayes*, Donne seems to go beyond this understanding of the book of creatures, quoting, with approval, the ideas of Raymond of Sebond:

> But of the third book, the book of *Creatures* we will say the 18th verse [of Is. 29], *The deaf shall heare the word of this book, and the eyes of the*

Herbert of Cherbury be regarded as a "deist"?', *Journal of Theological Studies* ns, 51:1 (2000), 113–49. **26** Cf. Bacon's *New Atlantis*, in which the inhabitants of the utopian island respond not to natural revelation, but to the canonical scriptures of the Old and New Testaments, miraculously revealed to them: Francis Bacon, *The advancement of learning; and, New Atlantis*, ed. Arthur Johnston (Oxford, 1974), pp 222–4.

blinde shall see out of obscurity. And so much is this book available to the other, that *Sebund*, when he had digested this book into a written book, durst pronounce, that it was an Art, which teaches al things, presupposes no other, is soon learned, cannot be forgotten, requires no books, needs no witnesses, and in this, is safer then the Bible itself, that it cannot be falsified by Hereticks. And ventures further after, to say, That because his book is made according to the Order of Creatures, which expresses fully the will of God, whosoever doth according to his book, fulfils the will of God. (*ED*, 9–10)

These claims are considerable, and Donne is slow to dismiss them, remarking only that Sebond 'may be too abundant in affirming, that *in libro creaturarum* there is enough to teach us all particularities of Christian religion'. Ultimately, Donne finds his solution in scripture itself, noting that 'St *Paul* clears it thus far, that there is enough to make us inexcusable, if we search not further'.[27] Natural revelation is not, then, an end in itself, but a prompt for further investigation; it points back to God, but onwards to the revelation of scripture. The fact of the Fall explains the necessity of scripture. Relenting somewhat on his criticisms of pre-lapsarian nature in Paradox VIII, Donne argues that if man had kept 'the first light of nature', 'he had needed no outward law; for then he was to himself a law, having all the law in his heart; as God promiseth for one of the greatest blessings under the gospel, when the law of nature is more cleerly restored: *I will make a new covenent, and put my law in their inward parts, and write it in their hearts'* (*ED*, 100). In this, Donne accords with Calvin's views on the knowledge of God imparted from nature:

> For, properly speaking, we cannot say that God is known where there is no religion or piety. I am not now referring to that species of knowledge by which men, in themselves lost and under curse, apprehend God as a Redeemer in Christ the Mediator. I speak only of that simple and primitive knowledge, to which the mere course of nature would have conducted us, had Adam stood upright. For although no man will now, in the present ruin of the human race, perceive God to be either a father, or the author of salvation, or propitious in any respect, until Christ interpose to make our peace; still it is one thing to perceive that God our Maker supports us by his power, rules us by his providence, fosters us by his goodness, and visits us with all kinds of blessings, and another thing to embrace the grace of reconciliation offered to us in Christ.[28]

27 Notably, Donne is, himself, making use of Romans 1:20 in this instance. It is significant that Donne stresses the closing clause of the verse, a clause omitted, as Screech points out, by Montaigne, *Apology*, pp vvii–xix, 10.   28 John Calvin, *Institutes of the Christian religion*, trans.

Donne continues to endorse this view of nature. While his statement, made in a Trinity Sunday sermon (tentatively dated to 1621) on II Corinthians 1:3, that 'there is an elder booke in the World then the Scripture; ... it is the World it selfe, the whole booke of Creatures; And indeed the Scriptures are but a paraphrase, but a comment, but an illustration of that booke of Creatures' (III, 264) appears to undermine the primacy of scripture, it is made in a context of the acknowledgment that 'there is nothing in Nature that can fully represent and bring home the notion of the Trinity to us' (III, 263–4). Subsequently, Donne articulates the same relationship that he outlined in the *Essayes*: 'Though God meant to give us degrees in the University, that is, increase of knowledge in his scriptures after, yet he sent us to Schoole in Nature before; ... That coming out of that Schoole, thou mightest profit the better in that University, having well considered Nature, thou mightest be established in the Scriptures' (III, 264).

This understanding underlies all of Donne's subsequent engagements with the book of Creatures. It is eloquent of Donne's theological pragmatism; it is an answer that works for his hearers, who are able to follow the promptings of nature to search further in revealed scripture. It does not solve the hard case of the 'savage' without written revelation, but Donne has little enough interest in pursuing philosophical speculation on their fate, and urges his congregation to leave them to God's 'unsearchable waies ... without farther inquisition' (IV, 78). God's unsearchable ways, however, allow for human involvement in the amelioration of the plight of scripture-less 'savages'. Donne's sermon 'Preached to the Honourable Company of the Virginian Plantation 1622' has been called 'the first English missionary sermon'.[29] Donne had a previous interest in the Virginian company, in his job search, before entering the ministry, and his sermon expresses a consciousness of the possibilities of the Virginian plantation. It also adumbrates a missionary motive for the Virginian endeavour.[30] A similar understanding of national responsibility to spread the gospel, in tandem with commercial endeavour had, however, been outlined in one of Donne's earliest sermons. This is, arguably, the first articulation of the concept of 'commerce and Christianity', later to become so important:

> The Lord reigneth let the Islands rejoice the Islands who by reason of their situation, provision and trading, have most means of conveying Christ Jesus over the world. He hath carried us up to heaven, & set us at the right hand of God, & shal not we endeavour to carry him to those nations, who have not yet heard of his name? Shall we still brag that we have brought our clothes, and our hatchets, and our knives, and

Henry Beveridge (Chicago, IL, 1990), pp 2–3. **29** Logan Pearsall Smith, ed. *Donne's sermons: selected passages* (Oxford, 1919), p. 249. **30** See Stanley Johnson, 'John Donne and the Virginia Company', *ELH* 14:2 (1947), 127–38; Paul W. Harland, 'Donne and Virginia: the ideology of conquest', *John Donne Journal* 18 (1999), 127–52.

> bread to this and this value amongst those poor ignorant Souls, and
> shall we never glory that we have brought the name and Religion of
> Christ Jesus in estimation amongst them? (I, 307–8)

No doubt Donne's audience was quite happy to be given this evangelical justification for the risky business of plantation. Nonetheless, his understanding of the
importance of this mission is underlined by an appreciation of the need of the
heathen:

> O, if you could once bring a cathechisme to bee as good ware amongst
> them as a Bugle, as a knife, as a hatchet: O, if you would be as ready
> to hearken at the returne of a Ship, how many Indians were converted
> to Christ Jesus, as what Trees, or drugges, or Dyes that Ship had
> brought, then ye were in your right way, and not till then. (IV, 269)

For the favoured members of English congregations, the hierarchy of nature,
reason and revelation is important.[31] Nature reveals God, Reason acts on this
natural revelation, but, ultimately, scripture surpasses both nature and reason;
'Gods Word is much better assurance, then the grounds of Nature, for God can
and does shake the grounds of Nature by Miracles, but no Jod of his Word shall
ever perish' (V, 292). We have, Donne suggests, 'light enough to see God by that
light in the theatre of nature and in the glass of creatures' (VII, 225). Indeed, this
light is so clear that 'the Atheist must pull out his eyes and see no creature before
he says he sees no God' (VIII, 225). To see God, however, is just a beginning,
and while 'man can teach us how to find God', a further hierarchy of revelation
is needed, and 'The natural man in the book of creatures', comes behind the
usefulness of 'the moral man in an exemplar life, the Jews in the Law, the
Christian, in general in the Gospel'. Ultimately, 'only the Holy Ghost enables us
to find God so as to make Him ours and enjoy Him' (VI, 128). Donne applies a
pair of telling images to the same hierarchy in his fourth Prebend Sermon:
'though there bee not a full meale, there is something to stay the stomach, in the
light of nature' (VII, 301). Nature, therefore, is a breakfast; the Law, dinner; and
in the church, the sufficiency of supper is found. Similarly, in the kind of
imagery that is the stuff of Donne's poetry,

> In the state of nature, we consider this light, as the Sunne, to be risen
> ... in the farthest East; In the state of the law, we consider it as the
> Sunne come to ... the first Quadrant; But in the Gospel, to be come
> to the Canaries, to the fortunate Ilands, the first Meridian. (VII, 310)

---

31 Notably, Donne uses this hierarchy to structure *Biathanatos* (written before 1619, published
1647), his 'mis-interpretable', paradoxical defence of suicide.

Donne pragmatically acknowledges that 'there may be some few examples given of men, enlightened by God, and yet not within that covenant which constitutes the Church' (VIII, 226). Nonetheless, while allowing for the sovereignty of God, we must remember that 'the ordinary place for degrees is the University', and 'the Church is our academy and university' (VIII, 226). Perhaps the best account of Donne's views of the possibilities and the limitations of this book of creatures is found in one of his later sermons:

> There is not so poor a creature but may be thy glasse to see God in. The greatest flat glasse that can be made, cannot represent any thing greater then it is: If every gnat that flies were an Arch-angell, all that could but tell me, that there is a God: and the poorest worme that creeps, tells me that. If I should aske the Basilisk, how camest thou by those killing eyes, he would tell me, Thy God made me so; And if I should aske the Slow-worme, how camest thou to be without eyes, he would tell me, Thy God made me so. The Cedar is no better a glasse to see God in, then the Hyssope upon the wall; all things that are, are equally removed from being nothing; and whatsoever hath any being, is by that very being, a glasse in which we see God, who is the roote, and the fountaine of all being. (VIII, 224)

Nature, all of Nature, is sufficient to prove the being of God. 'But then, for the other degree, the other notification of God ... the means is of a higher nature' (VII, 225). And that means is scripture.

Indeed, it is a part of the function of Nature to indicate to human reason the necessity of a more substantial, a more explicit revelation. For Donne, the revelation of Nature is only of use insofar as it refers us to the more complete revelation of scripture. Scripture is the word of God, and the garments in which God has 'apparelled, and exhibited his will' (V, 248). Additionally, it reveals the character of God: 'God is *Love*, and the *Holy Ghost* is amorous in his *Metaphors*; everie where his *Scriptures* abound with the notions of *Love*, of *Spouse* and *Husband* ...' (VII, 87). Since God 'hath declared himselfe in his Scriptures', it is of the first importance that this revelation be 'by Translations and Illustrations, made applicable to every understanding; all the promises of his Scriptures belong to all' (VIII, 122). This was one of the key battlegrounds of the Reformation and Donne explicitly re-visits this issue:

> Whether they or we, do best apply our practice to this rule, Preach all the Truth, preach nothing but the Truth, be this *lis contestata*, the issue joined between us, and it will require no long pleading for matter of evidence ... And here is the Latitude, the Totality, the Integrality of the meanes of salvation; you shall have Scripture delivered to you,

> by them the Holy Ghost shall teach you all things; and then you shall
> be remembred of all, by the explication and application of those
> Scriptures ... Now, is this done in the Roman Church? Are the
> Scriptures delivered, and explicated to them? so much of the
> Scriptures as is read to them their Lessons and Epistles, and Gospels,
> is not understood when it is read, for it is in an unknown language; so
> that, that way, the Holy Ghost teaches them nothing.[32] (VII, 401)

The ideal for Donne – and one which he feels that the English church has, in
good measure, attained – is for scripture to be freely accessible, 'explicated in
Sermons' and available for private consideration:

> But when men have a Christian liberty afforded to them to read the
> Scriptures at home, and then are remembred of those things at
> Church, and there taught to use that liberty modestly, to establish
> their faith upon places of Scripture that are plain, and to suspend
> their judgement upon obscurer places, till they may ... receive farther
> satisfaction therein, from them, who are thereunto authorized by God
> in his Church, there certainly is this Rule of our saviours, *Take heed*
> *what you hear*, preach *all* that you have received from me, likelier to be
> observed then there, where the body of the conveyance, the Scripture
> itself is locked up from us. (VII, 401)

Donne lays considerable stress on the policing role of ecclesiastical authority
(something we will have cause to investigate more closely). At the same time,
however, the availability of scripture to the individual has a significant role to
play in underwriting the explication of scripture by preaching.

   This quotation also emphasises the centrality of the Holy Ghost in the application of the text of scripture to the individual hearer. For Donne, the spirit is
intimately involved in the work of scripture. Revelation has been accomplished
by the agency of the Holy Spirit, with a view to being understood by men. 'God
speaks mens language, that is, the Holy Ghost in the scriptures descends to the
capacity and understanding of man, and so presents God in the faculties of the
minde of man and in the lineaments of the body of man' (IX, 135, see also IX,
142). Thus, the writers of scripture are the 'secretaries of the Holy Ghost' (*PM*,
14), writing 'by instinct of the Holy Ghost' (II, 269). A supernatural power,
then, pervades all of scripture. So, Donne, displaying his characteristic predilection for the Psalter, remarks that 'Any Psalme is Exorcisme enough to expell any
Devill, Charme enough to remedy any tentation, Enchantment enough to ease,

---

32 Donne is, perhaps, being less than completely fair to his opponents. A more scrupulous
honesty might have prompted him to make mention of the Douay Bible. Donne never refers to
this translation.

nay to sweeten any tribulation' (VI, 292). Donne allows for the role of the natural gifts of the authors, and traces the sweetness of scripture to this, accepting without endeavouring to reconcile the perennial paradox between revelation and personality. He sees no contradiction that he needs to address in speaking of the 'characteristic phrases' of authors who write by the dictation of the Holy Spirit (VIII, 293). Similarly, while he acknowledges that the gospel of John 'seems rather fallen from Heaven than written by a man' (V, 241), Donne allows for a limited role for natural ability and experience in the writing of scripture. In one of the sermons from his later series on the penitential Psalms, Donne uses David and the Psalms to exemplify this relationship:

> So in *Davids* Psalmes we finde abundant impressions, and testimonies of his knowledge in all arts, and all kinds of learning, but that is not it which he proposes to us. *Davids* last words are, and in that *Davids* holy glory was placed, That he was not onely *the sweet Psalmist*, That he had an harmonious, a melodious, a charming, a powerfull way of entring into the soule, and working upon the affections of men, but he was *the sweet Psalmist of Israel*, He employed his faculties for the conveying of the God of Israel, into the Israel of God; *The spirit of the Lord spake by me, and his word was in my tongue*; Not the spirit of Rethorique, nor the Spirit of Poetry, nor the spirit of Mathematiques, and Demonstration, But, *The spirit of the Lord, the Rock of Israel spake by me*, sayes he. (IX, 252)

In the context, Donne is deliberately using David is a paragon of preachers. Nonetheless, it is clear that for Donne, the aesthetic value of scripture, although always enjoyed and appreciated, remained secondary to their revelatory function. So, although 'of all Rhetoricall and Poeticall figures, that fall into any Art, we are able to produce higher straines, and livelier examples out of the Scriptures, then out of all the Orators and Poets in the world, yet we read not, we preach not the Scriptures for that use, to magnifie their Eloquence' (IX, 252).

CLARIFYING THE CANON

To acknowledge that a written divine revelation exists inevitably raises the question of the canon of sacred writings. Both as a controversialist and as a pastor, Donne engages with the issue of the canon of scripture. Donne addresses these questions by appeal to reason. Indeed, as Terry Sherwood has noted, 'The rational acceptance of Scripture is crucial in Donne's epistemology'.[33] Donne

33 Terry G. Sherwood, 'Reason in Donne's sermons', *ELH* 39:3 (1972), 355. For an earlier but equally valuable discussion of Donne's views of reason, which makes similar reference to this

stresses the importance of such human argument in the identification of scripture, dealing specifically with the issue of the canon:

> As for the whole body intirely together, so for the particular limbs and members of this body, the *severall books* of the Bible, we must accept *testimonium ab homine*, humane Arguments, and the testimony of men. At first, the Jewes were the depositaries of Gods Oracles; and therefore the first Christians were to ask the Jewes, *which* books were those Scriptures. Since the Church of God is the *Master* of those *Rolls*, no doubt but the Church hath *Testimonium à Deo*, The Spirit of God to direct her, in declaring *what Books* make up the Scripture; but even the *Church*, which is to deal upon men, proceedeth also *per testimonium ab homine*, by humane Arguments, such as may work upon the *reason* of man, in declaring the Scriptures of God. (IV, 217)

This insistence on the importance of reason, and Donne's confidence in the assistance provided to reason by the humanist project, is a distinctive feature of his thought. His 'insistence upon this rational justification of belief, as a means of suggesting reason's importance, shows that he found it an important paradigm for the way in which the mind first refers experience to rational scrutiny'.[34] And, Sherwood suggests, the importance of reason in this fundamental issue is indicative of a Thomist stress in Donne's thought. Given the Aristotelian stress on reason in Catholic theology, it is possible that Donne is demonstrating the influence of his upbringing, although this stress is an equally telling indication of the philosophical ground shared by Donne and Hooker. Certainly, the basic importance of reason in the delineation of scripture presents a significant challenge to Bredvold's marginalisation of reason in Donne's thought in favour of a scepticism built upon the mystical and fideistic elements of Augustinian thought.[35]

For all his insistence on the role of reason in identifying scripture, Donne acknowledges a residuum of aporia. Examining Donne's *oeuvre* in its entirety, it is noticeable that Donne's insistence that the canon can be reasonably derived by learning and reason alone is never quite backed up by concrete example or explication of how precisely reason may work. This quotation is typical:

> All those blessings by the Sacrament of Baptism, and all Gods other promises to his children, and all the mysteries of Christian Religion, are therefore believed by us, because they are grounded in the

passage see Irving Lowe, 'John Donne: the middle way', *Journal of the History of Ideas* 22:3 (1961), 389–97.   34 Sherwood, 'Reason', p. 356.   35 Louis I. Bredvold, 'The religious thought of Donne in relation to medieval and later traditions' in *Studies in Shakespeare, Milton and Donne* (New York, 1925).

> Scriptures of God; we believe them for that reason; and then it is not
> a worke of my faith primarily, but it is a worke of my reason, that
> assures me, that these are the Scriptures, that these Scriptures are the
> word of God. I can answer other Mens reasons, that argue against it,
> I can convince other men by reason, that my reasons are true: and
> therefore it is a worke of reason, that I believe these to be Scriptures.
> (V, 102)

Donne's protestations that his understanding of the canon is grounded in reason
have a tinge of stridency, and it is notable that he provides no evidence in support
of his asserted ability to 'convince other men by reason'. In this, he is reminis-
cent of Richard Hooker who, having conceded that the canon cannot be deduced
from scripture itself, argues from the premise that we are 'perswaded by other
meanes that these scriptures are the oracles of God' without outlining just what
those other means might be.[36] Understandably enough, Donne seems to wish
that the issue of canonicity was more clear-cut. On occasion, reason notwithstanding, he achives this clarity by handing the whole vexed issue over to the
authority of the church:

> Not that the Church is a Judge above the Scriptures (for the power
> and the commission which the Church hath, it hath from the
> Scriptures) but the Church is above thee, which are the Scriptures,
> and what is the sense of the Holy Ghost in them. (VIII, 228)

This awareness of the complexity of defining the canon does not prevent Donne
from invoking the topic controversially. Notably, when he does so, he approaches
the question on the basis of a largely stable and clearly defined body of canonical scripture. Quite explicitly, he regards the canon as the product of antiquity,
once problematic, but now determined. So, he remarks, somewhat caustically,
that he

> should hope better of their salvation, who in the first darker times,
> doubted of the Revelations of St *Iohn*, then of theirs, who in these
> cleare and evident times, accept, and enjoyne, and magnifie, so much
> as they doe in the Romane Church, the Revelation of St *Brigid*. (VIII,
> 137)

Donne's intentions in this quotation are intriguing; not only is it the case that,
while a degree of supernatural authority was ascribed to mystical books like the
revelations of Brigid, nobody seems seriously to have suggested that they take

36 Hooker, *Works*, I, 126.

their place alongside the canonical scriptures. Moreover, the fact that the canon-icity of the Apocalypse was questioned during the Reformation, most notably by Martin Luther, seems to call into question when in history Donne locates 'the first darker times'.[37]

For the most part, as in this quotation, Donne is more exercised by the dangers of addition to the canon, than by subtraction. While he touches briefly on the canonicity of Job, for example (III, 100), his chief concern, from a contro-versial point of view was the 'fathering' of 'Apocryphall and bastardly Canons' upon the Apostles (VII, 107). So, in one of his most substantial discussions of the canon, he adumbrates a view of a canon that progressed to sufficiency, but that has now been closed. The implication is that any such addition is not only wrong, but also unnecessary:

> [T]o adde to the Gospel, to adde to the Scriptures ... is a Diminution, a Dissolution, an annihilation of those Scriptures, that Gospel, that faith, and the Author, and finisher thereof. ... [T]he *Scriptures* grew ... the number of books grew; But they grew not to the worlds end, we know to how many bookes they grew. The body of man and the vessels thereof, have a certain, and a limited capacity, what nourish-ment they can receive and digest ... The soul, and soul of the soul, *Faith* and her faculties, hath a certain capacity too, and certain propor-tions of spirituall nourishments exhibited to it, in certaine vessels, certain measures, so many, these Bookes of Scripture. (VII, 399)

In this context, addition is worse than subtraction:

> Which of you can adde another booke to the Scriptures, *A Codicill* to either of [the] Testaments? The *curse* in the Revelation fals as heavy upon them that *adde* to the booke of God, as upon them that take from it: Nay, it is easie to observe, that in all those places of Scripture which forbid the taking away, or the adding to the Book of God, still the commandment that they shall not, and still the malediction if they do, is *first* placed upon the adding, and after upon the taking away. (VII, 399)

It is, Donne concludes, 'a more pernicious danger to the Church, to admit a book for *Canonicall*, which is *not* so, then to reject one that is so' (IV, 218). And, furthermore, this danger is a present one: on this issue that the battle remains to be won, for

---

37 For a discussion of the Reformation debate on the canonicity of Revelation, see Backus, *Reformation readings*, pp 3–36.

> though heretofore some Heretiques have offered at that way, to clip
> Gods coin in taking away some book of Scripture, yet for many
> blessed Ages, the Church hath enjoyed her peace in that point: None
> of the Books are denied by any Church, there is no subtraction
> offered; But for addition of Apocryphal Books to Canonicall, the
> Church of God is still in her Militant state, and cannot triumph: and
> though she have victory, in all the Reasons, she cannot have peace.
> (VII, 399–400)

We should remark that Donne's difficulty was not with the apocryphal books
per se. Indeed, he develops an ingenious strategy to accommodate the homiletic
benefits of the Biblical Apocrypha, arguing that 'because God foresaw that mens
curiosities would carry them upon Apocryphal books' (V, 280) he ensured their
usefulness. They are useful 'for applying our manners, and conversation to the
Articles of Faith; ... Canonicall for edification, but not for foundation' (VII,
385). As such, there is 'no occasion [for] an elimination, ... an extermination of
these Books' (VII, 386). But this usefulness does not give them the status of
scripture, a fact that Donne underscores when commenting on a conjectured
allusion to 2 Maccabees 7:7 in Hebrews 11. He again invokes divine sovereignty
in maintaining a clear differentiation between apocryphal and canonical
scripture:

> So then, there may be good use made of an Apocryphall Booke. It
> always was, and always will be impossible, for our adversaries of the
> Romane Church, to establish that, which they have so long endeav-
> oured, that is to make the Apocryphall Bookes equall to the
> Canonicall. It is true ... the blessed Fathers in the Primitive Church,
> afforded honourable names, and made faire and noble mention of
> those Books. So they have called them Sacred; and more then that,
> Divine; and more then that too, Canonicall Books; and more then all
> that, by the generall name of Scripture, and Holy Writ. But the Holy
> Ghost, who fore-saw the danger, though those blessed Fathers
> themselves did not, shed, and dropt, even in their writings, many
> evidences, to prove, in what sense they called those Books by those
> names, and in what distance they alwayes held them, from those
> Bookes, which are purely, and positively, and to all purposes, and in all
> senses, Sacred, and Divine, and Canonicall, and simply Scripture, and
> simply, Holy Writ. (VII, 385)

The moral pointed is clear, and resonates with what we have already seen of
Donne's efforts to foreground reason in the definition of a canon. There is no
reason to be confused about the identification of scripture.

Given that the question, as Donne chooses to see it, is as simple as this, why does a debate on the canon even exist? For Donne, it exists because the Church of Rome perpetuates it. They do so, not because they are stupid, but as part of a devious and malign project to undermine true scripture:

> It is not, principally, that they would have these Books as good as Scriptures; but, because they would have Scriptures no better then these Books: That so, when it should appeare, that these Bookes were weake books, and the Scriptures no better then they, their owne Traditions might be as good as either. (VII, 387)
>
> Their intention and purpose, their aime, and their end is, to under-value the Scriptures, that thereby they may over-value their owne Traditions, their way to that end may bee to put the name of Scripture upon books of a lower value, that so the unworthinesse of those additionall books, may cast a diminution upon the Canonicall books themselves, when they are made all one. (VII, 120)

Thus, disagreements about the identification of scripture serve to mask a more radical question about the nature and the value of divine revelation, and an agenda of deception and illusion.

Many of the issues that have been surveyed in this chapter come together in the sermon preached by Donne at St Paul's on Christmas Day 1621. As the Thirty Years War fizzled out in Europe, and as tensions within the English church mounted, Donne took as his text John 1:8 – 'he was not that light but was sent to bear witness of that light'. Right from the first sentence of the sermon, Donne is at pains to foreground the question of how scripture is known as the word of God: 'it is an injury common to all the Evangelists (as *Irenæus* notes) that all their *Gospels* were severally refused by one Sect of *Hereticks* or other. But it was proper to Saint *John* alone, to be refused by a Sect, that admitted *all the* other three Evangelists' (III, 348). The 'lime and branch of the *Arians*' who refused John's words did so because it is the way of sectaries to 'refuse all that they did not understand'. Quibbles over the content of scripture are the sort of thing that sects engage in. And such quibbles are far from incidental. Rather, they spring from the Arians' a priori commitment to mistaken doctrine.

Having established that the subject of canonicity is a concern of the sermon, Donne goes on to outline the first chapter of John's gospel, concluding, 'that the Gospel of Saint John contains all *Divinity*, this Chapter *all the Gospell*, and this Text all the *Chapter*'. Probably to the considerable relief of his hearers, he then outlined the more circumscribed engagement that was to occupy this sermon: 'Therefore it is too large to goe through at this time; at this time we shall insist upon such branches as arise out of that consideration, *what and who this light is*' (III, 351). Donne appears to answer this question very clearly and finally when he states, at the beginning of the following paragraph, that 'Christ is this light'. He then introduces the topic that though consistently disavowed seems to be the real focus of his preaching on this occasion: the place of reason in the life of the Christian. At first he deals with it negatively, disavowing the view that the light of John 1:8 is the light of reason. He acknowledges the antiquity of this interpretation, but concludes that

> Light is never (to my remembrance) found in any place of Scripture, where it must necessarily signifie the light of nature, *naturall reason*; but wheresoever it is transferred from the naturall to a figurative sense, it take a higher signification than *that*; either it signifies *Essentiall* light, Christ Jesus ... or it signifies the *supernaturall light* of *Faith* and *Grace*. (III, 352)

Donne bolsters the status of this reading in a way that is significant both for our present purpose and for the discussion of the next chapter:

> And therefore, though it be ever lawfull, and often times very usefull, for the raising and exaltation of our devotion, and to present the plenty, and abundance of the *holy Ghost* in the *Scriptures* ... yet this may not be admitted, if there may be danger thereby, to neglect or weaken the *literall sense* it selfe. (III, 353)

At this point, it seems clear that Donne is not interested in talking about reason in this sermon, and it is logical to expect that he will proceed by addressing the interpretation that best accords with the literal sense. And for a time that is precisely the route that Donne follows, discussing the ways in which light could be understood as being light essential, and contrasting the totality of divine light with the more dappled projection achieved by even the best of men. But Donne is working around to address the role of reason. Again he does so negatively – towards the end of his meditation on Christ as essential light, Donne voices a very typical warning against seeking to understand what has not been revealed. 'If we search farther into these points than the scripture hath opened us a way, how shall wee hope to unentangle, or extricate ourselves?' It is important, therefore to be aware of the danger that 'we may search so far, and reason so long of *faith* and *grace*, as that we may lose not onely *them*, but even our reason too, and sooner become *mad* than *good*' (III, 357).

Donne, however, is quick to balance this: 'not that we are bound to believe any thing *against* reason, that is, to believe, we know not why. It is but a slacke opinion, it is not *Beliefe*, that is not grounded upon reason' (III, 357). He illustrates this by imagining a heathen encountering the Gospel for the first time. The inept evangelist of Donne's imagination presents him with the facts of the

Christian message, and concludes with the uncompromising warning: 'believe all, or you burne in Hell'. Such a heathen 'would finde an easie, an obvious way to escape all; that is, first not to believe in *Hell* it selfe, and then nothing could binde him to believe the rest' (III, 358). The heathen has been let off the hook because the evangelist neglected to take advantage of the illustrative matter that God had provided in Nature. Using this resource, Donne unfolds the inexorable aetiology of conviction and conversion:

> The *reason* therefore of man must first be satisfied; but the way of such satisfaction must be *this*, to make him see, That this World, a frame of so much harmony, so much concinnitie and conveniencie, and such a correspondence, and subordination in the parts thereof, must necessarily have had a workeman, for nothing can make it selfe: That no such workeman would deliver over a frame, and worke, of so much Majestie, to be governed by *Fortune*, casually, but would still retain the Administration thereof in his owne hands: That if he doe so, if he made the World, and *sustaine* it still by his watchfull Providence, there belongeth a worship and service to him, for doing so: That therefore he hath certainly revealed to man, what kinde of worship, and service, shall be acceptable to him: That this manifestation of his Will, must be permanent, it must be *written*, there must be a *Scripture*, which is his *Word* and his *Will*: And that therefore, from that Scripture, from that word of God, all Articles of our Beliefe are to bee drawne. (III, 358)

The final result, presumably, one convinced heathen. Nature has a dual role, pointing backwards to the necessity of God, and forward to the necessity of scripture.

Nature is only a prompt, though, and its revelation is sufficient to indicate the necessity of written revelation. Donne's imagined heathen will very likely 'aske further proofe, how he shall know that *these Scriptures* accepted by the Christian Church are the true Scriptures' (III, 358). Donne addresses this issue in a very individual way:

> Let him bring any other Booke which pretendeth to be the Word of God, into comparison with these; It is true, we have not a Demonstration; not such an Evidence as that one and two, are three, to prove these to be Scriptures of God; God hath not proceeded in that manner, to drive our Reason into a pound, and to force it by a peremptory necessitie to accept these for Scriptures, for then, here had been no exercise of our Will, and our assent, if we could not have resisted. But yet these Scriptures have so orderly, so sweet, and so

> powerful a working upon the reason, and the understanding, as if any
> third man, who were utterly discharged of all preconceptions and
> anticipations in matter of Religion, one who were altogether neutrall,
> disinterested, ... should heare a Christian pleade for his Bible; the
> Majesty of the Style, the punctuall accomplishment of the
> Prophecies, the harmony and concurrence of the foure Evangelists,
> the consent and unanimity of the Christian Church ever since, and
> many other such reasons, he would be drawn to such an Historicall,
> such a Grammaticall, such a Logicall beliefe of our Bible, as to
> preferred it before any other, that could be pretended to be the word
> of God. (III, 358)

Very noticeably, Donne bases his defence of scripture, and its canon on an appeal
to reason.[38] Moreover, this reason is assisted by the humanist return *ad fontes*;
the eventual assurance of the heathen is based on a critical – and a literary critical
– approach to scripture.[39] Nor is the light of reason useful only for the heathen.
A little later in the sermon, Donne points out that the light of nature has a
function for those who sit in his congregation:

> This, though a fainter light, directs us to the other, *Nature to Faith*:
> and as by the quantitie in the light of the *Moone*, we know the position
> and distance of the *Sune*, how far or how neare the Sune is to her, so
> by the working of the light of *Nature* in us, we may discern (by the
> measure and virtue and heat of that) how near to the other greater
> light, the light of *Faith*, we stand. (III, 365)

Natural revelation still functions as an adjunct and complement to the
inscripturated word of God. But, just as natural revelation had to be properly
used, the reader of scripute had to approach them in the correct way. The
individual immersion in scripture was to be a humble one, undertaken for
pastoral profit and not to satisfy or stimulate an intellectual pride, a priority that
confirms Donne's status as a pastor, rather than a philologist:

> I am commanded *scrutari Scripturas, to search the scriptures*; now, that
> is not to be able to *repeat* any history of the Bible without booke, it is

---

38 As he does, with equal clarity, at I, 298.   39 This faith in historical research is echoed in J.B.
Leishman's interpretation of Donne's instruction, in 'Satire III' to 'ask thy father and let him ask
his' to identify true religion: 'This saving truth is, in a sense, factual rather than doctrinal, and to
be attained not in some beatific vision, but as a result of a long and laborious process of historical, or semi-historical, research': J.B. Leishman, *The monarch of wit: an analytical and
comparative study of the poetry of John Donne*, 5th ed. (London, 1962), p. 116. Cf. Irving Lowe's
contention, in a discussion of the place of reason in Donne's thought, that 'the sermons merely
make more explicit the grounds upon which Donne wrought from the beginning to the end of
his career': Lowe, 'Donne: the middle way', 396.

> not to *ruffle* a Bible, and upon any word to turne to the Chapter, and
> to the verse; but this is *exquisite scrudatio*, the true searching of the
> Scriptures, to finde all the *histories* to be *examples* to me, all the *prophe-
> cies* to induce a Saviour for *me*, all the *Gospell* to apply Christ Jesus to
> *me*. ... This is *Scrutari Scripturas, to search the Scriptures*, not as
> though thou wouldest make a *concordance*, but an *application*; as thou
> wouldest search a *wardrobe*, not to make an *Inventory* of it, but to
> finde in it something fit for thy wearing. (III, 367)

Reason and scripture alike must operate within clear boundaries. Donne
warns his listeners against allowing reason to lead them away from the observnce
of their religious duties:

> And therefore, as th Apostle saith, *Quench not the Spirit*, I say too,
> *Quench not the light of Nature*, suffer not *that* light to goe out; study
> your *naturall faculties*; husband and improve them, ad loce the *outward
> acts of Religion*, though an *Hypocrite*, and though a naturall man may
> doe them. ... He that undervalues *outward things*, in the religious
> service of God, though he begin at *ceremoniall* and *ritual* things, will
> come quickly to call *Sacraments* but outward things, in contempt. As
> some *Platonique* Philosophers, did so over-refine Religion and
> devotion, as to say, that nothing but the *first thoughts* and *ebullitions* of
> a devout heart, were fit to serve God in. (III, 368)

Care must be taken that the use of reason does not lead to the reasoning of
oneself away from the established order of the English church. And while
Donne singles out the sacraments for special mention in this context, he also
invokes sermons. His warning, then, applies to all parts of the ecclesiastical
spectrum – even though we might suspect that Donne sees greater danger at one
end than the other.

The established church with its rituall and ceremonial provides the parameters within which the light of reason ought to operate. And the nature of that
church is determined by scripture, by '*that faith which was once delivered unto the
Saints*' (III, 370). This rule of faith 'must not be *deformed*, it cannot be *Reformed*;
it must not be mard, it cannot be mended; whatsoever needs mending, and *reformation*, cannot be the rule of faith' (III, 370). Donne has alredy set this
conclusion in an anti-Roman context, and he goes on to develop the contrast
between the fixed and immutable light of faith, and the 'meteors' and 'comets'
produced by the Roman church. Donne is on familiar ground here, attacking
Rome for her additions to scripture, lamenting the evil effects of the Council of
Trent, which 'was brought to bed of *a new Creed*, not concieved before by the
holy Ghost in the scriptures, and (which is a monstrous birth) the child greater

then the Father, as soon as it is bourne, the new Creed of the *Councell of Trent* to containe more Articles, then the old Creed of the Apostles did' (III, 369).

This sermon, then, draws together many of the issues that we have surveyed in this chapter. Although Donne presents it as a Christological discourse, he has a great deal to say about scripture, reason, and their interrelationship. Donne's very high estimation of scripture emerges clearly, as does his belief in a religion that is demarcated only by scriptural precept. He sounds a recurring polemical note in his accusation that Rome has undervalued scripture in adding to it, and, in the Council of Trent, especially, has deformed essential Christianity. The sermon also demonstrates Donne's understanding of the role of natural revelation and of the natural reason upon which it acts. It also highlights the fact that neither reason or scripture operates in a vaccuum, and points the way to the interpretative concerns and implications that are the subject of the next chapter.

Interpretative authority and the authority of interpretation

Chapter one traced the way in which Donne identified scripture. This identification is only preliminary, laying the groundwork for engagement with, and
interpretation of the canon thus defined. Donne's work presents us with two
sorts of evidence about his interpretative measures. On one hand, the sermons
are instantiated interpretation, and inevitably reveal a great deal about the way in
which he interpreted scripture, but it is not the only or the most important type
of evidence. Donne is also at pains to record his own commentary on the task of
interpretation. This reflexive discussion of the business of interpretation is very
useful. This is especially the case because Donne preached in an atmosphere of
heightened textual awareness that foregrounded the theory of textual interpretation. It would be incorrect, however, to suggest that he was part of the
relatively confined group of scholars – Debra Shuger's 'republic of sacred
letters' – at the centre of Renaissance philology. His personal links to some of its
members were close enough; but Donne is separated from this group by his lack
of any deep linguistic scholarship. The precise extent of Donne's proficiency in
the original languages of scripture has been the focus of some debate. The
foundations had been laid for much of this work by Don Cameron Allen in 1943.
Allen's analysis of the sermons led him to the conclusion that

> There is no doubt that Donne knew enough Hebrew to find the place
> in the text of the Bible and to make reasonable translations. The fact
> that he seldom ventured beyond this and that he does not compare his
> text regularly indicates that his scholarship was extremely limited. He
> was undoubtedly better than the average preacher in his knowledge of
> Semitics, but he fell far below the standard set by Andrews and even
> by Hall.[1]

Allen does suggest that Donne makes the best possible capital of his limited
grasp of Hebrew: 'At no time does Donne seem to know as much Hebrew as
Andrews or even Hall although he is more ostentatious in his use of it than either
of them'.[2]

1 Don Cameron Allen, 'Dean Donne sets his text', *ELH* 10:3 (1943), 219.   2 Ibid., 213.

This broad picture has been challenged somewhat, and Anthony Raspa and Judith Herz have differed on the precise extent of Donne's facility in Hebrew.[3] Chanita Goodblatt has nuanced the picture, and offered a reconciliation. Goodblatt uses Matt Goldish's 'important conception of Christian Hebraism'. Within this taxonomy, Donne fits best into the rank of

> third-order Hebraists ... who could read *some* Hebrew, but who knew and used significant amounts of Jewish literature in Latin and vernacular translations. ... Such a conception realigns the terms of the debate to allow for both Raspa and Herz to be correct in their assertions; there is nothing contradictory, after all, about Donne's possessing a basic, lexical grasp of the Hebrew language while acquiring the more sophisticated semantic nuances from commentators such as Nicholas of Lyra ... as well as Johannes Reuchlin and Pietro Galatinus.[4]

The circumscribed nature of Donne's knowledge no doubt explains why 'Donne sometimes plunges into philological difficulties that are probably beyond his depth'.[5]

As far as Greek is concerned, Allen contends that the extent of Donne's ability and scholarship 'is far below that of the average preacher of his age'.[6] It was, however, typical of that age that Hebrew attracted more scholarly attention than Greek. During the period when Donne was at Oxford, 'Hebrew had more students than Greek, and there was great enthusiasm for the Hebrew among theologians' (X, 307). So, while Donne does make use of the variant readings provided by the King James Version and the earlier Geneva translations, his engagement with the Greek text of scripture does not go any deeper. Allen summarises his view of Donne's textual scholarship in a way that is eloquent of the nature of Donne's relationship with innovations in early modern Biblical scholarship:

> From these analyses we should gain some notion of Donne's scholarship as it applies to the setting of a text and to the care and accuracy with which he quotes the Scriptures to his parishioners. The result, it seems to me, is hardly a credit to Donne's scholarship. He knew some Hebrew and apparently some Greek, but he consults the original texts only when the mood is on him. ... He certainly lacked the scholarly

---

3 Anthony Raspa and Judith Scherer Herz, 'Response', *Renaissance and Reformation* 20 (1996), 97–8. 4 Christine Goodblatt, 'From "tav" to the cross: John Donne's Protestant exegesis and polemics' in *John Donne and the protestant reformation*, ed. Mary Arshagouni Papazian (Detroit, MI, 2003), pp 224–5. 5 Allen, 'Dean Donne', 217. 6 Ibid., 222. Allen fails to provide much evidence for this rather sweeping statement.

approach of the great divines to the Holy Word, but he undoubtedly was more careful in his inspection of texts than the average preacher. ... [I]f this study suggests anything, it is that we should be more cautious in applying the words *scholarly* or *learned* to Donne the divine.[7]

Donne had some aspirations to adopt the emerging trends in Biblical scholarship. Insofar as his learning permitted, he emulated the modes of this new school, and his approach to the issue is that of the highly educated man whose professional learning is primarily legal and theological.[8] Once again, however, we must recognise that Donne is a pastor, not a philologist, and remains only peripherally connected to the republic of letters.

The second distinctive innovation in the study of scripture in this period, can be seen, according to Shuger, as part of 'the Renaissance's scholarly fascination with the material culture of antiquity'.[9] This historicist strain in Biblical scholarship differed from the inflexion of the same ideas in classical history, which was largely 'political and biographical, dealing with generals, emperors, demagogues and statesmen'.[10] Biblical scholarship, by contrast,

> focuses on culture rather than on politics. Since the events of the New Testament are only marginally related to the vicissitudes of imperial power, exegesis turned instead to the exploration of social praxis and the fabric of ordinary existence, studying clothing, table manners, dishware, marital and burial customs, penal codes, kinship structures and ritual practice. ... Exegesis becomes less an explication of things (*res*) mentioned in the text than an inquiry into the codes and customary practices (*mos*) implicit in both the composition and content of scriptural narrative.[11]

Donne was very aware of these developments; the *Essayes in divinity* make clear his familiarity with some of the leading exponents of this scholarship, among them Reuchlin, Pietro Galatinus and Sebastian Münster. Donne was not a practitioner, and was, once again, removed by an appreciable distance from the cutting edge of this new investigation into scripture. This tendency does, however, leave its impress upon his preaching, less perhaps to aid exegesis than to further the hortatory purpose of his exposition.

Donne, then, was rather a pastor than a philologist, and this fundamental fact

---

7 Ibid., pp 227, 229.   8 The effects of Donne's legal education have been discussed in detail in Hugh Adlington, 'The preacher's plea: juridical influence in John Donne's sermons, 1618–1623', *Prose Studies* 26:3 (2003), 344–56.   9 Shuger, *Renaissance Bible*, p. 29.   10 Ibid., p. 32. 11 Ibid.

determines his priorities in engaging with scripture.[12] J.B. Haviland captured something of this:

> Before everything else he wants to understand and express … the experimental side of the Christian life and the role the Church plays in that experience. He is determined not to become entangled with mere words; … He is neither an etymologist nor a translator; he is a voyager into religious immensities which he believes beyond any doubt or question.[13]

It is this priority that explains why Donne values edification above exegesis, why, at times, he can disregard or dismiss questions of interpretation in order to allow him to make hortative use of a passage. Dennis Quinn is quite correct in stating that 'It is most historical and most accurate to think of Donne's sermons as spiritual or, specifically, tropological exegesis. Their central concern is the Christian soul'.[14] Indeed, Donne is disarmingly open about this practice. For example, in an Easter sermon, preached in 1624, on Revelation 20:6, Donne, having listed a number of exegeses of the verse, concludes it by stating:

> And then the occasion of the day, which we celebrate now, being the Resurrection of our Lord and Saviour Christ Jesus, invites me to propose a fourth sense, or rather use of the words; not indeed as an exposition of the words, but as a convenient exaltation of our devotion. (VI, 64)

The exaltation of his listeners' devotion reappears as the motive of overriding importance in a Christmas Day sermon preached in 1626. Here, its importance is sufficient to overcome the questionable nature of the sources upon which Donne relies:

> This assistance we have to the exaltation of our devotion, from that circumstance, that *Simeon* was an old man; we have another from another, that he was a priest, and in that notion and capacity, the better fitted for this epiphany, this Christmas, this Manifestation of Christ. We have not this neither in the letter of the story; no, nor so

---

12 Jeanne Shami, 'Squint-eyed, left-handed, half-deaf: *imperfect senses* and John Donne's interpretative middle way' in *Centered on the word: literature, scripture and the Tudor-Stuart middle way*, ed. Daniel W. Doerksen and Cristopher Hodgkins (Newark, DE, 2004), pp 173–92 identifies a similar priority in Donne's preaching, concentrating more particularly upon his treatment of controversy.　13 J.B. Haviland, 'The use of the Bible in the sermons of John Donne' (PhD, TCD, 1960), p. 14.　14 Dennis B. Quinn, 'John Donne's principles of Biblical exegesis', *Journal of English and Germanic Philology* 61 (1962), 326.

constantly in Tradition, that he was a Priest, as that he was an old
man: But it is rooted in Antiquity too. (VII, 285)

Likewise, preaching before King Charles, in 1626, on Isaiah 50:1, Donne
declined to rule definitively on the true meaning of his text, and rather makes
the greatest possible homiletical capital out of the scripture: 'And therefore, as
God hath opened himselfe to us, both wayes, let us open both eares to him, and
from one Text receive both Doctrines' (VII, 74). Indeed, this imperative towards
edification causes Donne to go beyond the use of readings lacking in textual
support, to the use of readings that are, beyond doubt, erroneous. So, for
example, in a discussion of 1 Corinthians 12:3 ('Wherefore I give you to understand, that no man speaking by the Spirit of God calleth Jesus accursed: and *that*
no man can say that Jesus is the Lord, but by the Holy Ghost') Donne makes
mention of

> those hereticall words of *Faustus* the *Manichean*, That in the Trinity,
> the Father dwelt ... In that light which none can attaine to, and the
> Son of God dwelt in this created light, whose fountaine and roote is
> the Planet of the Sun, And the Holy Ghost dwelt in the Aire, and
> other parts illumined by the Sun and, while rejecting their truth
> explains that 'we may make ... good use' of them. (VI, 126)

Similarly, even while disagreeing with the rendering of Psalm 77:11 in the
Vulgate,[15] Donne wishes 'wee could but take aright a mis-taken translation, and
make that use that is offered us in others error' (VIII, 304).

Clearly, the passages that Donne treats with such disregard for the niceties of
exact exegesis do not treat any fundamental doctrine, and thus are available for
the sort of pragmatic use to which Donne puts them. Donne is not alone in this;
indeed, he justifies this use of scripture by approving reference to Augustine's
observations on the difficulty of correctly understanding the Biblical account of
creation:

> If *Moses* were here, I would hold him here, and begge of him, for thy
> sake to tell me thy meaning in his words, of this Creation. But sayes
> he, since I cannot speake with *Moses* ... I begge of thee who art Truth
> it selfe, as thou enablest him to utter it, enable me to understand what
> he hath said. So difficult a thing seemed it to that intelligent Father,
> to understand this history, this mystery of the Creation. But yet
> though he found that divers senses offered themselves, he did not

15 Donne follows the Vulgate's verse numbering, but not its Psalm numbering. The Vulgate
renders the equivalent verse (Ps 76:11) as 'et dixi nunc coepi haec mutatio dexterae Excelsi' ('And
I said, Now have I begun: this is the change of the right hand of the most High'.)

> doubt of finding the Truth: ... What hurt followes, though I follow
> another sense, then some other man takes to be *Moses* sense? for his
> may be true sense, and so may mine, and neither be *Moses* his. (IX, 94)

Donne goes on to echo Augustine's dictum on the interpretation of contested
passages of scripture:

> Where divers senses arise, and all true (that is, that none of them
> oppose the truth) let truth agree them. But what is Truth? God; and
> what is God? Charity; Therefore let Charity reconcile such differ-
> ences. ... Let us use our liberty of reading Scriptures according to the
> Law of liberty; that is, charitably to leave others to their liberty, if they
> but differ from us, and not differ from Fundementall truths.[16] (IX,
> 94–5)

Donne's attitude to the interpretation of scripture is irenic where fundamental
truths are not concerned. In an earlier sermon, Donne cast a jaded eye back over
the history of reformation and counter-reformation, and alerted his congregation to the appalling consequences that an excessive insistence on doctrinal
unanimity had had for earlier generations of English men and women:

> From making infirmities excusable necessary (which is the bondage
> the Council of *Trent* hath laid upon the world) to make Problematicall
> things, Dogmaticall; and matter of Disputation, matter of faith; to
> bring the University into *Smithfield*, and heaps of Arguments into
> Piles of Faggots. (IV, 144)

Donne is conscious, throughout his writings, that no one man can claim to be an
authoritative interpreter of scripture: he was conscious that 'the best of men are
but Problematicall, Onely the Holy Ghost is Dogmaticall; Onely he ... seales
with Infallibility' (VI, 301). Accordingly, his own interpretation of scripture was
free from excessive dogmatism, and from the taint of arrogance.

   This notwithstanding, Donne took the interpretation of scripture very
seriously, and he was always at pains to stress the pastoral and practical implications of exegesis. Indeed, his excoriating attacks on the mis-reading of
scriptures, which have troubled some modern critics, can be better understood
when we remember just how serious, for Donne, were the stakes in play. So it is
that, in *Pseudo-martyr*, Donne dealing with the deliberate distortion of scripture
remarks that, if such readings 'carried them no further, than to simple and
childish actions', or to 'to stupid actions', 'sillinesse or some such disease might

16 On the role of this view in the rhetoric of Augustine and Donne, see Dennis B. Quinn,
'Donne's Christian eloquence', *ELH* 27:4 (1960), 277.

lessen the fault' (*PM*, 81–2). The reality, however, is infinitely more sinister than this: 'But then is there extreame horrour and abominations therein, when God and his Lieuetenants are at once injur'd, which is, when places of Scripture are malitiously or ridiculously detorted to the aviling of princes' (*PM*, 82). Donne greatly fears that his readers, and later his listeners, are being abused to their damnation. Later, in the sermons, Donne outlines a further consequence of incautious exegesis:

> It is a frequent infirmity among Expositors of scriptures, by writing, or preaching, either when men will raise doubts in places of scripture, which are plaine enough in themselves (for this creates a jealousie, that if the Scriptures be every where so difficult, they cannot be our evidences, and guides to salvation) Or when men will insist too vehemently, and curiously, and tediously in proving of such things as no man denies; for this induces a suspition, that that is not so absolutely, so undeniably true, that needs so much art, and curiosity, and vehemence to prove it. (V, 270)

Exegesis, for Donne, does not take place in a vacuum, and he cannot be an island insofar as Biblical interpretation is concerned. His exposition has consequences, and Donne never loses sight of this.

This attitude underpins Donne's interpretation of scripture. His exegesis is also dependent upon his belief that scripture was the result of divine inspiration, a work of revelation as remarkable, in its way, as the work of Creation. There followed from this belief, a view of scripture that stressed a basic unity of purpose, a homogeneity of intention that overrides the differences in the historical context and other circumstances attendant upon the writing of scripture. Donne states this very explicitly, even while acknowledging the assorted sources that make up canonical scripture:

> ... in the true Scriptures, we have a glorious sight of this *Mosaick*, this various, this mingled work; where the words of the Serpant in seducing our first parents, the words of *Balaams* Ass in instructing the rider himself, the words of prophane Poets, in the writings and use of the Apostle, the words of *Caiaphas* prophesying that it was expedient that one should dye for all, The words of the Divel himself (*Jesus I know, and Paul I know*). And here in this text, the words of a Thief executed for the breach of the Law; do all concur to the making up of the Scriptures, of the word of God. (I, 253)

This belief has clear implications for interpretation: 'It must bee Gods *whole Booke*, and not a fewe mis-understood *Sentences* out of that *Booke*, that must try thee. . . . That which must try thee is the whole *Booke*, the *tenor* and *purpose*, the *Scope* and *intention* of God in his *Scriptures*' (VII, 87). It leads Donne to ask 'but since our merciful God hath afforded us the whole and intire book, why should wee tear it into rags, or rent the seamless garment?' (*ED*, 16). In the immediate context, Donne is referring to the tendencies of Pico della Mirandella's cabbalism. Nonetheless, the query is indicative of Donne's understanding of scripture, and could apply with equal force to the proof-texting of the scholastics, and to the excesses of medieval exegesis. Donne repudiates this behaviour in very clear terms later in the *Essayes*:

> The Souldiers would not divide our Saviours garment, though past his use and his propriety. No garment is so neer God as his word: which is so much his, as it is *he*. . . . And in the Incarnation, the Act was onely of one Person, but the whole Trinity speaks in every word. The therefore which stub up these severall roots, and mangle them into chips, in making the word of God not such, . . . they, I say, do what they can this way, whose word it is pretended to be, no God. They which build, must take the solid stone, not the rubbish. (*ED*, 46)

This assumption of a pan-scriptural unity of intent also allowed Donne to stipulate certain universal principles of interpretation. Thus, there is no difficulty, for Donne, in stating that 'the first thing I look for in the Exposition of any scripture, and the nearest way to the literall sense thereof, is, what may most deject and vilifie man, what may most exalt and glorifie God' (IX, 361). In the same manner, Donne identified Christ as 'the subject of the Word of God, of all the Scriptures' (I, 287).

Donne's interpretation of scripture was underwritten by a pastoral imperative. This motivation for exegesis was a more important factor for Donne than the scholarly dictates of the humanist project. His lack of deep expertise in the Biblical languages was one factor limiting Donne's complete engagement in detailed *ad fontes* exegesis, and his assumption of the universal suitability of a Christological approach to the interpretation of scripture modified his commitment to a historicised reading of the Bible. But these interpretative possibilities, while of manifest relevance to our understanding of the detail of Donne's exegesis, were never the source of his most abiding interest in scripture. The exaltation of God and the instruction of man above all other considerations directed Donne's reading and exposition of the Biblical text.

THE LITERAL EMPHASIS OF DONNE'S EXEGESIS

The question of how exactly it was that Donne interpreted scripture has been the subject of some debate. Much of this discussion has identified Donne's exegetical options as mediaeval allegory, on the one hand, and modern literalism, on the other. Scholars have then attempted to situate Donne against this artificially polarised background. Anthony Raspa, dealing only with Donne's early (pre-ordination) prose works identifies Donne's chief method of interpretation as typological, a method that he, like Barbara Lewalski, extends into the poetry.[17] William Mueller acknowledges the place of allegorical interpretation in determining the structure of Donne's sermons, but ultimately contends that 'Donne seldom paid strict adherence to it in organizing his sermons'.[18] Dennis Quinn, presenting a rather fuller picture, stresses Donne's literal hermeneutic, and comes very close to denying that allegorical readings had any place in Donne's understanding of scripture. J.B. Haviland, in his earlier study of Donne's use of the Bible, seems unsure where precisely to position Donne, but on the whole attempts to understand his interpretation of scripture in relation to medieval and allegorical modes, concluding that 'his method was derived from the Church Fathers by way of medieval tradition'.[19] These debates tend, in practice, to boil down to discussions of just how modern, or how medieval, Donne was. There is legitimate importance in considering the question whether Donne's understanding of scripture was allegorical or literal. Indeed, Donne himself treats of this question extensively, as he speaks reflexively of his preferred manner of interpretation. To concentrate on this issue alone, however, is to miss the relevance of a good deal of more recent scholarship on Reformation and Renaissance hermeneutics, and thus to miss the opportunity to view Donne in relation to the developments that were taking place in this field.

Insofar, then, as the place of allegory in Donne's thought is concerned, we do well to remember that we have a range of works spanning twenty years. Moreover, these works were the product of a man noted for the investigative temper of his mind and for his wide engagement with new learning. It is should scarcely be surprising that Donne's views on scripture did develop. It is gratifyingly neat that the movement that Donne's hermeneutics display – away from the allegorical, and towards the literal – mirrors broader developments, over a much wider time span, in Biblical interpretation. This is not to suggest that we have earlier readings that are wholly allegorical, and later engagements that are entirely literal. Donne always laid considerable stress on the importance of the literal meaning; he never disdained the opportunity to make a point based on

---

17 Barbara K. Lewalski, *Protestant poetics*, esp. ch. 4: 'The biblical symbolic mode: typology and the religious lyric' and ch. 8: 'John Donne: writing after the copy of a metaphorical God'.
18 William R. Mueller, *John Donne: preacher* (Princeton, NJ, 1962), p. 90.   19 Haviland, 'Use of the Bible', p. 14.

allegory. But, as far as the dominant tenor of Donne's exegesis is concerned, there is a shift in emphasis from allegorical to literal interpretation.

Donne's use of the allegorical interpretation of scripture is inspired by a conviction that scripture is a text spiritually discerned, and therefore must contain more than a surface literal significance. To this conviction he gave clear expression; speaking of David's lament about the vexation of his bones in Psalm 6:2–3, he asked: 'Shall we, who have our conversation in heaven, finde no more in *Bones*, then an earthly, a worldly, a naturall man would doe?' (V, 353).[20] This use of spiritual meaning is most marked in the *Essayes in divinity*. Donne insists on the typical value of the record of Genesis, but stresses that there is also literal truth in the account. Further, the truth, while it is not on the surface and not available equally to all, is still easy to understand. 'There is then in *Moses*, both History and Precept, but evidently distinguishable without violence' (*ED*, 21–2). The application of this dictum is most clearly seen when Donne deals with the exodus of the Israelites from Egypt:

> Only to paraphrase the History of this Delivery, without amplifying, were furniture and food enough for a meditation of the best persever-ance, and appetite, and digestion; yea, the least word in the History will serve a long rumination. If this be in the bark, what is in the tree? If in the superficiall grass, the letter; what treasure is there in the hearty and inward Mine, the Mistick and retired sense? Dig a little deeper, O my poor lazy soul, and thou shalt see that thou, and all mankind are delivered from an Egypt; and more miraculously than these. (*ED*, 82)

This is a statement of the higher value of the spiritual, the allegorical, sense that accords very closely with medieval exegesis. It is very unusual, in Donne's inter-pretation, that he is so dismissive of the literal sense of the text – 'the superficiall grass' – and even this unflattering description is balanced by his insistence that the literal sense of the passage alone provides 'furniture and food' for a 'medita-tion of the best perseverance'.

Subsequently, Donne makes use of a more peculiarly typological mode of interpretation:

20 This view may help to explain Donne's statement, generally ignored by critics, that Philip and Mary Sidney had, in their translation of the Psalms 'both taught us what, and taught how to doe. /... /They tell us *why*, and teach us *how* to sing' (lines 20–2). Teaching how to sing is accounted for by Donne's clearly expressed views of the technical superiority of their translation. The teaching why to sing, qualified by the statement that the Sidneys had 'both translated, and apply'd' Psalm 97 (1.19), appears to involve the unveiling of a contemporary significance in the Psalms. We should note that we have already seen Donne apply this same Psalm, in his sermon to the honourable company of the Virginia Plantation (1622), to give it a contemporary relevance (see above, pp 37–8).

> Almost all the ruptures in the Christian Church have been occasioned
> by such bold disputations *De Modo*. ... But to decline this sad
> contemplation, and to further our selves in the Meditation of Gods
> justice declared in this History, let me observe to you, that God in his
> Scriptures hath Registred especially three symbols or Sacraments, of
> use in this matter. One in *Genesis*, of pure and meer *Justice*, vindica-
> tive and permanent; which is, The *Cherubim and fiery sword* placed in
> Paradise, to *keep out*, not only *Adam*, but his *Posterity*. The second in
> *Exodus*, of *pure* and *only Mercy*, which is the model and fabrick of the
> *Mercy seate*, under the shadow of the two Cherubims wings. The
> third, partaking of both *Mercy* and *Justice*, and a Memoriall and seal
> of both, is the *Rainebow* after the Deluge. (*ED*, 95–6)

These Old Testament types can, therefore, provide a trans-historical declaration
of the character of God, and by providing exemplars of the principles by which
God operates, short-circuit the bitter, and for Donne, ultimately purposeless
debates about the minutiae of God's operations, the questions *de modo* that he
consistently denounced. A similar dynamic is evident in Donne's identification
of Christ as the subject

> of all the Scriptures, of all that was shadowed in the Types, and
> figured in the ceremonies, and prepared in the preventions of the
> Law, of all that was foretold by the Prophets, of all that the Soule of
> man rejoiced in, and congratulated with the Spirit of God, in the
> *Psalms*, and in the *Canticles*, and the cheerefull parts of spirituall joy
> and exaltation, which we have in the Scriptures; Christ is the founda-
> tion of all these Scriptures, Christ is the burden of all those songs;
> Christ was in *sermone* then, then he was in the Word. (I, 287–8)

The centrality of Christ gives a unity to scripture that extends over all variations
of genre, and this unity both makes possible, and is itself made possible by, the
power of typology.

   The passage, quoted above, in which Donne speaks of the allegorical potential
of the Exodus, is the high-point of the allegorical mode of interpretation in his
oeuvre. Certainly, with the exception of the comment on the spiritual sense of
scripture quoted from the sermons, and of his acknowledgment, in the *Essayes*,
that scripture 'hath this common with all other books, that *words* signifie *things*;
but hath this particular, that all *things* signifie *other things*' (*ED*, 10). Donne does
not explicitly endorse allegorical interpretation of scripture. We can, however, see
him use this mode in his earlier sermons, and especially in those sermons preached
on the Psalms. Thus, in a sermon delivered at Lincoln's Inn, on Psalm 38:2,
Donne laid out his sermon based on a typological engagement with the passage:

> Which words we shall first consider, as they are our present object, as they are historically, and literally to be understood of *David*; And secondly, in their *retrospect*, as they look back upon the first *Adam*, and so concern *Mankind collectively*, and so *you*, and *I*, and all have our portion in these calamities; And thirdly, we shall consider them in their *prospect*, in their future relation to the *second Adam*, in *Christ Jesus*, in whom also all mankinde was collected ... for this Psalm, determin'd in *David*; some, a *Catholique*, and a *universall* Psalm, extended to the whole condition of *man*; and some a *Propheticall*, and *Evangelicall* Psalm, directed upon *Christ*. None of them inconveniently; for we receive help and health, from every one of these acceptations. (II, 75)

Donne uses this method throughout his earlier sermons on the Psalms, and this early use of allegorical interpretation is a little formulaic and even somewhat restrictive – the contrast with Donne's later sermons on the Psalms is marked.[21] Thus, it is clear that the effort to understand Donne's exegesis as an inflection of medieval hermeneutics is doomed to failure. The use that he makes of allegory is limited in its scope, and is influenced more by the developments in rhetorical awareness than by medieval exegesis. Certainly, it cannot be said to be a dominant feature of his interpretation of the Bible.

And this is true, even in the *Essayes*, where Donne's use of allegorical interpretation is most marked. Even in this relatively early work, Donne privileges a literal understanding of scripture above any allegorical or typological methods. So, Donne alerts his readers to the danger that Lyra is 'perchance too Allegorical and Typick' (*ED*, 10) and contends that Moses' purpose in writing Genesis was to provide 'such examples as might mollifie the Jews in their wandering', and therefore 'to put him in a wine-presse, and squeeze out Philosophy and particular Christianity, is a degree of injustice, which all laws forbid, to torture a man, *sine iudiciis aut sine probationibus*' (*ED*, 17). More explicitly, Donne states that:

> The word of God is not the word of God in any other sense then the literall, and that also is not the literall, which the letter seems to present, for so to diverse understandings there might be diverse literall senses; but it is called literall, to distinguish it from the Morall, Allegoricall, and the other senses; and is that which the Holy Ghost doth in that place principally intend. (*ED*, 46)

Donne is clearly stating his preference for the literal sense of scripture, but is careful to refine his definition of literal interpretation. He is, as Quinn states,

21 See I, 291; II, 97–8; II, 139.

rejecting 'both the literalistic and the fanciful without rejecting the services of either scholarship or spiritual insight'.[22]

One of the most fundamental debates of the Reformation centred on the issue of how precisely Christ's words 'this is my body' were to be interpreted and understood. Donne identified this issue as belonging properly to the debate on the figurative use of scripture. In the same sermon, he explicitly describes allegorical interpretations as a perfunctory and superficial reading of scripture, and demonstrated his awareness of the sort of biased interpretation that we have already seen:

> If a man read the scriptures a little, superficially, perfunctorily, his eyes seem straightwaies enlightened, and he thinks he sees everything he had pre-conceived, and fore-imagined in himselfe, as cleare as the Sun in the Scriptures. He can finde flesh in the Sacrament, without bread, because he findes *Hoc est Corpus meum*, *This is my body*, and he will take no more of that hony, no more of those places of Scripture, where Christ saies, *Ego vitis* and *Ego Porta*, that is he is *a Vine* and he is *a Gate*, as literally as he seems to say, *that that is his Body*. (V, 39)

Donne's non-controversial discussions of the correct method of understanding scripture all confirm his own personal predilection for a literal hermeneutic as the normative mode of engagement with scripture. In a later sermon, he again depicted allegorical interpretation as something that had been outgrown. Here he aligns it not with the Fathers, but with the Jewish interpreters of scripture:

> The Jews were as School-boys, always spelling, and putting together Types and Figures; which things typified and figured, how this Lamb should signifie *Christ*, how this fire should signifie a *holy Ghost*. The Christian is come from school to University, from Grammar to Logick, to him that is *Logos* it self, the Word; to apprehend and apply Christ himself; and so is at more liberty then when he had onely a dark law without any comment, with the natural man; or onely a dark comment, that is the Law, with a dimme light, and ill eys, as the Jews had: for though the Jew had the liberty of a Law, yet they had not the law of Liberty. (VIII, 351)

This comment is notable for its seemingly self-conscious use of the terms of contemporary philology. God's revelation has developed, and the changing nature of that revelation demands a like evolution of exegesis. The movement in

---

22 Quinn, 'Donne's principles of exegesis', 316.

both is from picture to word, from type to antitype, from allegory to text. The New Testament Christians, then, had progressed to that point where they were properly occupied with 'the right use of the true, and naturall, the native and genuine, the direct, and literall, and uncontrovertible sense of the words' (VII, 120).

The tensions informing Donne's preference for a literal understanding of scripture can also be seen in a sermon preached in St Dunstan's on the text Lamentations 3:1: 'I am the man, that hath seen affliction, by the rod of his wrath'. Donne spends some time at the beginning of the sermon attempting to define who the man primarily referred to in text is. He points out the affinity between this phrase and the words used in Pilate's presentation of the scourged Christ to the Jewish multitude, *Ecce homo*. This similarity has led 'many of the ancient Expositors [to] take these words *prophetically* of *Christ* himselfe; and that Christ himselfe who says, *Behold and see if there be any sorrow, like unto my sorrow*, says here also, *I am the man, that hath seen affliction* . . .' (X, 193). In this instance, Donne uses one typical reading to buttress another, and his objection is less that such a reading evacuates the literal meaning of the text, than that 'there are some other passages in this Chapter, that are not so conveniently appliable to Christ'. Donne rejects the suggestion that the text speaks of Jerusalem by a reference to the words used in the inspired text: 'but then it would not be expressed in that *Sex*, it would not be said of *Jerusalem, I am the man*'. He also rejects a reading that suggests the passage deals with 'any *particular*, that had his part in that calamity, in that captivity; that the affliction was so universall upon all of that nation of what condition soever, that *every man* might justly say, *Ego vir, I am the man*' (X, 193–4). Donne objects to this reading because it eliminates the possibility of understanding the text, and its wider context, literally:

> But then all this chapter must be *figurative*, and still, where we can, it becomes, it behoves us, to maintain a *literall sense* and interpretation of all Scriptures. And *that* we shall best do in this place, if we understand these words literally.

It is notable here that Donne appears to differentiate between a figurative reading, and a typical reading. The typical reading appears to have greater validity for Donne, because of his belief, already seen, that all scripture speaks of Christ. But just as telling is his insistence on the importance of context in validating the reading – he is following his own rules about maintaining the integrity of scripture.

Donne's interpretation of scripture, then, is not one that can be summarised in terms of simple polarities. The situation is more complicated than that. In the *Devotions*, Donne gives us an insight to the importance that a tension between the literal and the allegorical had for his theology, in its strictest sense:

> My *God*, my *God*, Thou art a *direct God*, may I not say, a *literall God*,
> a *God* that wouldest bee understood *literally*, and according to the
> *plaine sense* of all that thou saiest? But thou art also ... a *figurative*, a
> *metaphoricall God* too: A *God* in whose words there is such a height of
> *figures*, such *voyages*, such *peregrinations* to fetch remote and precious
> *metaphors*, such *extentions*, such *spreadings*, such *Curtaines* of
> *Allegories*, such *third Heavens* of *Hyperboles*, so *harmonious eloquutions*,
> so *retired* and so *reserved expressions*, so *commanding perswasions*, such
> *sinews* even in thy *milke*, and such *things* in thy *words*, as all *prophane*
> *Authors*, seeme of the seed of the *Serpant*, that *creepes*; thou art the
> dove, that flies. O, what words but thine, can expresse the inexpress-
> ible *texture*, and *composition* of thy *word*. (*D*, 99)

Away from the hortatory context of the sermons, Donne's balancing of the
literal and the allegorical is revealed as essential to his understanding of his God.
It is this God that breathed out scripture, scripture takes its character from him,
and a God who eschews the resources of figurative language is a God too prosaic
for Donne. The poet who expected and awaited eternal conformity to God, a
conformity that seemed imminent as he penned his *Devotions*, anticipated unity
with a greater, and not a lesser, poet. In general, then, Donne's preference is
clearly for a sensitive use of the literal sense that acknowledges, allows for, and
exults in the use of figurative language.

LOCATING INTERPRETATIVE AUTHORITY

Donne's treatment of scripture owed a good deal to the developments of the
Reformation. The most characteristically reformed element of that treatment
was the place that he gave to the individual engagement with scripture. Donne
trusted his lay readers, and never simply wanted them to rely on what they had
been taught, without the use of their own intellect and understanding. We can
see Donne's dynamic interplay of ecclesiastical and lay interpretation at work
right from his earliest prose works. In *Pseudo-martyr* and the *Essayes in divinity*,
Donne, then himself a layman, creates a freedom for his own engagement with
scripture. Once ordained, he allowed much of that same freedom to his congregations. The fact that Donne writes in these volumes as a layman appears to
trouble him, and he opens the *Essayes* with an apology for this fact:

> ... the holy Scriptures ... have these properties of a well provided
> Castle, that they are easily defensible, and safely defend others. So
> they have also this, that to strangers they open but a little wicket, and
> he that will enter, must stoop and humble himselfe. To reverend

> Divines, who by an ordinary calling are Officers and Commissioners
> from God, the great Doors are open. Let me with *Lazarus* lie at the
> threshold, and beg their crums. (*ED*, 7)

In coming to scripture, the private individual must be guided by 'outward interpretations', by expositions of the passages that fit within the general
understanding of the church. It is worthy of note that Donne, in the passage
quoted, links this preparation for exegesis with societal, as much as with ecclesiastical, authority.

This imbrication becomes more explicit in *Biathanatos*. In dealing with this
work, we must bear in mind its complexity in terms of its genre, its readership
and, more fundamentally, its intent. Remembering, then, that it is an odd book,
we may still observe some characteristic features of Donne's engagement with
scripture at work. Commenting, in the third division to this volume, on the
authority of scripture, Donne accords with the Roman church's traditional
reading of 2 Peter 1:20: 'That no prophesy in the Scripture is of private interpretation'. This means that 'the whole Church may not be bound and
concluded by the fancy of one, or of a few, who being content to enslumber
themselues in an opinion and a lazy preiudice, dreame arguments to establish
and to authorise that' (*B*, 110). This reading contrasts instructively with the
more Protestant understanding of the text that stressed the importance of
understanding scripture in context, of comparing scripture with scripture in
order to uncover its true meaning. Donne's appeal, by contrast, is to ecclesiastical authority. A little later, however, he broadens the scope of 'outward
interpretations' in a notable manner. Firstly, Donne instances Deuteronomy
32:39, 'I kill and I give Life'. From this, it 'is concluded, that all authority of
Life and death is from God, and none in our selues'. Donne rebuts this
assumption by reference to societial convention:

> But shall we therefore dare to condemne vtterly, all those States and
> Gouernments, where Fathers, Husbands and Masters had
> Iurisdiction ouer Children, Wifes and seruant's Lifes? If we dare, yet
> how shall we defend any Magistracy, if this be so strictly accepted?
> (*B*, 115)

He resorts to a very similar argument when dealing with the seventh
commandment:

> For though the Words be generall *Thou shalt not Kill*, we may kill
> beastes, Magistrates may kill Men; and a priuate Man in a Iuste warre
> may not onely kill, contrary to the sound of this Commandement, but
> he may kill his Father Contrary to another. (*B*, 116)

It is worthy of note that, rather than referring his readers to those parts of scripture that institute capital punishment, Donne directs us to the prevailing practice of the society in which he lives. This strategy is scarcely very risky, as Donne could rely on his readers' ability to trace that allusion for themselves. Nonetheless, the appeal to cultural practice gives Donne's contention force and emphasis, while stressing for us the importance that he attaches to an interpretative community by which scripture is mediated to the private individual.

In *Pseudo-martyr*, *Biatanathos* and, to a lesser extent, the *Essayes in divinity*, the interpretative community includes the ecclesiastical, the political and the legal authorities invoked and addressed in these works. In the sermons, Donne speaks as a man committed to the church in which he ministers and as a preacher conscious of his responsibility to address the varied religious needs of his congregation. Thus it is that his focus remains more firmly on the interpretative tradition provided by the church. As Shami has pointed out, Donne's interpretive middle way is

> a practice grounded in his understanding of the Church of England
> as a locus of Christian 'mediocrity' that enables the handling of sensi-
> tive controversial matter in the pulpit. It is a principle of exegesis
> developed in response to the extremes of Roman Catholicism on the
> one hand and separatism on the other, and it marks, for Donne, the
> rhetorical, spiritual and ecclesiological boundaries of what he calls
> 'our' church, the Church of England.[23]

There is need for nuance in understanding his use of this tradition: Donne, himself, was at pains to explicitly privilege scripture above any other source of religious authority. For Donne, as for other reformation divines, the church that interprets scripture remains subordinate to that scripture that validates her existence. This conviction he makes very clear, stating, for example, that 'the *foundations* of the *Church* are the *Scriptures*' (VIII, 73).

This does not sound like the Protestantism of Whig historiography. Where, we might ask, is the great reformation watch cry of *sola scriptura* in this appeal to the authority of the church? Questions of this sort indicate a certain naïvety about the teaching of scripture in the Protestant churches of the Reformation. In fact, *sola scriptura* never really meant that scripture would not be interpreted on the behalf of the individual believer. On the contrary, all the magisterial reformers and a great many of their followers were indefatigable commentators on scripture, constantly providing interpretative guidance. It is inaccurate to represent *sola scriptura* as a call for the radical abandonment of exegetical tradi-tion.[24] Such an understanding is excessively simplistic, and it is helpful to note Pelikan's nuancing of this historiographical truism:

23 Shami, 'Squint-eyed', 173.   24 See, for an example of this tendency, Bainton, 'Bible in the

It is a commonplace of theological and historical literature going back to the Protestant Reformers themselves that the sole authority of Scriptura, *Sola Scriptura*, was one of the fundamental principles of Reformation theology to which the authority of tradition had to yield, and that therefore, the Reformers no longer regarded Scripture and Tradition as two sources of divine revelation, nor even as a single source in two modalities. The confusions at work in this conventional wisdom have received helpful clarification through Heiko Oberman's 'two concepts of Tradition'.[25]

Rather than viewing a distinction between *sola scriptura* and tradition, Oberman posits two types of tradition:

> We call the single-source or exegetical tradition of Scripture held together with its interpretation 'Tradition I' and the two-sources theory which allows for an extra-biblical oral tradition 'Tradition II'.[26]

His remark, made in the specific context of his own work that 'the representatives of the first concept of Tradition by no means isolate Holy Scripture by divorcing it from Tradition understood as the history of the interpretation of scripture,' is equally valid in the context of the Reformation and of Donne's work.[27]

It would be wrong to portray Donne's understanding of the church's authority as simply a resource of homiletic convenience. He attached a great deal of importance to the precedent and order provided in ecclesiastical tradition. Always inclined to conservatism, Donne firmly believed that 'God loves not innovation', but 'old doctrines, old disciplines, old words and formes of speech in his service, God loves best' (II, 305). In Donne's understanding, reformation was renovation rather than innovation. Thus, in his sermon of valediction, preached before his departure for Germany in 1619, he drew a parallel between the actions of God in Creation, and in the church:

> ... here God raises up men to convey to us the dew of his grace, by waters under the firmament; by visible sacraments, and by the word

---

Reformation'. **25** Pelikan, *Reformation of the Bible*, p. 27. **26** Heiko A. Oberman, *The harvest of medieval theology: Gabriel Biel and late medieval nominalism* (Oxford, 1963), p. 371. This recognition that *sola scriptura* practically requires an exegetical tradition is at the heart of Richard Hooker's observation of Calvin: 'Of what accompt the Maister of sentences was in the Church of Rome, the same and more amongst the preachers of the reformed Churches Calvin had purchased ... His bookes almost the the very canon to judge both doctrine and discipline by': Hooker, *Works*, I, 11. **27** Oberman, *Dawn of the reformation*, p. 391.

> so preach'd, and so interpreted, as it hath been constantly, and unani-
> mously from the beginning of the Church ... God hath gathered all
> the waters of life in one place; that is all the doctrine necessary for the
> life to come, into his Church. ... And in this third daies work God
> repeats here that testimony ... he saw that it was good; good, that
> there should be a gathering of waters in one place, that is, no doctrine
> reciev'd that hath not been taught in the Church. (II, 242)

The church, therefore is the exemplar of doctrine, a body that determines the
truth, and hence the necessity, of doctrine. Antiquity is the yard-stick. The insistence upon the beginning of the church is vital, for it excludes, for Donne, the
accretion of tradition, and those 'interlineary doctrines, and marginal glosses',
which 'were but to vent the passion of vehement men, or to serve the turns of
great men for a time', and 'which were no part of the first text'. In eliminating
the teaching provided by paratextual apparatus Donne dismissed, at once, the
teaching of the Catholic Douay-Rheims translation and the Calvinistic notes to
the Geneva Bible.

It is crucial in our understanding of Donne's views of the status of scripture,
to note that the authority of the church is never mentioned without the place of
scripture also being stressed. Thus, in a defence of the practice of fasting, which
forms the opening to a sermon preached during Lent of 1625, Donne stresses
that the church cannot exist without the authority of scriptures:

> The Scriptures are Gods Voyce; The Church is his Eccho; a redou-
> bling, a repeating of some particular syllables, and accents of the same
> voice. And as we harken with some earnestnesse, and some admiration
> at an Eccho; so doe the obedient children of God apply themselves to
> the Eccho of his Church, when perchance otherwise, they would lesse
> understand the voice of God, in his Scriptures, if that voice were not
> so redoubled unto them. (VI, 223)

The figure of an echo is a telling one. Authoritative teaching originates with
scripture, and the church has no existence without it. The church, then, is a
mediator, and an interpreter of truth, and not its source. This mediatorial
function is something that Donne regularly stresses. Thus, in a later sermon, he
presents the church as the final link in the chain of divine manifestation: 'God
hath manifested himselfe to man in Christ; and manifested Christ in the scriptures; and manifested the scriptures in the Church' (VIII, 145). One year later,
Donne developed this point: 'we have a clearer, that is, a nearer light then the
written Gospell, that is, the Church' (VIII, 307). It is not that the church is
superior to scripture in its authority; it is clearer because nearer; it is the
mediator that makes the Word of God present and relevant. A similar imbrication of scripture and church is outlined by Donne in 1625:

> That which the *Scripture* says, *God* sayes (says St *Augustine*) for the Scripture is his word; and that which the *Church* says, the *Scriptures* say, for she is their word, they speak *in her*; they authorize her, and she explicates them; The *Spirit* of God *inanimates* the Scriptures, and makes them *his* Scriptures, the *Church actuates* the Scriptures, and makes them *our Scriptures.* (VI, 282)

Having thus safeguarded the extent of the church's authority, and having stressed again the primacy of scripture, Donne extols the benefits of submission to the church's teaching: 'There is not so wholsome a thing, no soul can live in so good an aire, and in so good a diet, ... Then still to submit a mans owne particular reason, to the authority of the Church expressed in the Scriptures'. The church, then, is 'the *Trumpet* in which God sounds his *Judgements*, and the *Organ*, in which he delivers his *mercy*' (VI, 283). Thus, if men 'will pretend to *heare Christ*, they must heare him there, where he hath promised to speake, they must *heare him in the Church*'.

For Donne, the mediation of scripture by the church is a safeguard against the danger of singularity and schism. It guarantees the integrity of the interpretative community; it underwrites the public and shared nature of scripture. So, he urges his hearers to

> Beleeve those things which the Saints of God have constantly and unanimely believed to be necessary to salvation: The Word is the Law, and the Rule, The Church is the Practice, and the Precedent that regulates thy faith; And if thou make imaginary revelations and inspirations thy Law, or the practise of Sectaries thy Precedent, thou doest but call Fancie and Imagination, by the name of Reason and Understanding, and Opinion by the name of Faith, and Singularity, and Schisme, by the name of Communion of Saints. The Law of thy faith is, That that that thou beleevest, be Universall, Catholique, believed by all. (VII, 263)

The polar opposite of this true Catholic is the 'Pharisee, that by following private expositions, separates himselfe from our Church' (IX, 169), seduced, by an excess of exegetical hubris, into severing the association that gives religious life its structure and meaning.[28] Donne plays on the possible meanings of Pharisee – separation and exposition – and identifies in a love of 'private interpretations' the separation from the teaching of the church, and 'a contempt of all antiquity; and not only an undervaluation, but a detestation of all opinions but his owne, and his, whom he hath set up for his idol' (IX, 168).[29] A propensity to doctrinal

---

28 See Franklin Hamlin Littell, *The origins of sectarian protestantism: a study of the Anabaptist view of the church* (New York, 1964). 29 Cf. Hooker, *Works*, I, 15–19, 44.

innovation and to schism corresponds for Donne with an organic unsuitability for communal religious life.

The ideal, for the conscientious Christian, was a humility that combined an awareness of personal limitations with a willingness to seek for help, and the wisdom to look for such help in the right place:

> And therefore, forebearing to make any interpretation at all, upon dark places of Scripture (especially those, whose understanding depends upon the future fulfilling of prophecies) in places that are clear, and evident thou maist be thine own interpreter; in places that are more obscure, goe to those men, whom God hath set over thee, and either they shall give thee that sense of that place, which shall satisfie thee, by having the sense thereof, or that must satisfie you, that there is enough for your salvation, though that remaine uninterpreted. (IV, 221)

It is typical that, in this sermon, Donne insists on the importance of an ecclesiastical calling to validate exegesis, even while stressing the need for each individual to possess and read scripture, and indeed, juxtaposes these two truths in as many sentences:

> It is not a bare *reading*, but a diligent *searching*, that is enjoyned us. Now they that search must have a warrant to search: they upon whom thou must rely for the sense of Scriptures, must be sent of God by his Church. (IV, 219)

The interpretative role of the church is, therefore, a flexible nexus, which has considerable power as an expository device and as a pastoral aid. This understanding falls firmly within Obermann's Tradition II. Donne's position is balanced and moderate and it is this moderation that he wants to inculcate in his congregation. In this respect, as in many others, Donne uses his commemorative sermon on Lady Danvers to describe the ideal parishioner, and, by extension, the paragon Christian:

> [S]hee govern'd her selfe, *according to his promises*; his promises, laid downe in his *Scriptures*. For, as the *rule* of all her *civill Actions*, was *Religion*, so, the *rule* of her *Religion*, was the *Scripture*; And, her *rule*, for her Particular understanding of the *Scripture*, was the *Church*. Shee never diverted towards the *Papist*, in undervaluing the *Scripture*; nor towards the *Separatist*, in undervaluing the *Church*. (VII, 90)

Ecclesiastical precedent and authority set the bounds of scriptural interpretation. For Donne, there is a fundamental importance to the interaction of the individual Christian with the words of Holy Scripture. Such an engagement was controlled, but crucial; it brought the risk of error, but remained indispensable. Donne wants his hearers to be readers and understanders of scripture. We have seen that it is the divine inspiration of scripture makes vernacular translations essential, a point that Donne emphasised as he preached the first sermon to the new King Charles in 1625.[30] This sermon is of considerable importance: in it we have Donne's survey of the English church at this significant point in her history. We have already seen Donne deal with the importance of ecclesiastical sanction in this sermon: it is notable then that this extract explicitly stresses the right of the lay man to try controversies by scripture:

> [T]he *foundation* it selfe is Christ himselfe in his *Worde*; his *Scriptures*. And then, certainly they love the *House* best, that love the *foundation* best: not they, that impute to the *Scriptures* such an *Obscuritie*, as should make them *in-intelligible* to us, or such a defect as should make them *insufficient* in themselves. To denie us the use of *Scriptures* in our vulgar *Translations*, and yet to denie us the use of them, in the *Originall* Tongues too, to tell us we must not trie *Controversies* by our *English*, or our *Latine Bibles*, nor by the *Hebrew Bibles* neither, To put such a Majestie upon the *Scriptures*, as that a Lay man may not touch them, and yet to put such a diminution upon them, as that the writings of men shall bee equall to them; this is a wrinching, a shrinking, a sinking, an undermining, a destroying of *Foundations*, of the *foundation* of this first *House*, which is the *Church*, the *Scriptures*. (VI, 253)

Likewise, in an earlier sermon, Donne had extolled the importance of a detailed private engagement with scripture:

> Thou art robbed of all, devested of all, if the Scriptures be taken from thee; Thou hast no where to search; blesse God therefore, that hath kept thee in possession of that sacred Treasure, the *Scriptures*; and then, if any part of that treasure ly out of thy reach, or ly in the dark, so as thou understandest not the place, *search*, that is, apply thy self to them that have warrant to *search*, and thou shalt lack no light necessary for thee. (IV, 219)

30 This sermon is discussed in some detail in Peter E. McCullough, 'Donne as preacher at court: precarious "inthronization"' in *John Donne's Professional lives*, ed. David Colclough (Cambridge, 2003), pp 179–204; Mark Sweetnam, 'Foundational faults: heresy and religious toleration in the later thought of John Donne' in *Heresy and orthodoxy in early English literature*, ed. Eiléan Ní Chuilleanáin and John Flood (Dublin, 2010), pp 113–26.

And this engagement was vital for all of God's people, regardless of age or sex:

> It is but a woman that Saint *Hierome* saith ... Love the Scriptures, and wisdom will love thee: The weaknesse of her *Sex* must not avert her from *reading* the Scriptures. It is instruction for a *Childe*, and for a *Girle*, that the same Father giveth, ... As soone as she is *seaven years old*, let her learn all the *Psalmes* without book; the tendernesse of her age, must not avert her from Scriptures. It is to the whole Congregation, consisting of all sorts and sexes, that Saint *Chrysostome* saith, ... I always doe, and always will exhort you, ... that at home, in your owne houses, you accustome your selves to a dayly reading of the Scriptures. (IV, 219)

It is important to recall that Donne did begin this section by cautioning his congregation that 'they that will search, must have a warrant to search; they upon whom thou must rely for the sense of the Scriptures, must be sent of God by his Church'. Thus, this engagement with scripture is set in a context controlled by the church. Nevertheless, his injunction that 'it is not a bare *reading*, but a diligent *searching* that is enjoyned us' (IV, 219) makes it clear that that this individual encounter with scripture is not merely to be a cosmetic exercise.

This theme resonates throughout Donne's career – he insisted, early in his career, that 'to beleeve implicitly as the Church believes, and know nothing, is not enough; know thy foundations, and who laid them' (III, 239). Later he stressed the same point: 'Blinde and implicite faith shall not serve us in matter of Doctrine, nor blinde and implicite obedience, in matter of practice' (VIII, 137). Even those who, like the un-ordained Donne, stand at the threshold 'see enough to instruct and secure [them]' (*ED*, 8). So, while it was given only to God's priests – fitted, by their ordination, to pass beyond the threshold – to see the 'treasure of saving mysteries', it was open to all, and incumbent upon all, to 'study God'. Such is the freedom and responsibility that Donne allows to the common reader of scripture. We may also observe his very characteristic endeavour to control that individual exegetical freedom – care is required that efforts to understand scripture do not transgress the bounds of curiosity, or that the individual does not aspire to a knowledge that is inappropriate to their position.

And these themes run right through Donne's sermons, revealing his willingness to allow his congregations the same freedom that he has appropriated to himself. This willingness is based firmly upon his conviction that there is a core of fundamental saving knowledge available to all – visible from the threshold. In this view, Donne was inflecting a long tradition in the understanding of scripture, a tradition that Hooker traced to Augustine himself:

> Some things are so familier and plaine, that truth from falsehood, and good from evill is most easily discerned in them, even by men of no deepe capacitie. And of that nature, for the most part are things absolutely unto all mens salvation necessarie, eyther to be held or denied, eyther to be done or avoided. For which cause Saint Augustine acknowledgeth that they are not only set downe, but also plainlely set down in Scripture: so that he which heareth or readeth may, without any great difficultie, understand.[31]

Donne stressed this point, in a Lent sermon, preached before the king, taking 1 Timothy 3:16 for his text. The two parts of the sermon highlighted manifestation and mystery, and in balancing these two, Donne stresses that the Apostle 'recommends to us such Doctrine as is without controversie: and truly there is enough of that to save any soule, that hath not a minde to wrangle it selfe into Hell' (III, 207). It was necessary for the Christian to know this doctrine: 'not to labour to understand the scriptures, is to slight God' (III, 208). In an image that called into question the exegetical purpose and helpfulness of the Calvinist annotations of the Geneva translation, he remarked that 'it is the Text that saves us; the interlineary glosses, and the marginal notes, and the *varie lectiones*, controversies and perplexities, undo us: the will, the Testament of God, enriches us; the Schedules, the Codicils of men, begger us' (III, 208).[32] Ironically, the matrix of hermeneutical control provided by the radical Protestants behind the Geneva version was impinging upon the status of scripture in a way potentially as harmful as Roman tradition or the marginal glosses of the Douay Bible. The ideal for his auditors was 'in ... all Mysteries of your Religion, to rest upon the onley word of God' (III, 212). Scripture alone provided the basis for the Christian life: 'upon the foundations laid by God in the scriptures, and not upon the super-edifications of men, in traditionall additions must wee build' (X, 109). Towards the end of his life, Donne was still encouraging his parishioners to engage with scripture, and was steadfast in his belief that 'the Scriptures were not written for a few, nor are to be reserved for a few' (IX, 123–4). This echoed his earlier expression that 'the hand of God hath written so, as a man may runne and read; walk in the duties of his calling here, and attend the salvation of his soul too' (III, 208). Similarly, in his Easter sermon for 1630, Donne, speaking on the visit of the faithful women to the tomb of Christ, stated that 'though all Scriptures be proposed to all, and Gods secret purposes proposed to none, yet the fundementall doctrines of the Christian faith

---

31 Hooker, *Works*, I, 13. 32 Donne was echoing royal policy, for the instructions to the translators of the 1611 King James Version, as reported to the Synod of Dort, clearly stated that 'no notes were to be placed in the margin, but only parallel passages to be noted': Alfred W. Pollard, ed. *Records of the English Bible: the documents relating to the translation and publication of the Bible in English, 1525–1611* (Oxford, 1911), p. 339.

are proposed to all, the weakest of all, These women had heard Christ' (IX, 212). Later, Donne exulted that saints of all abilities were able to benefit from reading scripture:

> Begin a *Lambe*, and thou will become a *Lion*; Reade the Scriptures modestly, humbly, and thou shalt understand them strongly, power-fully; for hence is it that Saint *Chrysostome*, more than once, and Saint *Gregory* after him, meet in that expression, That the Scriptures are a Sea, in which a *Lambe* may wade, and an *Elephant* may swimme. (IX, 124)

This quotation clearly illustrates Donne's belief that the scriptures are able to accommodate all abilities and capacities. But it also makes another point. Men and women of all abilities ought to be immersing themselves in scripture: there is no excuse for simply standing on the shore.

In spite of Donne's insistence on the simplicity of the scriptures when approached and used correctly, he still acknowledges that not all scripture is easy to understand. He admits this, in a Trinity Sunday sermon preached in St Dunstan's in 1627. He carefully couched this admission to maintain the revela-tory function of scripture, and, by virtue of a rather ingenious piece of exposition, gave it a characteristically pastoral twist:

> [T]he Apostle sayes, *Whatsoever things are written afore time, are written for our learning*; But yet, not so for our learning, as that we should think always to learne, or always to have a cleare understanding of all that is written; for it is added there, *That we, through patience, and comfort of the Scriptures, might have hope*; Which may well admit this Exposition, that those things which we understand not yet, we may hope that we shall, and we must have patience till we doe. For there may be many places in Scripture (especially in Propheticall Scripture), which, perchance, the Church of God her selfe, shall not understand, till those Prophecies be fulfilled, and accomplished. (VIII, 39)

He adopted a rather similar strategy in a sermon preached in 1622, remarking that 'It is true, in some places [the scriptures] are dark; purposely left so by the Holy Ghost ... lest we should think we had done when we had read them once' (IV, 220). This explanation for the obscurity of scripture is, as Dennis Quinn has pointed out, 'a venerable commonplace, traceable to Clement of Alexandria and Origen, and repeated by Christians down to and beyond Donne's time'.[33] A

---

33 Dennis B. Quinn, 'Donne and the wane of wonder', *ELH* 36:4 (1969), 630.

similar dynamic is at work, as Quinn also suggests, in Expostulation XIX of Donne's *Devotions*, where Donne places God's 'reserved' expressions alongside his plain and direct speech, and insists that there is a place for both (*D*, 99–103).

Donne's views on the interpretation of scripture are highly nuanced, and elude any attempt at polarised definition. The interplay of individual and church is lively and pastorally essential. By way of emphasising this point, it is useful to look at those passages where Donne speaks explicitly of reading scripture at home, for here those factors that we have already observed at work come into play in a very explicit way. It is interesting to note that these passages are clustered towards the end of Donne's preaching career. This is highly significant in light of the avant-garde conformist trend, remarked by Peter McCullough, towards 'increasing attempts to restrict the rights of Scriptural interpretation to the clerisy'.[34] It is true that the earlier discussions considered below occur before this tendency had fully developed. Nonetheless, Donne's persistence in it indicates his continuing commitment to facilitating the individual's engagement with scripture.

Possibly the earliest of these references to the private reading of scripture is found in a sermon conjecturally assigned, by Potter and Simpson, to 1623. In this extract, Donne stresses the importance of the church as the means of the application of scripture to the individual life in terms very consonant with those that we have already seen:

> You believe, because the great Angel Christ Jesus, hath left his history, his action and passion written for you; and that is historical faith. But yet salvation is nearer to you, in having all this applied to you, by them, who are like you, men, and there, where you know how to fetch it, the Church; That as you believe by reading the Gospels at home, that Christ died for the world, So you may believe, by hearing here, that he dyed for you.[35] (X, 50)

Curiously enough, it is in the communal context of the church that the individual is reached by this awareness of the personal relevance of Christ's saving work.

The second reference chronologically was made in a sermon preached in St Paul's in 1624/5. In this brief, almost glancing, reference, Donne does seem to be attempting the control of individual exposition. Speaking of the conversion of Saul, Donne stated:

---

34 McCullough, 'Donne as preacher', 201.   35 It is interesting that Donne uses Tyndale's concept of a historical faith – belief in the facts of the life of Christ – that must be distinguished from the feeling faith that resulted from the individual appropriation of the salvation that resulted from these facts: see William Tyndale, *The works of William Tyndale*, ed. G.E. Duffield (Appleford, 1964), pp 368–80.

> First then, what he was at that time, the Holy Ghost gives evidence
> enough against him, and he gives enough against himselfe. Of that
> which the Holy Ghost gives, you may see a great many heavy pieces,
> a great many applicable circumstances, if any time, at home, you do
> but paraphrase, and spread to yourselves the former part of this
> Chapter, to this text. Take a little preparation from me. (VI, 206)

Donne here is encouraging the private reading of the verses, encouraging his
congregation to unpack the truth of the passage in a way that the exigencies of
the sermon will not permit. However, rather than simply sending them off with
Bible in hand, Donne is interested in giving them some preparation. He is
adumbrating his guidelines for the most pastorally profitable understanding of
the passage. It is telling that, even when dealing with a very straightforward piece
of Biblical narrative, Donne desires to 'prepare' his congregation.

   In later sermons, Donne uses another strategy to safeguard the importance of
the church's role. In these extracts, teaching is seen as originating in the church,
and then being remembered by the individual at home, as he re-reads the scriptures that have previously been brought to his notice. So, in 1627, he told his
congregation:

> The Holy Ghost shall teach you *all things*, and bring *all things* to your
> remembrance: And here is the Latitude, the Totality, the Integrality
> of the meanes of salvation; you shall have Scriptures delivered to you,
> by them the Holy Ghost shall teach you all things; and then you shall
> be remembered of all, by the explication and application of those
> Scriptures, at Church, where lies the principall operation of the Holy
> Ghost. ... But when men have a Christian liberty afforded to them to
> read the Scriptures at home, and then are remembred of those things
> at Church, and there taught to use that liberty modestly, to establish
> their faith upon places of Scripture that are plain, and to suspend
> their judgement upon obscurer places, till they may, by due meanes,
> preaching or conference, receive farther satisfaction therein, from
> them, who are therteunto authorized by God in his Church. (VII,
> 401)

This extract serves as a neat summary of Donne's views on interpretative
authority. In addition, it is valuable to note the wider context of this extract – this
sermon constitutes an attack on the Roman church for denying the scriptures to
the layman and for failing to expound them by means of preaching. Thus, the
context of these remarks does depict the dialogue between church exposition
and private exegesis as a vital 'Christian liberty'. Joshua Scodel, in his discussion
of Donne's depiction of a truly desirable mean, expresses the bivalency of this

sermon, arguing, on the one hand, that, in the sermon as a whole, Donne 'applies the language of Pyrrhonist scepticism, in which he had articulated the individual's religious enquiry in Satire III, to urge the individual's deference to authority,' and, on the other, that it is notable in a sermon, addressed to Charles I, that Donne emphasises 'both the layman's reading of Scripture and the preaching of the Word'.[36] The fact that Donne was reprimanded for the sermon by Charles and Laud, indicates the delicate context in which Donne chose to deal with these issues, though Donne's apparent criticism of the Catholicism of Charles' wife Henrietta Maria is likely to have been what the monarch was principally concerned about.[37]

Similarly, in 1628, Donne is balancing the roles of public and private reading, although here, the private setting is rather the family circle than a truly individual engagement with scripture. Again, the order is explicit: learn at church, meditate at home.

> The most powerful meanes is the Scripture; But the Scripture in the Church. Not that we are discouraged from reading the Scripture at home: God forbid we should think any Christian family to be out of the Church. At home, the holy Ghost is with thee in the reading of the Scriptures; But there he is with thee as a Remembrancer (*The Holy Ghost shall bring to your remembrance whatsoever I have said unto you*, saies our Saviour). Here in the church, he is with thee, as a Doctor to teach thee; First learne at Church and then meditate at home, Receive the seed by hearing the Scriptures interpreted here, and water it by returning to those places at home. (VIII, 227)

Such were Donne's views on the interpretation of scripture by the private individual. These views implicitly privileged engagement with the Bible by ordained ministers, by those with a warrant from the church to search. Donne saw no difficulty with this; there were factors unique to the position of the minister that demanded a more sophisticated understanding of scripture. These factors were both pastoral and controversial and Donne outlined them very clearly:

> In the Wildernesse, every man had one and the same measure of Manna; The same Gomer went through all; for Manna was a Meat, that would melt in their mouths, and of easie digestion. But then for

---

36 Scodel, 'Religious politics', p. 63.   37 For a discussion of this censorship of Donne, see Annabel Patterson, *Censorship and interpretation: the conditions of writing and reading in early modern England* (Madison, WI, 1984), pp 110–11 and, on Donne's wider treatment of sensitive issues, see Marla Hoffman Lunderberg, 'John Donne's strategies for discreet preaching', *Studies in English Literature, 1500–1900* 44:1 (2004), 97–119.

> their Quailes, birds of a higher flight, meat of a stronger digestion, it is not said, that every man had an equall number: some might have more, some lesse, and yet all their fulnesse. Catechisticall divinity, and instructions in fundamentall things, is our Manna; Every man is bound to take in his Gomer, his explicite knowledge of Articles absolutely necessary to salvation; … But then for our Quails, birds of higher pitch, meat of a stronger digestion, which is the knowledge how to rectifie every straying conscience, how to extricate every entangled, and scrupulous, and perplexed soule, in all emergant doubts, how to defend our Church, and our Religion, from all the mines, and all the batteries of our Adversaries, and to deliver her from all imputations of Heresie, and schisme, which they impute to us, this knowledge is not necessary in all; In many cases a Master of servants, and a Father of children is bound to know more, than those children and servants, and the Pastor of the parish more than parishioners: They may have their fulnesse, though he have more, but he hath not his, except he be able to give them satisfaction. (V, 226–7)

The conscientious minister has to shoulder, *ex officio*, a heavier burden of interpretative responsibility, both to meet the challenge of religious controversy and to minister to the spiritual needs of his flock. And these are precisely those features that predominate in Donne's sermons. His account of the particular responsibility of the minister of the church echoes that expressed by Hooker. Having stated, as we have already noted, that he viewed doctrine essential for salvation as easily apprehended, Hooker goes on to delimit the special role of the minister:

> Other things also there are belonging … unto the offices of the Christian men: which, because they are more obscure, more intricate and hard to be judged of, therefore God hath appointed some to spende their whole time principally in the studie of things divine, to the end that in these more doubtfull cases their understanding might be a light to direct others.[38]

The concerns about the proper interpretation of scripture that hve been surveyed in this chapter come together in a particularly concentrated way in Donne's Easter 1624 sermon on Revelation 20:6, 'Blessed and holy is he that hath part in the first resurrection', preached in St Paul's. This sermon provides us with what is probably, apart from the *Essayes in divinity*, the longest discussion of hermeneutics in Donne's *oeuvre*. Beyond that, the sermon instantiates

38 Hooker, 13.

and exemplifies his approach to the interpretation of scripture in a way that helps us both to understand that approach and to appreciate why attempts to explain Donne's hermeneutic as either allegorical/medieval/Catholic or literal/modern/Protestant fail to offer any real illumination of his approach to scripture.

Indeed, it is a large part of Donne's purpose in this sermon to complicate precisely this binary. This is clear right from the opening sentence of the sermon:

> In the first book of the Scriptures, that of Genesis, there is danger in departing from the letter; In this last book, this of the Revelation, there is as much danger in adhering too close to the letter. (VI, 62)

This is an effective opening gambit: Donne could hardly have failed to arrest his audience's attention. But the sentence is more than an opening ploy – it summarises, with remarkable concision, the approach to scripture that underwrites this sermon, and all of Donne's other sermons. Now, as always, the stakes of Biblical interpretation are high for Donne – a failure correctly to interpret scripture is not merely wrong, it is dangerous. For all of the love of paradox that animates Donne's poetry, and in spite of the interest in the esoteric areas of kabbalistic interpretation that is evidenced in the *Essayes in divinity*, Donne in the pulpit felt, and consistently articulated, a sense of his responsibility to his congregation. But the opening of Donne's sermon also alerts us to the importance of nuance in Donne's interpretation of scripture, and its consequent importance to our understanding of it. All scripture cannot be interpreted the same way, considerations of genre have to control the appropriate hermeneutic.

The variable in this hermeneutic is closeness to the letter, and departing from and adhering to the letter sounds uncommonly like adopting an allegorical or a literal approach. But Donne is emphatic that he is not recommending the abandonment of literal interpretation:

> The literal sense is always to be preserved; but the literall sense is not alwayes to be discerned: for the literall sense is not always that, which the very Letter and Grammer of the place presents, as where it is literally said, *That Christ is a Vine*, and literally, *That his flesh is bread*, and literally, *That the new Ierusalem is thus situated, thus built, thus furnished:* But the literall sense of every place, is the principall intention of the Holy Ghost, in that place: And his principall intention in many places, is to expresse things by allegories, by figures; so that in many places of Scripture, a figurative sense is the literall sense, and more in this book than in any other. (VI, 60)

On one level, Donne is stating the obvious here, making the point that Protestant exegetes had been making all along, the point that Tyndale, to take one early example, made when he argued:

> Thou shalt understand therefore that the scripture hath but one sense which is the literal sense. And that literal sense is the root and ground of all, and the anchor that never faileth whereunto if thou cleave thoui canst never err or go out of the way. And if thou leave the literal sense thou canst not but go out of the way. Neverthelater the scripture useth proverbs, similitudes, riddles or allegories as all other speeches do, but that which the proverb, similitude, riddle or allegory signifieth is ever the literal sense which thou must seek out diligently[39]

And Tyndale illustrated the importance of a sensitivity to figurative language by reference to some of the same scriptures that Donne himself used, and acknowledged the special difficulties presented by Revelation in the same way:

> So in like manner the scripture borroweth words and sentences of all manner things and maketh proverbs and similitudes or allegories. As Christ saith (Luke 4), Physician heal thyself. Whose interpretation is do that at home which thou dost in strange places, and that is the literal sense. So when I say Christ is a lamb, I mean not a lamb that beareth wool, but a meek and patient lamb which is beaten for other men's faults. Christ is a vine, not that beareth grapes: but out of whose root the branches that believe suck the spirit of life and mercy and grace and power to be the sons of God and to do his will. The similitudes of the gospel are allegories borrowed of worldly matter to express spiritual things. The Apocalypse or Revelations of John are allegories whose literal sense is hard to find in many places.[40]

This is worth noting, for given that this is all a preamble to Donne's argument that the first resurrection of his text is not a literal resurrection at all, we might be tempted to dismiss his definition of the literal as semantics or special pleading.

Even if it is not special pleading, though, Donne's approach leaves us with the difficulty of identifying the Holy Ghost's intention, and thus the correct interpretation of the passage. It is important to notice Donne's insistence upon the objective: the task of recognising and then decoding figurative and metaphorical language may be challenging, but it is possible, for there is an objective truth being expressed in scripture. This is all well and good, but it leaves the reader

39 William Tyndale, *The obedience of the christian man*, ed. David Daniell (London, 2000), p. 136.
40 Ibid., p. 157.

and, a fortiori, the expositor of scripture with the difficulty of knowing how to approach a particular book, chapter or verse. Donne's solution to this conundrum is to look at the subjective experience that results from our interpretation. So, in the context of this sermon, he states that we know that it is wrong to interpret Genesis allegorically, we know, indeed, that it is dangerous to do so, because if we do 'we have no history of the Creation of the world in any other place to stick to' (VI, 62). Moreover, we have exemplars of the negative results of this misinterpretation to instruct us – 'the ... error of being too allegorical in Genesis, transported divers of the ancients beyond the certain evidence of truth'. Similarly, with more relevance to the case that Donne is making, 'to binde our selves to such a literall sense in [Revelation], will take from us the consolation of many spirituall happinesses, and bury us in the carnal things of this world'. Again, history has something to teach us:

> The ... error of being too literall in [Revelation], fixed many, very many, very ancient, very learned, upon an evident falshood; which was, that because here is mention *of a first Resurrection, and of a raigning with Christ a thousand years after that first Resurrection,* There should be to all the Saints of God, a state of happiness in this world, after Christs coming, for a thousand years; In which happy state, though some of them have limited themselves in spiritual things, that they should enjoy a kinde of conversation with Christ, and an impeccability, and a quiet serving of God without any reluctions, or concupiscences, or persecutions; yet others have dreamed on, and enlarged their dreams to an enjoying of all these worldly happinesses, which they, being formerly persecuted, did formerly want in this world, and then should have them for a thousand years together in recompense. (VI, 62–3)

Their error, then, is known for error because its results detracted from the focus on heavenly things that Donne wants to inculcate in his listeners. But, he also acknowledges that their error comes from their perspective, from where they are standing – the experience of worldly persecution and privation attracts them to this reading of scripture. Donne is not being relativistic here: he maintains the position that millennialism is wrong. However, he also demonstrates his awareness of the power of the subjective in deciding upon, if not in determining, the meaning of scripture. But the subjective must be constrained by reference to the results of interpretation. Or, as Donne himself puts it:

> In the figurative exposition of those places of Scripture, which require that way oft to be figuratively expounded, that Expositor is not to be blamed, who not destroying the literall sense, proposes such

> a figurative sense, as may exalt our devotion, and advance our edifica-
> tion. (VI, 63)

Perhaps aware that this provides rather too wide an opening for subjective interpretation (after all, the thought of a Millennium of compensation might well
exalt the devotion and advance the edification of a persecuted Christian), Donne
adds another doctrinal check:

> Neither do those Espositors ill, who with those limitations, that it
> destroy not the literall sense, that it violate not the analogy of the
> faith, that it advance devotion, do propose another and another such
> sense. So doth that preacher well also, who to the same end, and
> within the same limit, make his use of both, of all those expositions;
> because all may stand, and it is not evident in such figurative speeches,
> which is the literall, that is, the principall intention of the Holy
> Ghost. (VI, 63)

The concept of the analogy of faith had a long pedigree before and since the
Reformation, and Donne's reference to it here bolsters considerably his case for
regarding this resurrection as a spiritual experience. But it also complicates
Donne's hermeneutic. The balance and negotiation between the objective and
subjective meanings of scripture is still the relationship upon which Donne
wishes to focus, but this glancing reference reminds us that Donne's interpretation does not take place in a vacuum, a fact that is reinforced in this sermon when
he identifies 'persons of good note in the church' as the source of the interpretations that he wishes to offer.

Having provided this interpretive prologue, Donne turns to the exposition of
his text. And, claiming, as we have seen, the warrant of the church's esteem, he
offers three understandings of the verse and of the resurrection to which it
refers:

> First, that this first Resurrection, is a resurrection from that low
> estate, to which persecution had brought the Church; and so it
> belongs to this whole State, and Church ... Secondly, that it is a
> Resurrection from the death of sin, of actuall, and habituall sin; so it
> belongs to every penitent soul; ... And then thirdly, because after this
> Resurrection, it is said, *That we shall raign with Christ a thousand years*
> (which is a certain for an uncertain, a limited for a long time) it hath
> also been taken for the state of the soul in heaven. (VI, 63–4)

Clearly, then, Donne expects the listeners to find themselves in this portion of
scripture, both as a church and as individuals. The prophetic mirror of the

Revelation has devotional and edificational value for them, for it speaks to their past, their present and their future in a way that is both particular and personal.

The immediacy that Donne's exposition imparts to his exegesis emerges very clearly as he develops his first point. In emphasising the scale of the persecution of scripture, Donne reaches back into the Old Testament for illustration:

> We wonder, and justly, at the effusion, at the pouring out of blood, in the sacrifices of the old Law; that that little country scarce bigger then some three of our Shires, should spend more cattle in some few dayes sacrifice at some solemnities, and every yeare in the sacrifices of the whole yeare, then perchance this kingdome could give to any use. (VI, 65–6)

This extract is illuminating in two ways. On one hand, it reveals Donne's participation in a new emphasis in Biblical interpretation. This is, in fact, an outstanding instance of Donne's interest in the sort of Biblical scholarship identified by Debra Shuger as central to Renaissance exegesis.

But as the sermon continues, it emerges that the purpose for which Donne introduces this vivid account of sacrifice on an almost unimaginable scale in the past, is closely tied up with his hearers' present. The bloodshed of Jewish alters reminds us of the martyrdoms of the primitive church, and that leads us straight to 1624, and straight to St Paul's, where Donne reminds his audience of the present purpose of his sermonising:

> But beloved, the expressing the pressing of their depressions, does but chafe the Wax; the Printing of the seale, is the reducing to your memory, your own case: and not that point in your case as you were for a few years under a sensible persecution of fire, and prisons; that was the least part of your persecution; for it is a cheap purchase of heaven, if we may have it for dying ... but your greater affliction was, as you were long before, in an unsensiblenesse, you thought yourselves well enough, and yet were under a worse persecution of ignorance, and of superstition, when you, in your Fathers, were so farre from expecting a resurrection, as that ye did not know your low estate, or that you needed a Resurrection; And yet God gave you a Resurrection from it, a reformation of it. (VI, 67)

Donne has followed a fairly remarkable path here, from the sacrificial slaughter of animals – a remote historical example, given a contemporary immediacy and frame of reference – to the sufferings of the primitive church, past the fires and imprisonments of the Marian reign, on to the ignorance and superstition of the Catholic church and, it may be, of Donne's listeners. And this is all justified because, as Donne's typically apt metaphor reveals, the whole point of his exposition is to make an impression on his listeners, to bring history to bear to soften the wax, but scripture to bear to shape and mark their lives in a very immediate fashion, not even so little removed as 'a few yeares ago', but now, in the present. And Donne's use of the term reformation here is very typical. Repeatedly, he encourages his audiences not to regard reformation as a completed historical fact, but to understand it as an ongoing and continuous process in their own lives.

Donne's second section, interpreting the resurrection of the verse as a resurrection from sin, has a more immediately obvious personal application, but Donne is still keen to stress the immediate and the personal. And this immediacy influences Donne's preaching too. From a discussion of sin in general, he asks his listeners to 'be pleased to returne, and cast one halfe thought upon each of these: Sin is the roote of death; *Death by sin entered, and death passed upon all men for all men have sinned*'. The quotation from Romans 5:12 is an embrasive one, but Donne's insertion of the second 'men' serves to individualise it in a more marked way than the translators of either the Geneva Bible or the King James Version. And Donne's continuing treatment pushes relentlessly towards a personal and immediate understanding of the implications of his text:

> It is not evidence enough, to prove that thou art alive, to say, I saw thee at a sermon; that spirit, that knows thy spirit, he that knows whether thou wert moved by a Sermon, melted by a Sermon, mended by a Sermon, he knows whether thou be alive or no. (VI, 71)

Donne's view of the sermon as that which pre-eminently works a divine change in the life is typical of his very high estimation of the importance of the word preached. But here, as often in the sermons, the context of the sermon serves to heighten the tension between the individual and the collective. And Donne goes on to emphasise the individual effect of collective means:

> In the grave, which is the furnace, which ripens the body for the last resurrection, there is a putrefaction of the body, and an ill savour. In the Church, the wombe where my soule must be mellowed for this first resurrection, my soul, which hath the savour of death in it, as it is leavened throughout with sin, must stink in my nostrils, and I come to a detestation of all those sins which have putrified her. And I must not be afraid to accuse my selfe, to condemne my selfe, to humble my selfe, lest I become a scorne to men.

The agency of the self is clear here: it is the speaker who must himself accuse, condemn and humble. And the sphere of action too is individual – the repeated 'my selfe's individualise and separate Donne's congregation until they stand alone in relation to the word preached, in relation to the means of grace, in relation to the application of scripture.

It is remarkable, then, that when Donne turns to the third section of the sermon, and deals with the resurrection of the text as the restoration of the soul to the blessings of heaven, that he is at almost as great pains to emphasise the collectiveness of blessing and an eternal gregariousness that is entirely contrary to the sort of individualising that has occupied Donne so far:

> For, though that be not true, which *Origen* is said to say, That at last all shall be saved, nor that evident, which *Cyril* of Alexandria saies, That without doubt the number of them that are saved, is far greater then of them that perish, yet surely the number of them with which we have communion in Heaven is greater then ever lived at once upon the face of the earth. (VI, 76)

When Donne uses his prophetic mirror to reflect prophetic scripture into the present and on to his listeners, it is with the intention of finding the exposition that will encourage and edify the soul and exalt the devotion. His treatment of this scripture as future (for his listeners, at least, it remains prophetic) seems to indicate and to reiterate his view that prophecy, interpreted as prophecy simply does not provide the individual and targeted instruction that his listeners require.

Donne has, at this point, completed his discussion of the four heads into which he has divided his material. But he is not finished yet. And it is noteworthy that he is not finished, especially as he has been at some pains, in his discussion of his final point, to underscore 'the straitnesse of time' (VI, 75). Preachers do tend to know something about running out of time, but Donne wrote this comment into the text of his sermon: it is more than a throwaway remark. It works within the sermon to provide a contrast, between the straitness of the time available, and the expansive blessings that have to be discussed. But it is also interesting that Donne should conclude the point that he has described as his last, complaining of a lack of time to develop it fully, and then launch into another new section. This final section performs another interpretative act upon the words of Donne's text – a very self-conscious one, for Donne feels the need to deny that he is 'detorting' the text, or using 'any violence' upon it when he interprets it as speaking of 'Christ himself', *'the first fruits of them that sleep'* (VI, 77). Donne then retraces his hermeneutical steps to demonstrate that each interpretation he has offeres his hearers is, in fact, contained in this interpretation. Those who seek the resurrection in the 'first acceptation' must 'have [their] recourse to Christ' (VI, 78). Those who seek a resurrection from 'the fearfull death of heinous sin' must also go to Christ who bore 'all thy sins, and all thy

Fathers, and all thy childrens sins' (VI, 78). And those who desire the resurrection of the soul in the joys of Heaven desire, with the Apostle Paul, 'to be dissolved, and to be with Christ' (VI, 79). Christ is the whole purpose of Donne's interpretive endeavour, the whole point of his exposition:

> And therefore, as all that the naturall man promises himself without God, is impious, so all that we promise our selves, though by God, without Christ, is frivolous. God, who hath spoken to us by his Son, works upon us by his Son too; He was our creation, he was our Redemption, he is our Resurrection. And that man trades in the world without money, and goes out of the world that leaves out Christ Jesus. To be a good Morall man, and refer all to the law of Nature in our hearts is but ... the dawning of the day; To be a godly man, and refer all to God, is but ... A twilight; But the Meridionall brightnesse, the glorious noon, and height, is to be a Christian, to pretend to no spirituall, no temporall blessing, but for, and by, and through, and in our only Lord and Saviour Christ Jesus. (VI, 80)

Christ, then, is the focal point, where the objective and the subjective meet, and he is both the source and the aim of an accurate and edifying exposition of scripture.

And this is a point emphasised by the way in which Donne has chosen to construct his sermon. His introduction of a fourth division takes us, and would have taken his audience, back to his opening discussion on interpretative approaches. Medieval exegesis had focused on the four senses of scripture: the literal, tropological, allegorical and anagogical. These categories had homiletic, as well as a hermeneutic significance, for they were often used to lend structure to sermons. Donne's earlier sermons on the Psalms provide us with classic examples of this, as he offers the four readings of the verses under his consideration. In a sermon that has so explicitly foregrounded interpretative issues, and that so ostentatiously introduces a fourth division, it may well be that we see Donne self-consciously referencing this approach to scripture. If that is, indeed, his purpose, Donne's exegesis of the Revelation in this sermon becomes something more than occasional. Implicitly, his treatment of the difficult hermeneutical issues that Revelation raises allows him to adumbrate an understanding of scripture that has little real interest in interpretative categories like literal and allegorical. Rather, Donne's understanding of his own pastoral imperative, and his quest for the most appropriate application of scripture, leads him to develop a model of exegesis that holds both to the concept of an objective (and literal) truth, and to a subjective (but somehow not allegorical) application of that truth, an interpretative tension, or better, diplopia that ultimately finds its resolution in a Christological reading of scripture.

3

The authority of the church

Preaching, as was his custom, on the feast of the conversion of St Paul, in 1629, Donne took occasion from Paul's statement of his credentials as a Pharisee to make a statement that must have succeeded in arresting the attention of his auditors:

> Beloved, there are some things in which all Religions agree; The worship of God, The holinesse of life; And therefore, if when I study this holinesse of life, and fast, and pray, and submit my selfe to discreet, and medicinall mortifications, for the subduing of my body, any man will say, this is Papisticall, Papists doe this, it is a blessed Protestation, and no man is the lesse a Protestant, nor the worse a Protestant for making it, Men and brethren, I am a Papist, that is, I will fast and pray as much as any Papist, and enable my selfe for the service of my God, as seriously, as sedulously, as laboriously as any Papist. So, if when I startle and am affected at a blasphemous oath, as at a wound upon my Saviour, if when I avoid the conversation of those men, that prophane the Lords day, any other will say to me, This is puritanicall, puritans do this, It is a blessed Protestation, and no man is the lesse a Protestant, nor the worse a Protestant for making it, Men and Brethren, I am a Puritan, that is I wil endeavour to be pure, as my Father in heaven is pure, as far as any Puritan. (IX, 166)

This extract is striking, not only for its rhetorical effectiveness, but also for Donne's rejection of any simplistic and essentialist accounts of religious affiliation.[1] And Donne's suspicion of labels is not isolated to this extract. Earlier in his life, according to Walton, Donne had been reluctant to betroth himself to any 'religion that might give him any other denomination than a Christian'.[2] This statement comes to us with the uncertainty that we must ascribe to all of Walton's assertions, but it certainly accords closely with Donne's subsequent expression, in January of 1627, of the conviction that

1 This sermon is discussed in detail in Gregory Kneidel, *Rethinking the turn to religion in early modern English literature: the poetics of all believers* (London, 2008). See, for a valuable discussion of the use of these labels in Stuart religious writing, Thomas H. Clancy, 'Papist – Protestant – Puritan: English religious taxonomy, 1565–1665', *Recusant History* 13:4 (1976), 227–53. 2 Izaak Walton, *The lives of John Donne, Sir Henry Wotton, Richard Hooker, George Herbert and Robert Sanderson* (London, 1951), p. 32.

> If we will goe farther then to be Christians, and those doctrines, which
> the whole Christian Church hath ever believed, if we will be of
> *Cephas*, and of *Apollos*, if we will call ourselves, or endanger, and give
> occasion to others, to call us from the Names of men, Papists, or
> Lutherans, or Calvinists, we depart from the true glory and serenity,
> from the lustre and splendour of this Sunne. (VII, 310)

Donne's objection to any sort of sectarian and essentialist labelling of other
Christians continued unabated to the end of his career – in one of the sermons
from his undated sequence of the Penitential Psalms, Donne criticised hasty
conclusions about ecclesiastical affiliation based on behaviour or significantly on
the use of Laudian terminology:

> That man is affected when he hears a blasphemous oath, and when he
> lookes upon the generall liberty of sinning; therefore he is a Puritan;
> That man loves the ancient formes, and Doctrines, and Disciplines of
> the Church, and retaines, and delights in the reverend names of Priest
> and Altar, and Sacrifice, therefore he is a Papist, are hastie conclusions
> in Church affaires. (IX, 216)

It is important that we observe the consistency of the views expressed above,
spanning Donne's career. Stuart ecclesiology was a hotly contested nexus of
politics and religion, and Donne frequently preached in a very loaded political
context. As such, it is only to be expected that there will be variations of
emphasis in Donne's treatment of the authority of the church. What is remarkable, however, is the extent to which the core principles of his ecclesiology
remained constant throughout his career. This ecclesiology was shaped by a
consistent irenicism, by a refusal on Donne's part to see the church as an instrument of division, by his insistence that it was possible, rather, to define a limited
and essential ecclesiology that would unite, and not further divide, Christendom.
Thus, these extracts are paradigmatic of Donne's understanding of ecclesiastical
authority, emphasising not only his enduring lack of ease with the use of labels
other than Christian, but his continuing insistence on the surpassing importance
of the common and irreducible core of Christian religion. If nothing else, it
should make us very wary of attempts to pin Donne to any one ecclesiastical
position.

This is underscored for us when we contrast Donne's words with another
contemporary text. This document, from the hand of William Laud, in 1625 is
a list cataloguing the bishops of the English church, neatly labelled with 'P', for
Puritan, and 'O', for orthodox.[3] Laud felt able, for his own political purposes,

3 W. Scott and J. Bliss (eds), *The works of the most Reverend Father in God, William Laud DD* (7
vols, Oxford, 1847–60), III, p. 159. Cf. Jeanne M. Shami, 'Labels, controversy and the language

neatly to catalogue his colleagues, without ambiguity or ambivalence. Such certainty has been denied to historians of the period, and the primary historiographical debate has centred on the sort of division that Laud made. In this context, Donne's remarks serve not only as a warning against doing violence to his own conception of his position on the spectrum of Jacobean and Caroline Christendom, but also as a salutary reminder of the limited utility of labelling individuals, and the danger of over-simplification attendant upon such labelling. Thus, while it is important to bear in mind the heated historiographical debates about religious belief and practice in the period of Donne's ministry, it is, to say the least, unfortunate to reduce our engagement with Donne's understanding of the church to an attempt to determine the best pigeonhole to accommodate his views or to allocate them a conveniently totalising label. This sort of approach is especially unhelpful because in this area, as in all others, Donne refuses to accommodate himself neatly to any sort of rectilinear confines. Instead, throughout his life, he articulated an ecclesiology that was consistent, but not static, and that it is, in its individuality, expressive of the key stresses of his thought.

THEORISING THE REFORMED CHURCH

Donne is not unique in this – he takes his place in an English ecclesiological spectrum that was both broad and colourful. The central achievement of the revisionist history of recent decades has been the problematisation of simplistic binaries as the picture of English early modern religious history has become vastly more complicated.[4] This addition of nuance and the concomitant increase

of inclusion in Donne's sermons' in *John Donne's Professional lives*, ed. David Colclough (Woodbridge, 2003), pp 135–57. **4** For helpful surveys of developments in the historiography of the reformation, see Christopher Haigh, 'The recent historiography of the English reformation' in *The English reformation revised*, ed. Christopher Haigh (Cambridge, 1987), pp 19–33; Fincham, 'Introduction' in *The early Stuart church, 1603–1642*, pp 11–22; Nicholas Tyacke, 'Anglican attitudes: some recent writings on English religious history, from the reformation to the Civil War', *Journal of British Studies* 35 (1996), 139–67; Ethan H. Shagan, 'English Catholic history in context' in *Catholics and the 'protestant nation': religious politics and identity in early modern England* (Manchester, 2005), esp. pp 1–22. Peter Lake's summary of the effects of recent historiography is worthy of quotation: 'Now ... we had a situation that called the whole notion of mainstream and periphery into question; to appropriate and adapt Kevin Sharpe's phrase, not so much a common wealth as a polyphony, indeed at times of crisis, a veritable cacophony, of meanings, as a number of different groups and factions (puritans both radical and particularly moderate, evangelical Calvinist conformists, Whitgiftian conformists, avant-garde conformists, Laudians and proto-Laudians, various sorts of church papist and Catholic loyalist to name a few) manoeuvred within and in terms of the basic legal and institutional, the political, textual and ideological structures provided by the national Church, structures that, of course, they all hoped (to different extents) to change and even, in some cases and at some times, to transform in order to gloss and claim that Church as their own. In so doing the various parties very often tried to of complexity are especially relevant to Donne, whose ministry occurs at the nexus between the debates about the nature of the wider reformation project and the dynamics of the emergence of Laudian churchmanship. Both of these fundamental changes in the nature of the English church did involve opposing extremes, yet we must be careful of the impulse to see them simply in binary terms. There is, perhaps, an especial danger of this in light of the deliberately polarised account of events given by controversialists involved in contemporary debates, whose purpose was rather effective polemic than accurate history. Peter Lake, discussing the Admonition Controversy, and arguing that Cartwright and Whitgift shared more ground than has been usually recognised, provides an apposite account of the tendency

> of nearly all sixteenth-century religious polemicists to argue in terms of inversion and binary oppositions. Such exchanges employed a relatively limited number of ideal types or models of heterodoxy and unsoundness, among which, for respectable Protestants, both popery and Anabaptism held pride of place.[5]

The difficulty is, of course, that, while extremes did exist, and were often vigorously defended, most people were situated somewhere in the middle, deviating perhaps towards one end of the spectrum or the other, but still possessing a complicated and even contradictory range of views. It is vital, therefore, that we view the history of the Reformation, and of the Stuart church, as continua.[6]

achieve their ends by establishing some notion of the mainstream'. There is an entirely appropriate breathlessness to this extract that does as much as anything to establish the rich complexity of this issue. While we are about it, we would also do well to note Lake's warning that 'all this makes it doubly critical that historians trying to understand these interactions should adopt an attitude of critical distance, a more or less permanently suspended judgement about the "veracity" of the various renditions of the core and the periphery deployed by contemporaries': Peter Lake, 'Introduction: Puritanism, Arminianism and Nicholas Tyacke' in *Religious politics in post-reformation England: essays in honour of Nicholas Tyacke*, ed. Kenneth Fincham and Peter Lake (Woodbridge, 2006), p. 12.   5 Lake, 'Introduction: Puritanism, Arminianism and Nicholas Tyacke', p. 24. Shami, *Conformity in crisis*, pp 15–17 makes a similar point. For exceptionally helpful discussions of the dangers of simplistic binaries, and of other perils to which Reformation historiography is heir, see Peter Lake and Michael C. Questier, 'Introduction' in *Conformity and orthodoxy in the English church, c.1560–1660*, ed. Peter Lake and Michael C. Questier (Woodbridge, 2000), pp ix–xx and Debora Kuller Shuger, *Habits of thought in the English Renaissance: religion, politics and the dominant culture* (Toronto, 1997), pp 1–16. Milton, *Catholic and reformed* is of particular interest, because of its avoidance of binary oppositions. Peter Lake, 'Anti-popery: the structure of a prejudice' in *Conflict in early Stuart England: studies in religion and politics, 1603–1642*, ed. Richard Cust and Ann Hughes (London, 1989), pp 72–106 and Lake, 'Introduction: Puritanism, Arminianism and Nicholas Tyacke', provide valuable insights on the process by which these two opposing poles were constructed.   6 Kenneth Fincham, *The early Stuart church, 1603–1642* (Basingstoke, 1993) provides some very helpful overviews of the range of positions available to Stuart ecclesiastics. See, in particular, Fincham's 'Introduction' (pp 1–22) for a very useful taxonomy of positions within the English Church, and for the definition

This is especially important in the case of Donne, who consciously sought the middle ground on an array of issues and who, very often, held this middle ground less by eschewing elements from the extremes of the range of available belief than by accommodating elements from both ends of the continuum.[7] It is entirely possible for us to engage, as does Daniel Doerksen, in an attempt to pin Donne to one particular strand of the English church.[8] While there is little doubt that Doerksen is correct in his ultimate conclusion that Donne was a conformist, rather than a Laudian, this insight scarcely provides us with a light on his views in all their complexity – when the study concludes, we do not feel we know Donne much better, or understand him much more fully. Simply put, Doerkesen's treatment locates him in the context of a debate in which Donne was not terribly interested.

Debora Shuger, in her consideration of Richard Hooker and his construction of the Christian community in the *Lawes*, outlines an alternative way of understanding reformation history. She focuses less on the attempt to find a totalising meta-narrative, and concentrates instead on the individual case, allowing for the fact that these people did not conceptualise themselves in the categories of modern historiography, and certainly were at no pains to correspond directly with them. Shuger's point is made in the context of political history, but it applies with equal force to other historical paradigms:

> [The] tendency to resolve Tudor/Stuart religion into the dialectic of popular resistance and government repression renders invisible what it purports to illuminate: the role played by religion in early modern state formation. That the Crown attempted to reinforce political unification by imposing religious uniformity is evident. It is equally evident that this project met with opposition. The hagiographies, autobiographies, parish records, devotional manuals, theological polemics and pastoral handbooks written between the Middle Ages and the restoration document the ensuing conflicts. But they primarily document something else: the proliferation of local experiments in sacred community, experiments sometimes at odds with the laws of ecclesiastical polity, sometimes not. Book V of Hooker's *Lawes* is itself

of conformity used in this chapter. However, Fincham's consideration of the complexities of defining conformity in the period in Kenneth Fincham, 'Clerical conformity from Whitgift to Laud' in *Conformity and orthodoxy in the English church, c.1560–1660*, ed. Peter Lake and Michael C. Questier (Woodbridge, 2000), pp 125–58 ought also to be kept in mind. 7 Scodel, 'Religious politics' provides an outstanding and very valuable discussion of Donne's conception of the mean, and its importance to his thought. 8 Daniel W. Doerksen, *Conforming to the Word: Herbert, Donne and the English church before Laud* (London, 1997). The usefulness of Doerksen's work for students of Donne is also limited by his concentration on Herbert – his treatment of Donne appears almost an afterthought.

one such experiment, as is the imagined community of his
Presbyterian antagonists.[9]

Clearly there is a role for historical meta-narrative, and efforts to identify and
understand the grand plan of reformation history. For the purposes of this
study, however, we stand with Shuger on the importance of the individual
improvisation, and the imperative to understand the views of Donne in their
complexity.[10]

The consistency of Donne's views on the role of the church in relation to the
religious experience of the individual is remarkable. In light of Donne's conversion from Catholicism, it might well be unexpected; in view of his supposed guilt
about that 'apostasy' it seems impossible. Nevertheless, the texts that provide us
with the only reliable access to Donne's thought support it, and their endorsement must surely outweigh any psychological extrapolation from Donne's
biographical details. And this underlines the difficulties and the dangers of
approaches that rely on the critic's psychological insights to decode the 'hidden
meaning' of texts whose patent implications point in another direction.
Psychological criticism is always a risky endeavour: our inability to account for
the motives and actions of our own contemporaries ought to make us very wary
of dogmatic statements about the experience of those who occupied a milieu so
vastly different from our own. This is, perhaps, especially true of conversion.
Andrew Petegree opens his treatment of the culture of the Reformation with a
consideration of the process of conversion that raises pertinent and suggestive
questions but provides no certain answers. Rather, he reminds us how little we
know about the dynamics of this process:

> [The] recognition that the process of conversion was an extended and
> evolving process brings us up against the first and very substantial
> question. Are we right to assume that adherence to the Reformation
> was a conscious choice for more than a very small number of articu-
> late, educated individuals? Are we guilty of using a single word –
> conversion – to mask a complex process of psychological adjustment
> that requires far more careful analysis?[11]

9 Shuger, 'Imagined community', 325–7. 10 Powerful vindications of the illuminative value of
a careful study of idiosyncratic individuals are furnished, inter alia, by Patrick Collinson,
Archbishop Grindal, 1519–1583: the struggle for a reformed church (London, 1979); Peter G. Lake,
'Serving God and the times: the calvinist conformity of Robert Sanderson', *The Journal of British
Studies* 27:2 (1988), 81–116; Susan Holland, 'Archbishop Abbot and the problem of
"puritanism"', *The Historical Journal* 37:1 (1994), 23–43; Gary Jenkins, *John Jewel and the English
national church: the dilemmas of an Erastian reformer* (Aldershot, 2006); Peter Lake, 'Matthew
Hutton: a puritan bishop?', *History* 44 (1979), 182–204; Diarmuid MacCullough, *Thomas
Cranmer, a life* (New Haven, CT, 1996). 11 Andrew Pettegree, *Reformation and the culture of
persuasion* (Cambridge, 2005), p. 2. For a wide-ranging study of conversion in this period, see

Pettegree goes on to distinguish carefully between the experience of the first generation of the Reformation, for whom 'the religious alteration was one pregnant with consequences', a lonely choice to 'court calamity' and those who subsequently converted:

> Later, as the churches of the Reformation became institutionalised, it became possible to adhere to Protestantism with little real choice, and without any real mental engagement. Even here, however, there is reason to doubt whether such utter passivity would have been the normative experience.[12]

For Donne, these two situations might be said to overlap, and the complexities are correspondingly greater, for, if he lived in a society where Protestantism was the normative religious option, he also possessed a family noted for its Catholicism, a brother who was a *de facto* martyr to the cause of counter-reformation, Jesuit uncles and all the while, his mother, staunchly Catholic to her death, telling her beads in the background. Insofar as it is impossible that such complex circumstances could be replicated in our own experience, even the most hubristic of biographical critics would surely benefit from Donne's own insight on his experience.[13]

The difficulty is that Donne speaks very little about his conversion. We have, in fact, little beyond that strangely ham-fisted letter of explanation to his new and unwilling father-in-law, in which Donne goes out of his way to emphasise the slowness of his conversion, and the preface of *Pseudo-martyr*, where Donne presents his careful mental engagement with the teachings of the Roman and reformed churches as a paragon to his Catholic readers. Conversion, then, was an important experience in Donne's life, but it scarcely seems to have assumed the central and nagging importance that some critics have envisaged – the process, on Donne's own evidence, was painstaking and protracted, but it was also complete and completed. We ought to notice, at this point, that Donne's conversion concerned the choice of a 'local religion', and his conversion did not miraculously expunge every trace of his Catholic upbringing. Certainly, Donne never pretends that this is the case, and in his sermons, he takes spoil of the Egyptians at every opportunity, even as he plays with Roman doctrine and liturgy in his poetry. Conversion involved a change of allegiance, not of being.[14]

Michael C. Questier, *Conversion, politics and religion in England, 1580–1625* (Cambridge, 1996). Questier's reference to Donne (p. 56) is disappointingly slight, but the applicability of much of his material to Donne's experience is patent. Kathleen Lynch, *Protestant autobiography in the seventeenth-century anglophone world* (Oxford, 2012) provides a very helpful discussion of Donne's representation of the conversion process. 12 Pettegree, *Reformation*, p. 3. 13 Cummings, *Literary culture*, 365–417, provides an outstandingly nuanced and convincing account of Donne's conversion. 14 For a treatment of the literary dynamics of conversion in an even more complex set of circumstances, see Mark S. Sweetnam, 'Calvinism, counter-

The chronology of this change has proved a perpetual problem to Donne's critics. His marriage, or at any rate the letter of apology to Egerton, provides a *terminus ante quem*; there is no obvious *terminus post quem*. Typically, Satyre III, Donne's definitive documentation of the search for true religion, has been seen as representative of his frame of mind towards the beginning of the process of conversion, and there is little doubt that this poem is more a part of the ongoing process than a commentary on a past one. Nonetheless, the issues that Donne raises in the poem were to set the agenda for his ecclesiology and were consistently to provide the backbone of Donne's explication of the status and worth of the reformed Church of England.

SATYRE III: DONNE'S HOOKERIAN EXPERIMENT

An index of this consistency is the fact that the key elements of that ecclesiology all find their expression in some of Donne's earliest works, and re-echo throughout his career. In Satyre III the young Donne deals with preoccupations that telescope out of the poem and occur time and again throughout the prose works. For this reason, the Satyre is crucial to understanding Donne's ecclesiology. The reading of the Satyre that I wish to advance extends existing scholarship, which has a tendency to view the poem as embodying a political or, at most, a religio-political discussion.[15] There is manifest validity in such an approach, and to deny that the poem resounds with political attitudes and implications would be risible. Notwithstanding this, approaching Satyre III from a religious perspective sheds valuable new light on its knotty and intrinsically problematic matter. And the most challenging problems of the poem are intrinsic. In it we see a Donne who is somewhere on the path to embracing the local religion of the English church dramatising one particular understanding of that church. In the stanzas of the Satyre Donne adopts – or struggles to adopt – a version of Protestantism that owes a great deal to Richard Hooker. The experiment ultimately falters, but that Donne thought it worth his while to attempt it at all tells us a good deal about the sort of conversion he underwent and the sort of churchman that he became.

The evidence of a Hookerian dimension to Donne's ecclesiological thinking at this stage of his career lies in the Satyre's slight but exceedingly significant echoes of one of the most influential works of English ecclesiological theory, Book V of Richard Hooker's *Lawes of ecclesiastical polity*. These echoes, these

reformation and conversion: doctrinal palimpsest in Alexander Montgomerie's religious lyrics' in Crawford Gribben and David George Mullan (eds), *Literature and the Scottish reformations* (London, 2009), pp 143–60. 15 See, especially, Strier, 'Radical Donne'; Scodel, 'Religious politics'; M. Thomas Hester, *Kinde pitty and brave scorn: John Donne's Satyres* (Durham, NC, 1982).

structural resemblances, strongly argue for the centrality of Hooker's method and understanding of the nature of the English church to Donne's own episte- mology.[16] Before considering this claim in greater detail, it is necessary to look briefly at the dating of the Satyre. The general editorial consensus has dated the Satyre in the early to mid-1590s, a date that looks, at best, uncomfortably tight if we are to sustain the argument that Book V of the *Lawes*, first published in 1597, was a meaningful influence on the poem. However, as Paul Sellin points out,

> The date of 'Satyre III' has depended almost exclusively on specula- tive argument regarding Donne's spiritual biography rather than on historical or bibliographical facts. Unlike several of the other satires, the third has up to now yielded no easy historical allusions or similar clues by which scholars could establish even an indubitable *terminus a quo*, and it has never been possible to date the poem with precision.[17]

Having established the lack of any incontrovertible basis for dating, Sellin goes on to argue for a later date, based on events referred to in the poem. The first half of his argument relies on the imagery of polar exploration used earlier in poem, and he convincingly contends that this imagery used by Donne echoes reports of the third of the Dutch Barents expeditions, which returned from its polar hardships in November 1597. Sellin thus concludes that:

> 'Satyre III' clearly appears to be no earlier than November 1 1597 ... To assign the poem to so early a time, however, would assume that the news found its way to Donne directly from Amsterdam and that he reacted immediately. It therefore seems more likely that Donne's allusion stems from printed sources, in which case the earliest possible date is at least 1598. ... Because the story reached the height of its popularity between 1599 and ... 1600–1 ... it is reasonable to conclude that the likeliest *terminus a quo* for 'Satyre III' ranges from middle or late 1598 to 1602, with mid-1598 as the earliest moment feasible.[18]

Such a dating would, clearly, allow us to visualise Donne writing the poem with Book V of the *Lawes* fresh in his mind. To be sure, Sellin does go on to argue,

16 The theological relationship between Donne and Hooker has already been investigated by Elizabeth de Volin Tebeaux, 'John Donne and Anglicanism: the relationship of his theology to Richard Hooker's' (PhD, Texas A&M U, 1977). This study is suggestive, but lacking in historical and theological nuance. Tebeaux assumes a very unproblematic 'Anglicanism', and sees Hooker and Donne as contributors to this ideal *via media*. She also fails to address Hooker's reinterpre- tation of *adiaphora*. 17 Paul R. Sellin, 'The proper dating of John Donne's "Satyre III"', *The Huntington Library Quarterly* 43:4 (1980), 275. 18 Ibid., 281.

on the basis of resemblances between the image of Truth on a hill, later in the poem, and the medal struck to commemorate the Synod of Dort, that the correct dating of the Satyre may be as late as 1620, but this later argument lacks the conviction of the earlier, and makes some questionable assumptions. Dating, then, does not eliminate the possibility that the Satyre was influenced by Hooker's work, and indeed it makes it likely that Hooker's work was fresh in Donne's mind as he wrote the poem.

It would, of course, be very helpful if we could point to incontrovertible evidence that Donne had, in fact read Book V of the *Lawes*. Such evidence is lacking from Donne's *oeuvre* – his works, indeed, contain no direct reference to Hooker. However, this is also true of other contemporary English works of religious controversy of such relevance and importance that it is unthinkable that Donne, with his theological and controversial proclivities, had not read them.[19] Thus, this lack of direct allusion ought not, perhaps, discourage us too much. We could argue on the grounds of probability that Donne was familiar with Hooker. Happily, a marginal note in a tract entitled *A Iust and Temperate Defence of the Five Books of Ecclesiastical Policie: written by M. Richard Hooker*, by William Covell, presently held in the Harvard College Library, provides us with clearer evidence. The tract was published in 1603, while Donne was employed by Bishop Morton.[20] The page opposite the title contains the following Latin epigram, in Donne's handwriting, and bearing Donne's signature:

Ad Autorem
Non eget Hookerus tanto tutamine; Tanto
Tutus qui impugnat sed foret Auxilio.

[Hooker does not need such great protection; but he who attacks such great help would be safe.]

The comment is typically and frustratingly cryptic, but Donne appears to be expressing an appreciation for Hooker and a rather less flattering estimation of Covell. George Field summarises the weight of this evidence succinctly:

19 This is especially so in light of Walton's account of Donne's attention to contemporary occurrences: '[A]ll businesses that passed of any public consequence, either in this or any of our neighbour-nations, he abbreviated either in Latin, or in the language of that nation, and kept them by him for useful memorials' (p. 87). *Ignatius, his conclave* also furnishes us with ample evidence of Donne's familiarity with current affairs and discoveries. 20 The tract, and the collection in which it is found, are described by R.E. Bennett, 'Tracts from John Donne's library', *Review of English Studies* 13 (1937), 333–5. The content of Covell's *defence* is summarised in some detail in Peter Lake, 'Business as usual? The immediate reception of Hooker's *Ecclesiastical polity*', *Journal of Ecclesiastical History* 52:3 (2001), 462–81. Given the overtly ceremonial and sacramental direction in which Covell pushed Hooker's argument, Doone's distaste for it is a telling confirmation of his views as discussed in this chapter.

Such a judgment would hardly seem possible were Donne not familiar
with Hooker's *Laws*, as well as being in such substantial agreement as
to be provoked into writing this epigrammatic comment – a unique
action by Donne unparalleled in any of the other books known to be
from his library.[21]

In the light of this regard for Hooker, it is not excessive to argue that resemblances between the very influential Book V and Donne's radical discussion of
the search for true religion are more than a matter of coincidence or of shared
sources.

What, then, are these resemblances, and what is their significance in Donne's
thought? The poem opens with Donne weighing the respective value, in eschatological terms, of 'fair Religion' and of the 'vertue' of the first blinded age. It is
instructive to note that Hooker begins Book V in precisely the same way, for his
argument that 'true religion is the roote of all true virtues and the stay of all well
ordered common-wealthes' leads him inevitably to the question of the virtuous
pagan, the 'blind philosophers'. Hooker's reference to 'pure and unstained
religion' resonates with the opening section of Donne's poem, as well as with
later allusions to images of sexual purity. Also noticeable is the motive to which
both writers ascribe the virtue of those for whom 'heavens joyes' are not a goal.
Hooker instances those who commend the

> felicitie of that innocent world, wherein it is said that men of theire
> own accorde did imbrace fidelitie and honestie, not for feare of the
> magistrate, or because revenge was before theire eyes, if at any tyme
> they should doe otherwise, but that which helde the people in awe was
> the shame of ill doinge, the love of equitie and right it selfe a barre
> against all oppressions which greatnes of power causeth. (19)

This motivation for virtue could be summarised in Donne's words on the
subject: 'earth's honour'.

A twin repudiation of rash courage and cowardice forms the basis from which
Satyre III approaches the search for true religion. Donne lists examples of excessive and intemperate zeal:

> Dar'st thou ayd mutinous Dutch, and dar'st thou lay
> Thee in ships woodden Sepulchers, a prey
> To leaders rage, to stormes, to shot, to dearth?
> Dar'st thou dive seas, and dungeons of the earth?
> Hast thou couragious fire to thaw the ice

21 George C. Field, 'Donne and Hooker', *Anglican Theological Review* 48 (1966), 307–9.

> Of frozen North discoveries? and thrise
> Colder then Salamanders, like divine
> Children in th'oven, fires of Spaine, and the line,
> Whose countries limbecks to our bodies bee,
> Canst thou for gaine beare? and must every hee,
> Which cryes not, 'Goddesse,' to thy Mistresse, draw,
> Or eate thy poysonous words? (lines 17–28)

He goes on, as Richard Strier and Joshua Scodel have both helpfully argued, to identify such intemperate zeal as disguised and suicidal, cowardice:

> O desperate coward, wilt thou seeme bold, and
> To thy foes and his (who made thee to stand
> Sentinell in his worlds garrison) thus yeeld,
> And for forbidden warres, leave th'appointed field? (lines 28–32)

Before giving the instruction that would equip the reader to find a middle way between Rome and Geneva, then, Donne wishes to inculcate a suitable frame of mind; a medium between intemperate zeal, and excessive, even suicidal, cowardice.

When we turn, then, to Hooker, we find an answer to Donne's preparatory laying aside of zeal and fear in the third chapter, entitled 'Of superstition and the root thereof, either misguided zeal, or ignorant fear of divine glorie':

> [T]wo affections there are, the forces whereof, as they beare the greater or lesser sway in mans harte, frame accordinglie the stampe and character of his religion; the one zeale, the other feare. Zeale, unless it be rightlie guided, when it endeavoureth most busily to please God, forceth upon him those unseasonable officies which please him not. ... Zeal, except it be ordered aright, when it bendeth it selfe unto conflict with things either in deed, or but imagined to be opposite unto religion, useth the razor many times with such eagerness, that the verie life of religion it selfe is thereby hazarded, through hatred of tares the corne in the field of God is pluckt up. (27)

Hooker then turns to the complementary vice of fear, and argues that, while a reverential fear of God is a necessary and a healthy thing, an excessive and a cringing fear prevents the sort of reasonable consideration of religion that Hooker is conducting. Such fear is, in fact, the first step towards superstition:

> Feare is a good solicitor to devotion. Howbeit sith feare in this kinde doth growe from an apprehension of deitie indued with irresistible

> power to hurte, and is of all affections (anger excepted) the unaptest
> to admit any conference with reason, for which cause the wise man
> doth saie of feare that it is the betrayer of the forces of reasonable
> understandinge, therefore except men knowe before hand what
> manner of service pleaseth God, while they are fearful they try all
> thinges which phancie offereth. (28)

Hooker's explanation of the way in which these dispositions impede the search
for true religion amply accounts for and unpacks Donne's preliminary determi-
nation to eschew them both.

At this point, it must be acknowledged that neither discussion of the virtue of
the Golden Age nor the identification of wisdom in the Aristotelian medium
between zeal and fear are particularly recherché, and certainly they are not
unique to Donne or to Hooker.[22] So much is true. Nonetheless, there is a
congruence of arrangement and of the intent underlying that arrangement that
seems to call for an explanation more convincing than happenstance. This
conviction can only be strengthened when we come to Mirreus and Crants.
Here, Donne sets up the second of two middle ways – firstly between intemperate zeal and cowardice, and secondly between Rome and Geneva. We have
already considered the importance of the first of these, but the significance of
the second should be noted, especially in light of Peter Lake's contention that

> Hooker was the first conformist to locate the English church between
> Rome on the one hand and an image of Presbyterian and Genevan
> extremism on the other. ... In constructing that image Hooker was
> trying to sever the close links of belief and identity which, as men like
> Bridges and Whitgift had acknowledged, had always bound the
> church of England to the foreign reformed churches. If a crucial
> element in the ideology of 'anglicanism' was the claim to have
> maintained a middle path between Rome and Geneva then Hooker
> deserves considerable credit for having been the first divine to formu-
> late that proposition in as many words.[23]

Donne is following Hooker when he personifies the two extremes that demar-
cate the middle way in the figures of Mirreus who thinks religion

> ... unhous'd here, and fled from us,
> Seekes her at Rome: there, because hee doth know
> That shee was there a thousand yeares agoe,
> He loves her ragges so, as wee here obey
> The statecloth where the Prince sate yesterday.

22 The classic statement, and the source for Hooker, was, of course, Aristotle's *Ethics*.
23 Lake, *Anglicans and Puritans*, 159–60.

The other extreme is represented by Crants who

> ... to such brave Loves will not be inthrall'd
> But loves her onely, who'at Geneva's call'd
> Religion, plaine, simple, sullen, yong,
> Contemptuous, yet unhandsome.

Donne, then, is determined to navigate his way between a religion that can point only to past glories, on the one hand, and one having no past on the other. The balance that he seeks is less in terms of doctrine than in order and beauty – his objection to Geneva concentrates on its lack of beautifying order. Graius, on the one hand, and Phrygius and Graccus, on the other, also dramatise an opposition – they function as exemplars of excessive credulity and of two types of excessive scepticism respectively. All five religious seekers function as counter examples, and Donne turns from them to directly address his audience, and, it seems, himself:

> but unmoved thou
> Of force must one, and forc'd but one allow;
> And the right; aske thy father which is shee,
> Let him aske his; though truth and falshood bee
> Neare twins, yet truth a little elder is. (lines 69–73)

With 'force' comes the sceptre of cohersion, but Donne seems simply to be stating the truth (contra Graccus) that the individual must choose one religion, and cannot simply among the available options.

It also seems at least possible that Donne, with his own traumatic conversion not so very far behind him, is regretting the necessity to choose a particular religion. In light of that conversion, the advice to 'ask thy father' and to 'let him ask his' seems a little odd – this is precisely what Donne, for all his pride in his illustrious and thoroughly Catholic lineage, did not do.[24] It is, however, precisely the course that Hooker, quoting Deuteronomy 32:7, urged upon his readers:

> Neither may we in this case lightlie esteeme what hath bene allowed as fitt in the judgment of antiquitie and by the longe continewed practise of the whole Church, from which unnecessarelie to swarve experience hath never as yet found it safe. ... [L]ett no man ... neglect the instructions, or dispise the ordinances of his elders, sith he whose guift wisdome is hath said, *Aske thy father and he will show thee, thine Ancients and they shall tell thee.*[25]

24 Donne's reference, in Satyre III, was echoed in Holy Sonnet VIII: 'If faithfull soules be alike glorifi'd': See also Sweetnam, 'Reformation of the eucharist', 14–15. 25 Richard Hooker, *The Folger Library edition of the works of Richard Hooker, 2: Of the laws of ecclesiastical polity*, ed. William Speed Hill (Cambridge, MA, 1977), pp 34–5.

There are, then, some striking and suggestive congruencies between Donne's record of the search for true religion, and Richard Hooker's defence of the English settlement as just such a true and fair religion. These suggest an endorsement by Donne of the elements of Hooker's approach to the subject of ecclesiastical polity. Clearly, the possibility of Hooker's influence on Donne does not entirely depend on the respective dates of Book V and Satyre III – Hooker had dealt with general issues of the relationship between scripture and ecclesiology in Books III and IV, and the resemblances between Hooker's and Donne's stances on a range of issues are indicative of a shared viewpoint. However, the correspondences between Book V and the Satyre indicate a basic consonance of approach, and suggest that Donne found in Hooker's method insights crucial to the formation of his ecclesiology. We will consider the shared elements of this ecclesiology shortly, but Satyre III is concerned less with details than with fundamental questions of approach. Arguably, Hooker's most enduring contribution to the emerging Anglicanism was his emphasis on the role of reason as a balancing influence on both Roman tradition, and, more especially, puritan Biblicism. *The lawes of ecclesiastical polity* was, prima facie, a reasoned and reasonable defence of the Elizabethan and Jacobean settlements. The primacy of reason in Hooker's approach was attractive to Donne, and of fairly obvious importance in a poem that begins with an attempt to set aside emotion as an essential preliminary for the finding of true religion.[26]

Donne's wish to proceed by reason is established by his instruction to the reader to 'doubt wisely' and to 'stand enquiring right'; but also by 'the long and laborious process of historical, or semi-historical, research' implied in Donne's instruction to 'ask thy father' and 'let him ask his'.[27] Similarly, the painstaking ascent towards Truth, is gradual, not the product of a swift or sudden revelation, but the winning of 'hard knowledge', by means of the 'mindes indeavours'. Satyre III, then, is expressive of Donne's desire to follow Hooker's method, to be convinced by his reason of the identity of true religion. Indeed, it just such an approach that Donne records as he describes his own conversion in *Pseudo-martyr*. This account stresses the role of careful research and the reasoned weighing of the opposing claims of the Roman and English churches. However, the Satyre also seems to dramatise the failure, for Donne, of this reasoned approach. His commitment to reason leaves him less than fully satisfied. The whole point of Hooker's work was that reason could give the assurance of the possession of true religion, and Hooker is apparently serene in his confidence in

26 On the role of reason in Hooker's epistemology, and the tensions implicit in his dependence upon reason, see 'Richard Hooker, Lancelot Andrewes and the Boundaries of Reason' in Shuger, pp 17–68. For reason in Donne's epistemology, see Lowe, 'John Donne'; Sherwood, 'Reason in Donne's serons'; Terry G. Sherwood, *Fulfilling the circle: a study of John Donne's thought* (Toronto, 1984); Elizabeth de Volin Tebeaux, 'John Donne and the problem of religious authority: "Wranglings that tend not to edification"', *South Central Bulletin* 42:4 (1982), 29–44.
27 Leishman, *Monarch of wit*, p. 116.

the possibilities of reason.[28] Donne, in spite of his reliance on the 'mindes indevour' to win 'hard knowledge', seems unable, at this point, wholly to share Hooker's serenity. Reason fails to identify true religion beyond debate, and so he 'stand[s] inquiring right' and feels unable to 'run', in the pursuit of religion, to pursue a *via media*, a way and not a place.

Towards the end of the poem, the breakdown of Donne's Hookerian experiment becomes acute. In spite of the fine intellectual independence expressed in Donne's scornful reference to uselessness of simply relying upon the dictates of 'a Philip, or a Gregory, a Harry, or a Martin' as a reliable basis for identifying 'true religion', the poem ends in anger and not in peace:

> As streams are, Power is; those blest flowers that dwell
> At the rough streames calme head, thrive and do well,
> But having left their roots, and themselves given
> To the streames tyrannous rage, alas are driven
> Through mills, and rockes, and woods, and at last, almost
> Consum'd in going, in the sea are lost:
> So perish Soules, which more chuse mens unjust
> Power from God claym'd, than God himselfe to trust. (lines 103–10)

At the end of the Satyre, Donne is expressing both his sense that Hooker's approach to religion is ultimately unsatisfactory, and an acute realisation that it is rendered unsatisfactory by the *realpolitik* of Tudor religion. At this stage in his life, Donne is still deeply conscious of having lost hold of his roots, and fears that he has done so to his damnation.

Donne ultimately found a religion in which he could run, but he cannot be said to have remained a Hookerian. His more important difference with Hooker was on the issue of rites and ceremonies. Donne did not, in general, follow Hooker in defending these observances on the ground of their necessity. Rather, he preferred to echo earlier generations of conformist apologists. This reluctance to over-determine the adiaphoric is of a piece with the picture of Donne's ecclesiology that will emerge in our study.

CATHOLIC YET REFORMED: DONNE AND
ALLEGIANCE TO THE ENGLISH CHURCH

A crucial element in Donne's understanding of the church appears in *Pseudo-martyr*, his earliest controversial work. It emerges in the context of Donne's discussion of the relative origins of magistracy and of ecclesiastical authority. As

---

28 Hooker largely maintains this serenity in the *Lawes*. As Shuger, *Habits of thought*, points out, consideration of the Hooker *oeuvre* in its entirety reveals some telling tensions (pp 17–68).

such, it forms a vital element in Donne's defence of the king's right to impose the oath of allegiance. Additionally, however, it is very revealing of Donne's conception of the nature of ecclesiastical authority. We have already alluded to this passage in relation to Donne's appreciation of the necessity of divine revelation, but it bears quotation here at greater length, noting its echo of Satyre III in the first sentence:

> Certainely all power is from God; And as if a companie of *Savages*, should consent and concurre to a civill maner of living, Magistracie & Superioritie, would necessarily, and naturally, and Divinely grow out of this consent. ... And into what maner and forme soever they had digested and concocted this Magistracie, yet the power it-selfe was *Immediately* from God: So also, if this Companie, thus growen to a *Commonwealth*, should receive further light, and passe, through understanding the Law written in all hearts, and in the Book of creatures, and by relation of some instructers, arrive to a saving knowledge, and Faith in our blessed Saviours Passion, they should also bee a *Church*, and among themselves would arise up, lawfull Ministers for Ecclesiastical function, though not derived from any other mother Church, & though different from all the divers hierarchies established in other Churches: and in this State, both Authorities might bee truly said to bee from God. (*PM*, 79)

There are a number of elements to note in this extract. First of all, it provides us with a crucial insight into Donne's views of ecclesiastical polity. In this connection, we should notice that, the establishment of civil rule, as part of created order, is anterior to the emergence of ecclesiastical hierarchy, and validates the members of that hierarchy – they are 'lawfull Ministers'. Ecclesiastical rule, as much as the civil, originates with God as a principle. Divine ordinance does not, however, extend so far as to cover the precise manifestation of that hierarchy. This statement of Donne's understanding of hierarchy is important, not least because of the scarcity of reference to the subject in the sermons. Rather than just compensating for this paucity, however, the statement accounts for it: for Donne, church polity is divinely established, mediated through existing civil power structures, and not, therefore, up for debate. As a member of the Established hierarchy, preaching to members of the church by law established, Donne has little reason to debate something that ought, in his view, to be taken entirely for granted.

The sermons are not entirely devoid of such discussions, and one of the most important occurs in Donne's Trinity Sunday sermon for 1621. There is much in the contemporary context to explain why Donne choose to address this issue: the period leading up to the publication of James I's *Directions* was marked by considerable ferment – negotiations over the Spanish match, and concern about the fate of the Palatinate conspired to create an atmosphere of heightened tension.[29]

> Donne's sermons of this period contrast the excessive zeal of those who would reform abuses outside the law with the normal processes available for such improvement. Many of the analogies he uses reinforce his sense that the legally constituted institutions of England, in both church and state, are the only legitimate means through which to effect further reform. ... Virtually all of Donne's sermons in these controversial times articulate a doctrine of callings focusing primarily on their spiritual as well as their social necessity.[30]

This analysis is borne out by Donne's sermon on 1 Peter 1:17: 'And if ye call on the Father, who without respect of persons judgeth according to every man's work, pass the time of your sojourning here in fear'. The closing section of the sermon commences with a warning not to

> thinke that power, by which the world is governed, is but the resultance of the consent, and the tacite voice of the people, who are content, for their ease to bee so governed, and no particular ordinance of God: It is an undervaluing, a false conception, a misapprehension of those beames of power, which God from himself sheds upon those, whom himselfe cals Gods in this World. (III, 289)

In this context, with its obvious similarity to that outlined in *Pseudo-martyr*, Donne discusses the office and duties of priest and king:

> We sin then against the Father, when we undervalue God in his Priest. God hath made no step in that perverse way of the Roman Church, to prefer, as they doe, the Priest before the King; yet, speaking in two severall places, of the dignity of his people, first, as Jews, then as Christians, he sayes in one place, That they shall be *a Kingdome*, and *a Kingdome of Priests*; and he sayes in the other, They shall be *Sacerdotium*, and *Regale Sacerdotium*, *Priests*, and *royall Priests*: In one place, *the King*, in the other, *the Priest* mentioned first, and in both places, both involved in one another: The blessings from both so great, as that the Holy Ghost expresses them by one another mutually. (III, 289)

There is, then, an imbrication of authority and of office, and both are to be given their allotted due: if the Christian is to 'abstaine from violating the power of God

29 Donne's sermons for this period are discussed in Shami, *Conformity in crisis*, pp 75–101. For a helpful discussion of the rather intractable complexities of the Spanish Match, see Glyn Redworth, *The Prince and the Infanta: the cultural politics of the Spanish match* (New Haven, CT, 2003).   30 Shami, *Conformity in crisis*, pp 90–1.

the Father, in dis-esteeming his power thus planted in the Priest' (III, 289), he must also avoid sinning 'against the Father, the roote of power, in conceiving amisse the power of the Civill Magistrate' (III, 290). Donne still sits very lightly on the precise detail of the hierarchy in which the priest functions; crucially, however, he is a 'lawfull minister'.

For Donne, then, civil and church authority are closely related. But though closely related they are distinct, and in a sermon preached to the royal household in 1626, Donne cautions any attempt to use civil means to religious ends:

> Christ beats his Drum, but he does not Press men; Christ is serv'd with Voluntaries. There is a *Compelle intrare*, A forcing of men to come in, and fill the house, and furnish the supper: but that was an extraordinary commission, and in a case of Necessity: Our ordinary commission is *Ite, prædicate; Go, and preach the Gospel*, and bring men in so: it is not, *Compelle intrare*, Force men to come in: it is not, Draw the Sword, kindle the Fire, winde up the Rack: for, when it was come to that, that men were forc'd to come in (as that Parabolical story is reported in this Evangelist) *the house was fill'd*, and the supper was furnisht (the Church was fill'd and the Communion table frequented) but it was *with good and bad too:* for men that are forc'd to come hither, they are not much the better in themselves, nor we much the better assur'd of their Religion, for that: Force and violence, pecuniary and bloudy Laws, are not the right way to bring men to Religion, in cases where there is nothing in consideration, but Religion meerly. (VII, 156–7)

As the last clause quoted suggests, it is not always the case that 'Religion meerly' is in question, and Donne goes on to argue a role for the State when men's 'allegience is complicated with their Religion' (VII, 157). Thus, the imbrication of civil and ecclesiastical authority has a negative, as well as a positive aspect.

Returning to the quotation from *Pseudo-martyr*, there are further details of significance to remark. We have already noted at some length the evidence, in this extract, of the radical importance of scripture to Donne's ecclesiology. What is equally significant, however, is Donne's belief that adherence to scripture as the source of the church's authority still allows considerable freedom and flexibility in the details and minutiae of ecclesiastical practice. Donne therefore stands in contrast to Biblicist puritans, like Cartwright, who contended that adherence to scripture should be absolute and excluded any room for variation in ecclesiastical practice. This accommodation of variety in practice was, and remained, fundamental to Donne's understanding of ecclesiastical authority. It is also entirely consonant with Donne's interest in contemporary developments in the state of Venice, which seemed, for a time, to have the potential to result in further secession from the sovereignty, if not from the doctrine, of the Roman church. *Pseudo-martyr* resounds with Donne's fascination with these events, and it seems probable that the chapters originally planned by Donne to close the book would have further developed these ideas.

A similar conception of the possibility of differing manifestations of ecclesi-astical polity appears in the *Essayes in divinity*. In the *Essayes*, this account emerges in the context of Donne's discussion of the significance of the diversity in names found in scripture. The reasons for this lack of uniformity had exercised the ingenuity of cabbalists, and Donne is dismissive of their tendency to 'observe in every variety some great mystick signification' (*ED*, 54–5). He offers '*It is so, because God would have it so*' as an accurate, if a 'lazy', explanation. However, Donne makes characteristic use of this debate to emphasis the ireni-cism of his own ecclesiology:

> I encline to think that another usefull document arises from this admitting of variety; which seems to me to be this, that God ... fore-seeing, I say, that this his dearly beloved Spouse, and Sister, and Daughter, the Church, should in her latter Age suffer many convul-sions, distractions, rents, schisms and wounds, by the severe and unrectified Zeal of many, who should impose necessity upon indif-ferent things, and oblige all the World to one precise forme of exterior worship and Ecclesiastick policie; averring that every degree and minute and scruple of all circumstances which may be admitted in either belief or practice is certainly, constantly, expressly and obliga-torily exhibited in the Scriptures; and that Grace and Salvation is in this unity and no where else; his Wisdome was mercifully pleas'd, that those particular Churches, devout parts of the Universall ... should from this variety of Names in the Bible it selfe, be provided of an argument, *That a unity and consonance in things not essentiall, is not so necessarily requisite as is imagined.* (*ED*, 55–6)

While this argument is essentially the same as that outlined in *Pseudo-martyr*, we should observe one important development. In the earlier work, Donne spoke in terms of different churches developing in isolation, among unconnected savages. In this quotation the concept of a Catholic church emerges. This is to some degree a consequence of the belief that scripture allows room for diversity in the practice of true churches. Each individual church is validated as a church, not by external matters of polity, but because of its membership in this universal Catholic Church, a membership that, itself, springs from adherence to the core doctrines of Christianity. Donne expanded upon this understanding of catholicity in a sermon preached in 1619. The origin of this sermon is noteworthy – it is one of the two into which Donne 'digested' a single sermon preached at The Hague.[31] It is somewhat frustrating that we do not, therefore, know of a certainty that this section was preached on that occasion, but its appeal to the reformed church in the Netherlands is patent:

> The Church loves the name of Catholique; and it is a glorious, and an harmonious name; Love thou those things wherein she is Catholique, and wherein she is harmonious, that is, ... Those universall, and fundementall doctrines, which in all Christian ages, and in all Christian Churches, have beene agreed by all to be necessary to salvation; and then thou art a true Catholique. Otherwise, that is, without relation to this Catholique and universall doctrine, to call a particular Church Catholique (that she should be Catholique, that is, universall in dominion, but not in doctrine) is such a solecism, as to speak of a white blacknesse, or a great littlenesse; A particular Church to be universall, implies such a contradiction. (II, 280)

The respective etymologies of 'Catholic' and 'Protestant' gave the Roman church an unfair semantic advantage. Donne here participates in the effort to regain the broader sense of the term, a sense that accommodated the reformed communions. In the following year, he engaged in further careful redefinition of terms that the Roman church sought to monopolise. 'Every Church is a Supreme Church, and every Church is an Apostolicall Church ... as long as they agree in the unity of that doctrine which the Apostles taught, and adhere to the supreme head of the whole Church, Christ Jesus' (III, 138). And, in a sermon preached at Paul's Cross in 1627, Donne expressed his wish that all of Christendom might be united in the sort of Catholic Church that he longed to see:

> Blessed be that God, who, as he is without change or colour of change, hath kept us without change, or colour of change, in all our foundations; And he in his time bring our Adversaries to such a moderation as becomes them, who doe truly desire, that the Church may bee truly *Catholique, one flock, in one fold, under one Shepherd*, though *not all of one colour*, of one practise in all outward and disciplinarian points. (VII, 433)

Donne is careful not to deny the possibility of a participation in this re-defined Catholicism by the Roman church.[32] In the *Essayes*, as later in his career, Donne,

---

31 For a detailed discussion of this sermon and the circumstances surrounding its delivery, see Paul R. Sellin, *So doth, so is religion: John Donne and diplomatic contexts in the Reformed Netherlands, 1619–1620* (Columbia, MO, 1988), esp. pp 109–34. 32 The status of the Roman church had been the subject of broad agreement in the earlier reformation: see Anthony Milton,

while insisting on the necessity for reformation, is unwilling to deny that the Roman church is, essentially, still a church. In this, Donne's echoes Hooker's statement that the Church of Rome ought 'to be held and reputed a part of the howse of God, a lime of the visible Church of Christ'.[33] Likewise, with a somewhat odd derangement of mammalian imagery, Donne allows for the validity of both Eastern and Western, Roman and separatist churches, a gesture that echoed one of James' preoccupations:

> Therefore that Church from which we are by Gods Mercy escaped, because upon the foundation, which we yet embrace together, Redemption in Christ, they had built so many stories high, as the foundation was, though not destroyed, yet hid and obscured; And their Additions were of so dangerous a construction, and appearance, and misapplyableness, that to tender consciences they seem'd Idolatrous, and are certainly scandalous and very slippery, and declinable into Idolatry ... And though these points be not immediately fundementall points of faith, yet radically they are, and as neer the root as most of those things wherein we and they differ ... yet though we branch out *East & West*, that Church concurs with us in the root, and sucks her vegetation from one and the same ground, *Christ Jesus*; who, as it is in the *Canticle*, lies between the brests of his Church, and gives suck on both sides. And of that Church which is departed from us, disunited by an opinion of a necessity that all should be united in one form, and that theirs is it, since they keep their right foot fast upon the Rock Christ, I dare not pronounce that she is not our Sister. (*ED*, 56–7)

In this quotation we have progressed beyond matters merely of external procedure, which, in Donne's view, are the result of 'the ground and state wherein God hath planted' a particular church, to those of doctrine (*ED*, 57). We will have more to say on this distinction later, but for the present, it is important to note that Donne regards both polity and non-fundamental doctrine as areas in which difference can be tolerated. And Donne, with his enduring ability to find the telling image, goes on to give memorable expression to this dichotomy between the external and the essential:

> As naturall, so politick bodies have *Cutem & Cuticulam*. The little thin skin which covers al our body may be broken without pain or danger, and may re-unite it selfe, because it consists not of the chief

'The Church of England, Rome and the true church: the demise of a Jacobean consensus' in *The early Stuart church, 1603–1642*, ed. Kenneth Fincham (Basingstoke, 1993), pp 187–210. [33] Hooker, *Works*, II, 355.

and participant parts. But if in the skin it self, there be any solution or division, which is seldome without drawing of blood, no art nor good disposition of Nature, can ever bring the parts together again and restore the same substance, though it seem to the ey to have sodder'd it self. It will ever seem so much as a deforming Scar, but is in truth a breach. Outward Worship is this *Cuticula*: and integrity of faith the skin it self. (*ED*, 57)

It is as well, perhaps, that the image is a memorable one, for the concept that it represents is crucial to our understanding of the Donneian ecclesiology. If it appears, at times, inadequate, it is because Donne seems to locate so many issues on the thin outer skin, and relatively few on the inner. This problem diminishes, however, when we recollect that while the articles of non-negotiable faith may be few in number, they are vast in significance – for Donne, they compose essential Christianity.

This contrast between the internal and essential, and the external and optional endured throughout Donne's career, and, indeed, its clearest articulation in the sermons is found in the series on the Penitential Psalms.[34] Donne adopts the Pauline image of treasure in earthen vessels, from II Corinthians 4:7:

> Consider the Church of God collectively, and the Saints of God distributively, in which Babylon you will, in the Chaldean Babylon, or in the Italian Babylon, and these waters doe come nigh us, touch, and touch to the quick, to the heart. But yet, ..., they touch not us, they come not nigh us; for *wee have treasures in earthen vessels*; They may touch the vessel, but not the Treasure. And this literally expressed in the Text it selfe, ... not that they shall not come neare his house, or his lands, or his children, or his friends, or his body, but *non eum*, they shall not come nigh him. For, for the Church, the peace of the Church, the plenty of the Church, the ceremonies of the Church, they are *sua*, but not *illa*, they are hers, but they are not she. And these things, riches and ceremonies, they may be washed off with one tide, and cast on with another, discontinued in one Age, and re-assumed in another, devested in one Church, and invested in another, and yet the Church is, she in her fundamentall Doctrines, never touched. (IX, 332)

---

34 The dating of these sermons on the penetintial Psalms has proved problematic. Potter and Simpson have generally adopted a later date. P.G. Stanwood, 'Donne's earliest sermons and the penitential tradition' in *John Donne's religious imagination*, ed. Raymond-Jean Frontain and Frances M. Malpezzi (Conway, AR, 1995), pp 66–84 argues for an earlier date, although he does suggest that Donne may have revised and re-used some of these sermons – a telling indicator of the consistency of some of Donne's views.

To take these views on the nature of the church to their logical conclusion would be to suggest that differences in polity or liturgy could simply be disregarded; that the issue of ecclesiastical affiliation was a matter of indifferency. Donne is conscious that his views could be caricatured in this way, and guards against this interpretation. While Donne emphasises common ground and shared belief, he is also adamant in his conviction that one ought not and cannot 'shuffle religions together, and make it all one which you chuse' (IV, 196). And this conviction is re-stated throughout the sermons. Like other of the key elements of Donne's ecclesiology, however, its most memorable expression occurs in Satyre III.

The over-riding preoccupation of the Satyre might be summarised as the choice of religion. The opening lines site this consideration in an eschatological context – the issues of Heaven and Hell are introduced early, and the Satyre, even in its more ironic moments, never quite allows us to forget this. Thus, it is scarcely surprising that Donne emphasises his firm belief, already noted, that the choice of church is not a matter of indifferency. Donne expresses his repudiation of those who view the Church of England as the only valid church:

> Graius stayes still at home here, and because
> Some Preachers, vile ambitious bauds, and lawes
> Still new like fashions, bid him thinke that shee
> Which dwels with us, is onely perfect, hee Imbraceth her.
>
> (lines 55–9)

But the poem, in its pursuit of the mean, is equally critical of those who regard all religions as equally valid. So, he also criticises those like Graccus, one of the other counter-examples in the poem, who

> ... loves all as one, and thinkes that so
> As women do in divers countries goe
> In divers habits, yet are still one kinde,
> So doth, so is Religion; and this blind-
> nesse too much light breeds. (lines 65–8)

An indifference that regards all variation in religious practice simply as a matter of externals, is to be avoided. And Donne restates this conviction throughout the sermons, pronouncing, for example, in an undated Lincoln's Inn sermon:

> [W]o unto him that is so free from all offences, as to take offence at nothing; to be indifferent to any thing, to any Religion, to any Discipline, to any form of Gods service; That from a glorious Masse to a sordid *Conventicle*, all's one to him. (III, 166)

It is of particular interest to observe Donne take up this subject in his sermon preached in defence of James' *Directions for preachers*.[35] This was an intensely political sermon, perhaps the most political that Donne ever preached, and, in light of the proposed Spanish marriage and James' diplomatic negotiations, the Direction's instruction that 'no preacher of what title or denomination soever, shall consciously and without invitation from the text, fall into bitter invectives, and indecent railing speeches against the person of either papists or puritans,' it is not, perhaps, surprising that Donne does stress the possibility of compromise with those who differ in some points.[36] Nonetheless, we should note that Donne took occasion to stress the impossibility of compromising on fundamental principles:

> First then we are in Contemplation of *a Spirituall warre*: now, though there be a *Beati Pacifici*, a blessing reserved to *Peace-makers*..., yet there is a *Spirituall Warre*, in which, *Maledicti Pacifici*; Cursed bee they that goe about to make Peace, and to make all one, The warres betweene *Christ* and *Belial*. *Let no man sever those whom God hath joined*, but let no Man joyne those whom *God* hath severed neyther. ... God hath put *Truth* and *Falshood*, *Idolatrie* and *Sinceritie* so farre asunder, and infused such an incompatibilitie, and imprinted such an implacability betweene them, as they cannot flow into one another: And therefore, there, *Maledicti Pacifici*, It is an opposition against God, by any colourable Modifications, to reconcile opinions diametrically contrary to one another, in fundamentall things ... There are points, which passions of men, and vehemence of disputation, have carried farther a sunder than needed: and these indeed have made the greatest noyse ... But then there are matters so different, as that a Man may sit at home, and weepe, and wish, prayse God that hee is in the right, and pray to God for them that are in the wrong, but to thinke that they are indifferent, and *all one*, *Maledicti Pacifici*, hee that hath brought such a Peace, hath brought a curse upon his owne Conscience, and layd, not a *Satisfaction*, but a *Stupefaction* upon it. (IV, 192–3)

In a later sermon, preached in 1622, that dealt with the similarly divisive issues of images and iconoclasm, Donne stressed that, while compromise for the sake of friendship was by no means unthinkable, it could never be on fundamental beliefs:

> Problematicall things are our *silver*, but fundementall our *gold*; problematicall our *sweat*, but fundementall our *blood*. If our

---

35 This important sermon, and the considerable body of related scholarship, are discussed in greater detail in ch. 5, below. 36 Milton, *Catholic and reformed*, p. 59.

> Adversaries would be bought in, with our silver, with our sweat, we
> should not be difficult in meeting them halfe way, in things, in their
> nature *indifferent*. But if we must pay our Gold, our Blood, our *funda-*
> *mentall* points of Religion, for their friendship, A Fortune, a Liberty,
> a Wife, a Childe, a Father, a Friend, a Master, a Neighbour, a
> Benefactor, a Kingdome, a Church, a World, is not worth a dramme
> of this Gold, a drop of this Blood. (VII, 433)

For all Donne's emphasis on the importance of essential Christianity, and his
willingness to stress the role of ecumenism and the possibility of more cordial
inter-church relationships, he consistently argued the insufficiency of personal
religious practice based upon a sparing or grudging commitment to the tenets of
Protestant Christianity in general, and the Church of England in particular:

> Doe not say, I will hold as much of Jesus, as shall be necessary, so
> much as shall distinguish me from a *Turk*, or a *Iew*, but if I may be the
> better, for parting with some of the rest, why should I not? Doe not
> say, I will hold All, my self, but let my wife, or my son, or one of my
> sons, goe the other way, as though *Protestant*, and Papist were two
> severall callings; and as you would make one son a Lawyer, another a
> Merchant, you will make one son a Papist, another a Protestant. (IV,
> 263)

The fact that Donne spoke these words in the 1622 sermon commemorating the
discovery of the Powder Treason plot, intended for the very public arena of
Paul's Cross, is, once more, an important reminder of the vital political dimension to this debate. Thus, it is valuable to note the similarity of Donne's thought
in an undated christening sermon. In this context, less public and political, more
intimate and pastoral, Donne closed his remarks with an account of the nature
of the church into which the infant had been baptised. In this domestic context,
he stressed not so much the choice between different churches, but rather the
danger of attempting to overlook or to minimise the differences between
conformity to the Church of England, and those who diverged to either side:

> To come as neere Christ as we can conveniently, to trie how neare we
> can bring *two Religions* together, this is not to preserve *Integritatem*
> *Jesu*: In a word, Intirenesse excludes deficiency, and redundancy, and
> discontinuance; we preserve not intirenesse, if we preserve not the
> dignity of Christ, in his Church, and in his *discipline*, and that
> excludes the defective *Separatist*; we doe not preserve that entirenesse
> if we admit *traditions*, and additions of Men, in an equality to the
> word of God, and that excludes the redundant *Papist*; neither doe we

> preserve the entirenesse, if we admit a discontinuence, a slumbering
> of our Religion for a time, and that excludes the *temporisers*, the
> *Statist*, the *Politician*. (V, 150)

So, while Donne's comprehension of the church as a core of essential beliefs
overlaid by non-essential ceremonies that vary with time and place is fundamental to his ecclesiology, and remained so throughout his career; he balanced
this by insisting that all churches were not equally valid, and, specifically, that
the Church of England, which he had chosen after careful deliberation, was the
correct place for English Christians to be.

Donne spends less time explaining why this should be so than we might
expect. There are, essentially, three reasons that Donne offers to explain his
conviction that the Church of England is not be abandoned by members of his
congregations. The first of these is, simply, its antiquity. For Donne, the ability
of the English church to trace its heritage back beyond the reformers and
ultimately to the primitive church, was vital to its claim for allegiance. He was
firm in his belief that 'God loves not innovation' but 'old doctrines, old disciplines, old words and formes of speech in his service, God loves best' (II, 305).
This appeal to antiquity validated both doctrine and liturgical practice. So, in an
undated sermon on Christ's instruction to Simon Peter and Andrew to 'Follow
me', Donne emphasised the value of the true church as a doctrinal template, and
hence as a necessary means to follow Christ:

> [I]n Doctrinall things, There must have gone some body before, else
> it is no following; Take heed therefore of going on with thine owne
> inventions, thine owne imaginations, for this is no following; Take
> heed of accompanying the beginners of Heresies and Schismes; for
> these are no followings where none have gone before: Nay, there have
> not gone enow before, to make it a path to follow in, except it have
> long continuance, and beene much trodden in. And therefore to follow
> Christ doctrinally, is to embrace those Doctrines, in which his Church
> hath walked from the beginning, and not to vexe thy selfe with new
> points, not necessary to salvation. That is the right way, and then thou
> art well entred; but that is not all; thou must walke in the right way to
> the end, that is to the end of thy life. (II, 298–9)

This appeal to antiquity was also Donne's recourse when addressing the puritan
enemies of the established church, in an undated Trinity Sunday sermon. He
took occasion to defend the fact of that antiquity, as well as its virtues:

> [I]n his Religion, and outward worship, we have enemies that deny
> God his House, that deny us any Church, any Sacrament, any

> Priesthood, any Salvation, as Papists; And enemies that deny Gods house any furniture, any stuffe, any beauty, any ornament, any order, as non-Conformitans; ... For our refactary, and schismaticall enemies, I call not upon them to answer me ... Let them answer the Church of God, in what nation, in what age was there ever seen a Church, of that form, that they have dremt, and believe their own dream? (III, 257)

Secondly, and as we have already seen, Donne contends that the established church deserves the allegiance of his auditors precisely because it is Established, because of its relationship with civil government. This point he develops in an undated sermon preached at Lincoln's Inn:

> When our whole Land is in possession of peace and plenty, and the whole Church in possession of the Word and Sacraments, when the Land rejoices because the Lord reigns; ... every man that is encom-passed within a Sea of calamities in his estate, with a Sea of diseases in his body ... may yet open his eyes above water, and find a place in the Arke above all these, a recourse to God, and a joy in him, in the Ordinances of a well established, and well governed Church, this is truly Regnum Dei, the Kingdome of God here ... This then is the blessed state that wee pretend to, in the Kingdome of God in this life; Peace in the State, peace in the Church, peace in our Conscience. (III, 127)

Civil and religious peace, then, are interrelated, and their correspondence is guaranteed by the special status of the national church.

Thirdly, Donne reminds his listeners that they had been born into the English church, and argues, consequently, that they owe her their continued love and allegiance. Donne makes only sparing use of the biblically validated imagery of the church as a woman, and when he does use it, uses it most often to depict the English church as a mother deserving of her children's love and obedience.[37] Preaching in 1625 in the presence of the body of the king who was so largely responsible for his position in that church, he applied the words of Canticles 3:11: 'Go forth, O ye daughters of Zion, and behold king Solomon with the crown wherewith his mother crowned him in the day of his espousals, and in the

---

37 This is an interesting contrast with the sleazily sexual imagery that permeates Satyre III. Even in that poem, however, the language of debased sexuality is reserved to the misguided efforts of those who fail in the search for true religion. 'True religion' in the poem is not a bawd or a strumpet, but a mistress. That term is intriguingly polyvalent, but she is, at any rate, a woman commanding the 'soul's devotion', rather than sordid misapprehension.

day of the gladness of his heart'. It is highly significant that, in praising the dead king, Donne chooses to eulogise the English church:

> And therefore you daughters of Sion … quarrel not your mothers honor, nor her discretion: Despise not her person nor her apparel: Doe not say, *she is not the same woman, she was heretofore, nor that she is not so well dressed, as she was then*; Dispute not her *Doctrine*, Despise not her *Discipline;* that as you *sucked her breasts* in your *Baptism*, and in the *other Sacrament*, when you entred, and whilst you stayd in this life, so you may *lie in her bosome*, when you goe out of it. (VI, 284)

In light of the love due to this mother, in light, too, of the gratitude due to her for her ministry of nourishment, it is a serious betrayal to look elsewhere:

> [W]hen we are bid to *Go forth*, it is not to go so far, as *out* of that Church, in which God hath given us our station; for, as *Moses* says, That *the word of God is not beyond the Sea*; so the Church of God, is not so *beyond Sea*, as that we must needs seek it *there*, either in a *painted Church*, on one side, or in *a naked Church*, on another; a Church in a *Dropsie*, overflown with *Ceremonies*, or a Church in a *Consumption*, for want of such Ceremonies, as the primitive Church found usefull, and beneficiall for the advancing of the glory of God, and the devotion of the congregation. (VI, 284)

The possibility that English Christians might look elsewhere for the pattern of the ideal church was troubling to Donne. His belief that the English church was a complete and adequate church made such an investigation both superfluous and a betrayal, and, in a sermon preached to the earl of Carlisle and his company, he was clear in his instruction that his auditors ought not to trouble themselves

> to know the formes and fashions of forraine particular Churches; neither of a Church in the lake, nor a Church upon seven hils; but since God hath planted thee in a Church, where all things necessary for salvation are administred to thee, and where no erroneous doctrine (even in the confession of our Adversaries) is affirmed and held. (V, 251)

This was also a useful rhetorical device, identifying religious with national loyalty, and suggesting that both puritans and papists were less than loyal in their commitment to the English state, a charge with considerable bite in the prevailing political and diplomatic environment.

These arguments for continued loyalty to the English church are noticeably based more upon political and, it might be said, sentimental reasons. Donne is strikingly slow to make any sweeping doctrinal claims for his church. One of the most outstanding occasions when Donne did engage in this sort of defence comes relatively late in his career, in a sermon preached before Charles in 1627, a sermon that got Donne in trouble with the King and Archbishop Laud. Maura Lunderberg argues cogently that it was Donne's remarks about the possibility that the wives of religious kings might 'have retained some tincture, some impressions of errour, which they may have sucked in their infancy, from another Church' that offended Charles (VII, 409).[38] Certainly, it seems unlikely that either Charles or Laud would have been offended by Donne's defence of the *via media* of the reformed church:

> From extream to extream, from east to west, the *Angels* themselves cannot come, but by passing the middle way between; from that extream impurity, in which the Antichrist had damped the Church of God, to that intemerate purity, in which Christ had constituted his Church, the most Angelicall Reformers cannot come, but by touching, yea, and stepping upon some things, in the way … It is the posture reserved for heaven, to sit down, at the right hand of God; Here our consolation is, that God reaches out his hand to the receiving of those who come towards him; And nearer to him, and to the institutions of his Christ, can no Church, no not of the *Reformation*, be said to have come, then ours does. It is an ill nature in any man, to be rather apt to conceive jealousies, and to suspect his Mothers honour, or his sisters chastity, then a strange womans. It is an irreverent thankfulnesse, to think worse of that Church, which hath bred us, and fed us, and led us thus far towards God, then of a foreign Church, though *Reformed* too, and in good degree. (VII, 409)

Donne's conception of a continuum of reform, along which the English church has found just the right place to stop, is an interesting one. It emphasises for us the importance of the *via media* in Donne's thought. As in Satyre III, Donne is searching for a church that combines antiquity of practice, with the reinvigoration of reform. This characterisation of the *via media* continues throughout the sermons, as when, for example, Donne exhorted his readers to thankfulness that their church suffered neither 'a dropsy nor a consumption, neither overflowing with unnecessary, nor lacking beneficial ceremonies' (VI, 284). Donne's desire for his congregations was that they, with him, might be 'content to consist in moderate, and middle wayes in the Reformed Church' (VIII, 135).

---

38 Lunderberg, 'Strategies for discreet preaching', 97–119.

4

Defining Christianity: Donne's
essentialist ecumenism

That Donne, throughout his life, self-consciously sought a *via media* is one of the oldest truisms of his biography. It shares with most truisms the quality of not really telling us anything terribly useful. The concept of a middle way is inherently referential, and also inherently dependent on the way in which extremes are identified and percieved. This chapter examines more closely Donne's ecclesiology, the way in which he understood the nature and role of the English church after the Reformation. Donne adopted an essentialist definition of Christianity that looked back beyond both the turmoil of the Reformation and the corruption of the Roman church to Apostolic teaching, the early councils and the belief of the primitive church. These elements, agreed upon by Roman and reformed churches, form the core of Donne's ecclesiology. Roy Battenhouse, in one of the best available treatments of Donne's understanding of Christianity, identified this trend in Donne's thought, arguing that 'he seeks Christian unity by reducing dogma to a common minimum' and that 'his whole faith moves within the bounds of the creed of Nicea'.[1] Battenhouse uses the term 'fundamentalism' to label this tendency in Donne's ecclesiology. His choice of terminology is curious. The term 'Fundamentalism' emerged in the United States in the 1920s, with the publication of a number of Biblicist and intensely anti-modernist tracts defending core Christian values.[2] These tracts were collectively entitled *The Fundamentals*. From this, the movement whose ideas they represented became known as fundamentalism. Since then, the use of the term has evolved, and it has come to have definite overtones of intransigence and even of extremism. These associations render it singularly inappropriate to describe Donne's essentialist rendering of Christian dogma. We might more accurately, if less elegantly, speak of Donne as adopting an essentialist ecumenism. This stance was irenic, stressing the unifying potential of agreement on the essential core of Christian doctrine. This view is consistently articulated in the sermons, but it is worthwhile to remark its practical expression in Donne's friendship with

---

1 Roy W. Battenhouse, 'The grounds of religious toleration in the thought of John Donne', *Church History* 11:3 (1942), 229–31. 2 See Ernest R. Sandeen, *The roots of fundamentalism: British and American millenarianism, 1800–1930* (Chicago, IL, 1970); George M. Marsden, *Fundamentalism and American culture: the shaping of twentieth-century evangelicalism, 1870–1925* (New York, 1980).

individuals from all parts of the ecclesiastical spectrum in England, as well as his interest in and links to Gallicans, Paolo Sarpi and other Venetian reformers, and the proceedings of the Synod of Dort.[3]

This essentialist ecumenism can be seen most clearly in those sermons in which Donne attempts capsule definitions of the truth of Christianity. In his Whitsunday sermon for 1628, he does so by appealing to primitive creeds, endorsing a version of Christianity stripped down even further than the Church of England's creed:

> Truly I had rather put my salvation upon some of those ancient Creeds, which want some of the Articles of our Creed (as the *Nicene* Creed doth, and so doth *Athanasius*) than upon the *Trent* Creed, that hath as many more articles as ours hath.[4] (VIII, 263)

At other times, he provides his own confession, stating, for example, that:

> The simplest man, as well as the greatest doctor, is bound to know that there is one God in three persons, that the second of those, the Sonne of God, tooke our nature, and dyed for mankinde; and that there is a Holy Ghost, which in the Communion of Saints, the Church established by Christ, applies to every particular soule the benefit of Christs universall redemption. (V, 276)

In the sermon preached to the earl of Carlisle, he turned the attention of his congregation to the three cornerstones of this essential Christianity:

> the Ten Commandments, which is the sum of all that we are to doe; The Lords Prayer, which is the summe of all that we are to ask; and the Apostles Creed, which is the summe of all that we are to believe. (V, 247–8)

Donne also adopted the minimalist definition of the church outlined in the Thirty-Nine Articles, itself echoing the Augsburg Confession, and according closely with Calvin's own definition: 'the true Church is that, where the word is truly preached, and the Sacraments duly administred' (VIII, 309).[5] He did, however, go on to qualify this definition by stressing that the word so preached

---

3 See also Shami, *Conformity in crisis*, pp 10, 20, 23.   4 Note that the continued use of this Creed was objected to by Cartwright, on the basis that the demise of the Arian heresy made it both superfluous and irrelevant. Hooker, in Chapter 42 of Book V, gave an account of its origin, and argued in favour of its retention as part of the liturgy of the Reformed Church.   5 Calvin, *Institutes*, 4.1.9. See Hirofumi Horie, 'The Lutheran influence on the Elizabethan settlement, 1558–1563', *Historical Journal* 34:3 (1990), 519–37.

must be 'the word inspired by the holy Ghost; not Apocryphall, not Decretall, not Traditionall, not Additionall supplements', and that the Sacraments administered must be those 'instituted by Christ himself, and not those super-numerary sacraments, those posthume, *post-nati* sacraments, that have been multiplied after'.

The ecumenical implications of this view of Christianity emerge clearly in Donne's treatment, in a sermon preached in Lincoln's Inn, of Matthew 18:7: 'Wo unto the world because of offences'. Donne used this text to issue a very typical call for consideration for those who differ in non-essentials, stressing that 'wee are forbidden to scandalize any person' (III, 174). But Donne qualifies this call, and limits the range of possible offence proscribed by scripture, to allow for the defence and statement of the verities of this essential Christianity:

> [Paul] was as carefull not to scandalize, not to give just occasion to Jew, nor Gentile, as not to the Church of God; so must we be towards them of a superstitious religion among us, as carefull as towards one another, not to give any scandal, and just cause of offence. But what is to be called a just cause of offence *towards* those men? Good ends, and good ways, plain and direct, and manifest proceedings, these can be called no scandal, no just cause of offence, to Jew, nor Gentile, to Turk, nor Papist; nor does Saint *Paul* intend that we should forbear essentiall and necessary things, for fear of displeasing perverse and peevish men. To maintain the *doctrinall truths* of our religion, by conferences, by disputations, by writing, by preaching to avow, and to prove our religion to be the same, that Christ Jesus and his Apostles proposed at the beginning, the same that the generall Councels established after, the same that the blessed Fathers of those times, unanimely, and dogmatically delivered, the same that those glorious Martyrs quickned by their death, and carryed over all the world in the rivers, in the seas of their blood, to avow our religion by writing, and preaching, to be the same religion, and then to preserve and protect that religion which God hath put into our hearts, by all such meanes as hee hath put into our hands, in the due execution of *just Laws*; this is no scandal, no just cause of offence to Jew nor Gentile, Turke nor Papists. (III, 175)

This identification of Protestant doctrine with Apostolic and Patristic teaching addressed the Catholic depiction of reformed doctrine as innovation. Indeed, Donne's appeal to primitive and patristic Christianity reaped rhetorical dividends, for it allowed him to characterise the Roman church in general, and the council of Trent, more particularly, as forces of innovation, and to upbraid them for their failure to perceive or to respect the sufficiency of this fundamental doctrine. Donne stated this position forcibly in his 1621 Christmas sermon, dealing with John 1:8: 'He was not that Light, but was sent to bear witness of that Light'.

> As in the heavens the stars were created at once, with one *Fiat*, and then being so made, stars doe not beget new stars, so the *Christian doctrine necessary* to salvation, was delivered at once, that is, intirely, in one spheare, in the body of the Scriptures. And then, as stars doe not beget stars, Articles of faith doe not beget Articles of faith; so, as that the *Councell of Trent* should be brought to bed of *a new Creed*, not conceived before by the *holy Ghost* in the Scriptures, and (which is a monstrous birth) the child greater then the Father, as soon as it is borne, the new Creed of the *Councell of Trent* to containe more Articles, then the old Creed of the Apostles did. Saint *Jude* writing of the *common salvation* ... exhorts them to *contend earnestly for that faith, which was once delivered unto the Saints. Semel, once;* that is, *at once, semel, simul, once altogether.* (III, 369–70)

The polemical thrust of this extract is patent, and Donne goes on to underscore the culpability of the Roman church in adding to this once-delivered faith. Inevitably, transubstantiation and '*quotidian miracles*' come in for a mention, but Donne has spleen to spare for Rome's political innovations, as he summarises and re-states his position:

> To contract this, their *occasionall Divinity*, doctrines to serve present occasions, that in *eighty-eight*, an Hereticall Prince must necessarily be excommunicated, and an Heriticall Prince excommunicated must necessarily be deposed, but at another time it may be otherwise, and *conveniencies*, and *dispensations* may be admitted, these, and such as these, *traditionall, occaisionall, Almanack Divinity*, they may bee *Comets*, they may be *Meteors* ... but they are not *lux æternorum corporum*, the light of the stars and other heavenly bodies, for, they were made *at once*, and diminish not, encrease not. *Fundamentall articles* of faith, are always the same. And that's our application of this *lux æternorum corporum*, the light of those heavenly bodies, to the Light of our Text, Christ working in the Church. (III, 370–1)

Donne was revisiting a theme that he had already examined in an undated sermon, preached on Job 19:26, at Lincoln's Inn, dealing with the theme of resurrection. Here Donne pauses in his discussion of the church's unique role in propagating the doctrine of bodily resurrection to distinguish carefully between the creation and the declaration of articles of faith. Notably, he also takes the opportunity to stress that doctrine must be in accordance with reason to the extent that it must not contradict what reason grasps of the character of God:

> For, though articles of faith be not *facta Ecclesiæ*, they are *dicta Ecclesiæ*, though the Church doe not *make* articles, yet she *declares* them. In the Creation, the way was, *Dixit & facta sunt*, God spake, and so things were made; In the Gospell, the way is, *Fecit, & dicta sunt*, God makes articles of faith, and the Church utters them, presents them. That's *manifestè verum*, evidently, undeniably true, that Nature, and Philosophy say nothing of articles of faith. But, even in Nature, and in Philosophy, there is some preparation *A priore*, and much illustration *A posteriore*, of the Resurrection. For, first, we know by naturall reason, that it is no such thing, as God cannot doe; It implies no contradiction in it selfe, as that new article of *Transubstantiation* does; It implies no defectiveness in God, as that new article, *The necessity of a perpetuall Vicar upon earth*, does. (III, 94–5)

In addition, then, to its very considerable possibilities as a means of promoting Christian unity, Donne's essentialist ecumenism allowed him room for some very effective polemical manoeuvre against the Roman church and her adherents. In a funeral sermon for William Cokayne, preached in December of 1626, Donne made it an equally effective weapon against those at the other extreme of the religious spectrum. Interestingly, as in the Christmas Day sermon, Donne is dealing explicitly with the theme of the faith. As befits the more lugubrious occasion, Donne calls for introspection and self-examination: there is a far stronger sense in this sermon of obedience to the faith embodied in the teaching of the church as an individual exercise and responsibility.

> There is a Law of faith; a rule that ordinates, and regulates our faith; by which law and rule, the Apostle cals upon us, To examine our selves whether we be in the faith, or no; not onely by the internall motions, and private inspirations of his blessed Spirit, but by the Law and the Rule, which he hath delivered to us in the Gospell. The Kings pardon flowes from his mere grace, and from his brest; but we must have the writing and the Seale, that we may plead it: so does faith from God; But we must see it our selves, and shew it to others, or else we do not observe the Law of faith. ... So that it is not enough to say, I feele the inspiration of the Spirit of God, He infuses faith, and faith infused cannot be withdrawne; but, as there is a Law of faith, and a practice of faith, a Rule of faith, and an example of faith, apply thy

selfe to both; Regulate thy faith by the Rule, that is the Word, and by
Example, that is, Beleeve those things which the Saints of God have
constantly and unanimely believed to be necessary to salvation: The
Word is the Law, and the Rule, The Church is the Practise, and the
Precedent that regulates thy faith; And if thou make imaginary
revelations, and inspirations thy Law, or the practise of Sectaries thy
Precedent, thou doest but call Fancie and Imagination, by the name of
Reason and Understanding, and Opinion by the name of Faith, and
Singularity, and Schisme, by the name of Communion of Saints. (VII,
262–3)

Donne is in pastoral, as well as polemical, mode here, and he can be found in a
similar vein as he discusses the same issue towards the end of his career, in the
Christmas Day sermon for 1629. In this, he stressed not only the simplicity of
the essence of Christianity – now reduced to the two commandments given by
Christ – but also his reprehension of those who, by their 'wrangling' complicate
Christianity:

> Whereas the Christian Religion, is ... a plaine, an easie, a perspicuous
> truth, but that the perverse and uncharitable wranglings of passionate
> and froward men, have made Religion a hard, an intricate, and a
> perplexed art; so that now, that Religion, which carnall and worldly
> men, have, by an ill life, discredited, and made hard to be believed, the
> passion, and perversness of Schoole-men, by Controversies, hath
> made hard to bee understood. Whereas the Christian Religion, is of it
> selfe *Iugum suave*, a sweet, and an easie yoak, and *verbum abbreviatum*,
> an abridgement and a contracted doctrine; for, where the Jews had all
> abridged in *decum verba* (as *Moses* calls the ten Commandements, *ten
> words*) the Christian hath all abridged in *duo verba*, into two words,
> *love God, love thy neighbour.* (IX, 150)

Donne's distaste for the heated debate of doctrinal minutiae echoes throughout
the sermons, often in just such a pastoral context. At times, too, Donne's repudiation, or even disgust, is motivated by the purposelessness of 'all such
controversies which are all but forced diseases of hot brains and not sound
minds' (V, 123). But beyond the pointless nature of such debate, Donne alerted
his congregations to the tragic potential that such discussions had to weaken the
defence of orthodox Christianity by dividing its forces. So, in a court sermon
preached to King Charles in 1629, Donne warned of the possibility that
internecine Christian controversy distracted attention from the true enemies of
the gospel:

> Truly it is a sad Contemplation, to see Christians scratch and wound
> and teare one another, with the ignominious invectives, and unchari-
> table names of Heretique, and Schismatique, about Ceremoniall, and
> Problematicall, and indeed but Criticall, verball controversies: and in
> the meane time, the foundation of all, the Trinity, undermined by
> those numerous, those multitudinous Anthills of *Socinians*, that
> overflow and multiply every where.[6] (IX, 52–3)

This concern about misplaced use of 'heretic' as a convenient and emotive
pejorative label is typical of Donne. It was an important, and deliberate, implication of his ecumenical essentialism that it made heresy much more difficult to
achieve, and far more serious when it did occur. Donne spelled this out quite
explicitly, in another sermon before Charles:

> I shall better answer God for my mildenesse, then for my severity.
> And though anger towards a brother, or a *Raca*, or a foole, will beare
> an action: yet he shall recover lesse against me at that bar, whom I have
> called weake, or mislead (as I must necessarily call many in the *Roman
> Church*) then he whom I have passionately and peremptorily called
> *heretick*: for that consists much in the manner. It must be matter of
> faith, before the matter be heresie. (IX, 77)

In this extract, Donne adopts an accommodating attitude to Roman Christians,
something that, undoubtedly, has a good deal to do with its audience and its
context in court. Earlier in his career, the threat against which Donne called for
English Christians to unite was this same Roman church. As he outlined this in
a Lincoln's Inn sermon, he articulated a principle fundamental to his vision of
an accommodating and tolerant church:

> He is a good Christian that can ride out ... a storme, that by industry,
> as long as he can, and by patience, when he can do no more, over-lives
> a storm and does not forsake his ship for it, that is not scandalized
> with that State, nor that Church, of which he is a member, for those
> abuses that are in it. The Arke is peace, peace is good dispositions to
> one another, good interpretations of one another; for, if our
> impatience put us from our peace, and so out of the Arke, all without
> the Arke is sea; The bottomlesse and boundlesse Sea of Rome, will

6 See for an extended discussion of this important sermon, see 'Donne as preacher at court:
precarious "inthronization"' in *John Donne's Professional lives*, ed. Colclough (Cambridge, 2003),
pp 179–206; Mark Sweetnam, 'Foundational faults: heresy and religious toleration in the later
thought of John Donne' in Eiléan Ní Chuilleanáin and John Flood (eds), *Heresy in early English
literature* (Dublin, 2010), pp 113–26.

> hope to swallow us, if we dis-unite our selves, in uncharitable mis-
> interpretations of one another; The peace of God is the *peace that
> passeth all understanding*; That men should subdue and captivate even
> their understanding to the love of this peace, that when in their
> understanding they see no reason why this or this thing should be
> thus or thus done, or so and so suffered, the peace of God, that is,
> charity, *may passe their understanding*, and goe above it; for, howsoever
> the affections of men, or the vicissitudes and changes of affairs may
> vary ... howsoever I say, various occasions may vary their Laws,
> adhere we to that Rule of the Law, which the Apostle prescribes, that
> we always make ... *The end of the Commandment charity.* (III, 185)

Christian peace, then, is a peace that passes understanding: a peace built upon an understanding of the limitations of reason. At times, then, it may be necessary to 'doubt wisely'. Again, this is a facet of Donne's thought identified by Roy Battenhouse, who summarises Donne's views on the value of human reason in this context by suggesting that, for Donne, 'the mind's effort in pursuit of definitions produces results that are suggestive but not substantial, pertinent but not essential'.[7] Battenhouse identifies this strain in Donne's thought with the doctrine of 'learned ignorance' as taught by Erasmus and other Renaissance humanists, but taking its inspiration from Nicholas of Cusa. Ultimately, however, he identifies Donne's limitation of the utility of reason as a species of pietism, and briefly contends that this 'anti-intellectual' impetus can be traced 'back through St Bernard to Gregory the Great, Augustine, Jerome, Chrysostom and the Greek Fathers generally'.[8] Battenhouse is, perhaps, going to the very outer limits of the evidence by describing Donne's methods as anti-intellectual. In addition, he seems to underestimate the importance of another, more immediate source of this appreciation of a peace passing understanding. This emphasis in Donne's ecclesiology follows the approach taken by Hooker in *The lawes of ecclesiastical polity*.

Sacramental theology had a vital importance in Hooker's view of the church. The Eucharist was of special importance in the cultivation of church community. The precise mode of operation of the sacrament had been a subject of much discussion; central to the debate between the Roman and the reformed churches, but of similar import in inter-reformed debate. The battle between Roman transubstantiation, Lutheran consubstantiation and Zwinglian memorialism was always intractable and frequently divisive. In spite of the importance that Hooker ascribes to the Eucharist, he views this battle as vastly unproductive and, ultimately, unnecessary. He argues that the correct response to this central sacrament of the church was rather a personal appropriation of spiritual benefit,

---

7 Battenhouse, 'Grounds of religious toleration', 224.   8 Ibid., 225.

and not a desire to investigate the nuts and bolts of sacramental operation. Hooker is not entirely accommodating of every perspective – like Donne, he resists Zwingli's idea, later adopted in the Westminster Confession, that the species of the Eucharist were simply signs, and not channels, of grace. Beyond this qualification, however, Hooker is not prepared to pronounce on the mode of sacramental operation:

> This was it that some did exceedinglie feare, least *Zwinglius* and *Oecolampadius* would bringe to passe, that men should accompt of this sacrament but only as of a shadowe, destitute emptie and void of Christe. But seeinge that by opening the severall opinions which have bene held, they are growen (for ought I can see) on all sides at the lengthe to a generall agreement, concerninge that which alone is materiall, Namelye the *reall participation* of Christe and of life in his bodie and bloode *by means of this sacrament*, wherefore should the world continewe still distracted and rent with so manifold contentions, when there remainethe now no controversie savinge onlie about the subjecte *where* Christ is? Yea even in this point noe side denieth but that the *soule of man* is the receptacle of Christes presence. Whereby the question is yeat driven to a narrower isshue, nor dothe anie thing rest doubtfull but this, whether when the sacrament is administred, Christ be whole *within man onlye*, or els his bodie and bloode be also externallye seated in the verie consecrated elementes them selves, which opinion, they that defende, are driven either to *consubstaniate* and incorporate Christe, with elementes sacramental or to *transubstantiate* and change substance into his. ... All thinges considered and compared with that successe, which truth hathe hitherto had, by so bitter conflictes with errours in this point, shall I wishe that men would more give themselves to meditate with silence what wee have by the sacrament, and lesse to dispute of the manner how.[9]

Similarly, for Donne, the issue of importance is 'what wee have by the sacrament', and not the insoluble and divisive question of 'the manner how'. He expressed this belief very clearly in his Christmas Day sermon for 1626, which 'contains ... his most explicit treatment of sacramental doctrine':[10]

9 Hooker, II, pp 331–2.   10 Robert Whalen, 'Sacramentalizing the Word: Donne's 1626 Christmas sermon' in *Centered on the Word: literature, scripture and the Tudor–Stuart middle way*, ed. Daniel W. Doerksen and Cristopher Hodgkins (Newark, DE, 2004), p. 192. This sermon is also discussed in some detail in Robert Whalen, *The poetry of immanence: sacrament in Donne and Herbert* (Toronto, 2002), pp 83–109; Eleanor McNees, 'John Donne and the Anglican doctrine of the eucharist', *Texas Studies in Literature and Language* 29:1 (1987), 94–114.

> When thou commest to this seale of thy peace, the Sacrament, pray
> that God will give thee that light, that may direct and establish thee,
> in necessary and fundamentall things; that is, the light of faith to see,
> that the Body and Bloud of Christ, it is applied to thee, in that action;
> But for the manner, how the Body of Bloud of Christ is there, wait his
> leisure, if he have not yet manifested that to thee: Grieve not at that,
> wonder not at that, presse not for that; for hee hath not manifested
> that, not the way, not the manner of his presence in the Sacrament, to
> the Church. A peremptory prejudice upon other mens opinions, that
> no opinion but thine can be true, in the doctrine of the Sacrament,
> and an uncharitable condemning of other men, or other Churches
> that may be of another perswasion then thou art, in the matter of the
> Sacrament, may frustrate and disappoint thee of all that benefit,
> which thou mightst have, by an humble receiving thereof, if thou
> wouldest exercise thy faith onely, here, and leave thy passion at home,
> and referre thy reason, and disputation to the Schoole. (VII, 290–1)

In this extract, as is typical of Donne's Christmas sermons, it is the pastoral
imperative that is stressed, and Donne alerts his congregation to the danger that
an attitude of sacramental curiosity may nullify the personal and spiritual benefit
of the sacrament. Curiosity, for Donne, often leads to a lack of charity, and true
Christian charity should be able to accommodate differences of opinion in
matters of 'probability'. Donne stresses the function of charity in his discussion,
in his Easter sermon for the same year, of the importance of 'allowing another
man his probability' on issues where scripture is silent:

> Where two contrary opinions are both probable, they may be
> embraced, and believed by two men, and those two be both learned,
> and discreet, and pious, and zealous men. And this consideration
> should keep men from that precipitation of imprinting the odious and
> scandalous names of Sects or Sectaries upon other men who may
> differ from them, and from others with them, in some opinions.
> Probability leads me in my assent, and I think thus; Let me allow
> another man his probability too, and let him think his way in things
> that are not fundamentall. They that do not believe alike, in all
> circumstances of the manner of the Resurrection, may all, by Gods
> goodnesse, meet there, and have their parts in the glory thereof, if
> their own uncharitablenesse do not hinder them: And he that may
> have been in the right opinion, may sooner misse heaven, then he that
> was in the wrong, if he comes uncharitably to condemne or contemne
> the other: for, in such cases, humility, and love of peace, may, in the
> sight of God, excuse and recompense many errours and mistakings.
> (VII, 97)

As we have already noted, sacramental debate was not just a matter of pastoral importance: it was an issue of central polemical interest. Later in the Christmas sermon quoted above, Donne acknowledged this aspect of the question. The imagery he uses expresses very acutely Donne's impatience with the taking up of positions simply to take a position:

> And so, diving in a bottomlesse sea, they poppe sometimes above water to take breath, to appeare to say something and then snatch at a loose proposition, that swims upon the face of the water; and so the Roman Church hath catched a *Trans*, and others a *Con* and a *Sub*, and an *In*, and varied their poetry into a Transubstantiation, and a Consubstantiation, and the rest, and rymed themselves beyond reason, into absurdities, and heresies, and by a young figure of *similiter cadens*, they are fallen alike into error, though the errors that they are fallen into, be not of a like nature, nor danger. We offer to goe no farther, then according to his Word; In the Sacrament our eyes see his salvation, according to that, so far, as that hath manifested unto us, and in that light wee depart in peace, without scruple in our owne, without offence to other mens consciences. (VII, 296)

This extract is dismissive of theological debate – the endorsement of different positions on the Eucharist is seen less as a matter of careful thought than a desperate grasping at seemingly random ideas. It is this extract, perhaps, that comes closest to justifying Battenhouse's use of the term pietism to describe Donne's theology.

This treatment of the operation of the sacrament is paradigmatic of Donne's approach to a wider range of doctrinal debates. He outlined this approach, and some of the issues to which it was pertinent, in one of the undated sermons from his series on the penitential Psalms:

> But still we continue in that humble boldnesse, to say, God is best found, when we seeke him, and observe him in his operation upon us. God gives audiences, and admits accesses in his solemne and publike and out-roomes, in his Ordinances: In his Cabinet, in his Bed-chamber, in his unrevealed purposes, wee must not presse upon him. ... We must abstaine from enquiring *De modo*, how such or such things are done in many points, in which it is necessary to us to know that such things are done: As the maner of Christs presence in the Sacrament, and the maner of Christs descent into Hell, for these are *arcana Imperii*, secrets of State, for the maner is secret, though the thing bee evident in the Scriptures. But the entring into Gods unrevealed, and bosome-purposes, are *Arcana domus*, a man is as farre

from a possibility of attaining the knowledge, as from an excuse for offering it. (V, 298–9)

In another undated sermon, preached at a christening, he added to the list of *Arcana domus* another insoluble mystery:

> Now since the Holy Ghost, that is the God of unity and peace, hath told us at once, that the satisfaction for our sins is Christ himselfe, and hath told us no more, Christ entirely, Christ altogether, let us not divide and mangle Christ, or tear his Church in pieces by forward and frivolous disputations, whether Christ gave his divinity for us, or his *humanity;* whether the divine Nature, or the humane Nature redeemed us; for neither his divinity nor his humanity, is *Ipse*, He himselfe, and *Dedit seipsum*, He gave himselfe: Let us not *subdivide* him into lesse pieces, then those, *God*, and *Man*; and enquire contentiously, whether he suffered in *soul*, as well as in *body* ... He gave himselfe; let us least of all shred Christ Jesus into lesse scruples and atoms then these, Soul, and body; and dispute whether consisting of both, it was his *active*, or his *passive* obedience that redeemed us ... Let us abstain from all such curiosities, which are all but forc'd dishes of hot brains, and not sound meat, that is, from all perverse wranglings, whether *God*, or *Man* redeemed us. (V, 123–4)

Among these unplumbable mysteries, Donne also reckoned the controverted points of predestinarian theology, urging his listeners:

> let no Man be too curiously busie, to search what God does in his bedchamber; we have all enough to answer, for that, which we have done in our bedchamber. (V, 160)

We may, then, observe Donne summarising this approach to these issues of theology in another of his sermons on the Penitential Psalms, even as he introduces a related but distinct issue in the life of the English church:

> When the Lord is working in his Temple, in his Ordinances, and Institutions, let not the wisdome of all the world dispute why God instituted those Ordinances, the foolishnesse of preaching, or the simplicity of Sacraments in his Church. Let not the wisdome of private men dispute, why those whom God hath accepted as the representation of the Church, those of whom Christ sayes, *Dic Ecclesiæ, Tell the Church*, have ordained these, or these Ceremonies for Decency, and Uniformity, and advancing of Gods glory, and mens

> Devotion in the Church; Let all the earth be silent, *In Sacramentis*,
> The whole Church may change no Sacraments, nor Articles of faith,
> and let particular men be silent *In Sacramentalibus*, in those things
> which the Church hath ordained, for the better conveying, and
> imprinting, and advancing of those fundamentall mysteries; for this
> silence of reverence which is an acquiescence in those things which
> God hath ordained, immediately, as Sacraments, or Ministerially, as
> other Rituall things in the Church. (IX, 281–2)

The doctrinal issues that we have already mentioned were enormous in their intrinsic import. Less inherently important in doctrinal terms, but of equal, if not greater, impact to the experience of church life, and the practical implementation of ecclesiastical authority, were the 'Ceremonies for Decency, and Uniformity' mentioned in this extract – matters of ritual and liturgy indifferent in themselves, but endorsed by the church. These matters were hotly contested between those who conformed – with whatever degree of enthusiasm – to the form of the *Book of Common Prayer*, and the puritan and proto-Presbyterian elements of English Protestantism. A long history of debate between conformists and separatists had focused on these issues: the fashion of churches, the form of public prayer and the use of the *Book of Common Prayer*, the use of the cross in baptism the observance of holy days.[11] Not all of these issues are of equal importance for Donne, but many do occur in the sermons. Donne is concerned not to prove that the acceptance of these adiaphora was essential, but that it was possible without violence to the conscience to follow the direction and ordinance of the church in matters not essential. Donne justifies the retention of contested ceremonies, on which scripture is silent, by appeal to 'Decency and Uniformity' in the praxis of the English church.

The objection raised to these matters of ritual, and thus requiring to be addressed by their apologists, was that they came to close to the observance of the Roman church, and hence had no place in reformed polity. Hooker had summarised the complaints of the puritan party, stating that the ritual of the English church 'hath in their eye too great affinitie with the forme of the Church of Rome; it differeth too much from that which Churches elsewhere reformed allowe and observe'.[12] It fell to the lot of apologists of conformity to argue that similarity to Rome was not, in and of itself, a basis to reject matters of observance otherwise indifferent. Donne expressed this conviction clearly in the sermon that he preached in 1628, marking the conversion of St Paul:

> I doe not intend, that we should decline all such things, as had been
> superstitiously abused, in a superstitious Church; But, in all such

11 For a helpful discussion of the accommodation of common prayer and images in Donne's theology, see Jeffrey Johnson, *The theology of John Donne* (Cambridge, 1999), pp 37–88.
12 Hooker, *Works*, II, p. 119.

things, as being in their own nature indifferent, are, by just commandment of lawfull authority, become more then indifferent (necessary) to
us ... (for, though salvation consist not in Ceremonies, Obedience
doth, and Salvation consists much in Obedience) That in all such
things, we always informe our selves, of the right use of those things
in their first institution, of their abuse with which they have been
depraved in the Roman Church, and of the good use which is made of
them in ours. That because pictures have been adored, we do not
abhor a picture; Nor sit at the Sacrament, because Idolatry hath been
committed in kneeling. ... For this is a true way of shutting out
superstition, Not always to abolish the thing it selfe, because in the
right use thereof, the spirituall profit and edification may exceed the
danger, but by preaching, and all convenient wayes of instruction, to
deliver people out of that ignorance, which possesses people in the
Roman captivity. (VIII, 331)

Similarly, in his Trinity Sunday sermon for 1624, Donne explicitly addressed
those who questioned the value of any extra-Biblical ritual. In the context, his
immediate concern is the justification of the liturgical use of scripture, the application of certain passages to particular days. His defence of this practice,
however, goes beyond this particular adiaphoron, to embrace the whole range of
external practices in the life of the church:

It hath been the custome of the Christian Church to appropriate
certaine Scriptures to certaine Dayes, for the celebrating of certaine
Mysteries of God, or the commemorating of certaine benefits from
God: They who consider the age of the Christian Church, too high or
too low, too soone or too late, either in the cradle, as it is exhibited in
the Acts of the Apostles, or bed-rid in the corruptions of Rome, either
before it was come to any growth, when Persecutions nipped it, or
when it was so over-growne, as that prosperity and outward splendour
swelled it, They that consider the Church so, will never finde a good
measure to direct our religious worship of God by, for the outward
Liturgies, and Ceremonies of the Church. But as soon as the
Christian Church had a constant establishment under Christian
Emperours, and before the Church had her tympany of worldly
prosperity under usurping Bishops, in this outward service of God,
there were particular Scriptures appropriated to particular days.
Particular men have not liked this that it should be so: And yet that
Church which they take use to take for their patterne (I meane
Geneva) as soone as it came to have any convenient establishment by
the labours of that Reverend man, who did so much in the rectifying

> thereof, admitted this custome of celebrating certaine times, by the
> reading of certaine Scriptures. (VI, 132–3)

Donne's appeal to the practice of the primitive church is very typical, but we
should also notice his citation of the practice of Geneva in support of the
practice of the English church – a move calculated to impress upon his congregation the validity of this practice. This is a device that Donne used whenever
possible: Calvin is routinely empanelled to speak for the continued use of images
and the considered preservation of ceremonies in the life of the church. So, for
example, in a sermon preached on Candlemas day, close to the end of his life,
Donne concludes his very frank acknowledgment that the celebration of
Candlemas is a Protestant perpetuation of a Roman ceremony that originated in
pagan practice by appealing to Calvin's three dicta on appropriate ceremonies,
approving his requirement that ceremonies used in the reformed church should
be 'few in number; . . . easie for observation; [and] . . . clearly understood in their
signification' (X, 90).

Donne's essentialist ecumenism, then, and his approach to both doctrine and
ceremony emphasised a form of Christianity, a view of church authority calculated to appeal to as wide a range of opinion as possible. In no matter is this
intent more clear than Donne's treatment of the Council of Trent.[13] Anti-
Tridentine polemic was something of a Protestant staple. With Donne's interest
in controversy, he was likely to be familiar with many of these writings against
Trent. At the very least it is virtually certain that he would have known the work
of Paolo Sarpi, the most prominent and prolific exponent of the genre, in whom
Donne had a clear interest.[14] These works of polemic drew the reader's attention
to a large array of shortcomings in the instantiation, deliberations and decrees of
Trent. With such a wide range of weapons at his disposal, it is very noticeable
that Donne repeatedly returns to one central complaint: the Council of Trent
had over-determined Christian doctrine, and had made 'Problematical things,
Dogmatical; and matter of Disputation, matter of Faith' (IV, 144). Donne's
disagreement was not simply with the outcomes of Trent, but its very premise:

> We charge them with *Heresie* in the whole *new Creed* of the *Councell*
> *of Trent* (for, if all the particular doctrines be not *Hereticall*, yet, the
> doctrine of inducing new Articles of faith is *Hereticall*, and that

---

13 For a wider discussion of Donne's views on Trent, see Jeffrey Johnson, 'John Donne and
Paolo Sarpi: rendering the Council of Trent' in *John Donne and the protestant reformation*, ed.
Mary Arshagouni Papazian (Detroit, MI, 2003), pp 90–112. 14 Sarpi's *History of the Council of
Trent* was published in England in 1619. See Frances A. Yates, 'Paolo Sarpi's "History of the
Council of Trent"', *Journal of the Warburg and Courtauld Institutes* 7 (1944), 123–43. Johnson,
'Donne and Paolo Sarpi' provides a valuable discussion of the correspondences, and discontinu-
ities between the thought of Sarpi and Donne.

> doctrine runs through all the Articles, for else they could not be
> Articles). (III, 132)

And, while Donne adverts from time to time to specific determinations of Trent
(such as the status it gave to the Vulgate, and its use of the 'unanime consent' of
the Fathers as the gold standard for the interpretation of scripture)[15] it is a
repudiation of its unnecessary codification of Christian belief that most consistently occupies him.

So it is that, in his first sermon before Charles, preached in April 1625,
Donne includes, as a part of his discussion of the state of the English church, a
very typical criticism of the Tridentine additions to the fundamentals of
Christian religion:

> [T]hey have made *Salvation* deare; Threescore yeares agoe, a man
> might have beene sav'd at halfe the price hee can now: Threescore
> yeares agoe, he might have beene saved for believing the *Apostles
> Creed*; now it will cost him the *Trent Creed* too. Evermore they will
> presse for all, and yield nothing; and there is indeed their
> *Specification*, there's their *Character*, that's their *Catholique*, their
> *Vniversall*; To *have all*; ... It would not be granted at *Rome*, if we
> should aske a *Church* for a *Church*. In a word, wee charge them with
> *uncharitablenesse* (and *Charitie* is without all Controversie, a
> *Foundation* of *Religion*) that they will so peremptorily exclude us from
> Heaven, for matters that doe not appertaine to *Foundations*. For, if
> they will call all *Foundations*, that that *Church hath*, or *doth*, or *shall*
> decree, wee must learne our *Catechisme* upon our *Death-bedd*, and
> inquire for the Articles of our Faith, when wee are going out of the
> world, for they may have decreed something that morning. (VI, 249)

Later, in another sermon preached before the king, Donne deals tellingly with
Trent's unnecessary additions. In proof that these additions are undesirable, as
well as unnecessary, Donne goes on to instance the realisation of the 'sad and
sober' men within the Roman church who have come, ruefully, to recognise that
they have committed themselves to an over-defined and inflexibile Christianity:

> [W]hen we have *Primogenitum Ecclesiæ*, The eldest son by the
> Primitive Church, The Creed of the Apostles, they will super-induce
> another son, by another *venter*, by a step-mother, by their sick and
> crazy Church, and ... will then make the portion of the later, larger
> than the elders, make their Trent-Creed larger then the Apostles. ...

---

15 See, for example, III, 176; III, 316; IV, 61; VIII, 205; VIII, 358.

But the mystery of their Iniquity is easily revealed. ... All this is not because they absolutely oppose the Scriptures, or stiffly deny them to be the most certaine and constant rule that can be presented. ... But because the Scriptures are constant, and limited, and determined, there can be no more Scriptures, And they should be shrewdly prejudiced, and shrewdly disadvantaged, if all emergent cases arising in the Christian world must be judged by a Law, which others know beforehand, as well as they; Therefore being wise in their own generation, they choose rather to lay up their Rule in a cupboard, then upon a Shelfe, rather *in Scrinio pectoris*, in the breast and bosome of one man, then upon every deske in a study, where every man may lay, or whence every man may take a Bible. Therefore have so many sad and sober men among them, repented, that in the Councell of Trent, they came to a finall resolution in so many particulars; because how incommodious soever some of those particulars may prove to them, yet they are bound to some necessity of a defence, or to some aspersion if they forsake such things as have been solemnly resolved in that matter. (VII, 124–5, cf. VI, 300–1)

By way of a contrast that clearly points up Donne's objection to Trent, and that articulates an alternative conciliar model that appealed to his essentialism, we must give consideration to his views of the Synod of Dort, expressed in the same sermon.[16] We are less interested in Donne's view of the theology of Dort than in his endorsement of the method of Dort:[17]

In the last forraine Synod, which our Divines assisted, with what a blessed sobriety, they delivered their sentence. ... That we must

16 A very suggestive discussion of Donne's wider views of Dort is provided in Jeanne M. Shami, '"Speaking openly and speaking first": John Donne, the Synod of Dort and the early Stuart church' in *John Donne and the protestant reformation*, ed. Mary Arshagouni Papazian (Detroit, MI, 2003), pp 35–65. See also Shami, *Conformity in crisis*, pp 154–7. 17 It is also significant that a commitment to councils of the church, as a means of resolving doctrinal differences, had a long history in English Protestantism and was, furthermore, of considerable importance in Hookerian ecclesiology. See, on the role of councils in general, the overview of scholarship provided by Francis Oakley, 'Natural law, the *Corpus Mysticum* and consent in conciliar thought from John of Paris to Matthew Ugonis', *Speculum* 56:4 (1981), 786–810 and, on the pre-reformation background, Bruce Gordon, 'Conciliarism in late mediæval Europe' in *The reformation world*, ed. Andrew Pettegree (London, 2000), pp 31–50. Specifically on Hooker's consiliarism, see W.B. Patterson, 'Hooker on ecumenical relations: conciliarism in the English refomation' in *Richard Hooker and the construction of Christian community*, ed. A.S. McGrade (Tempe, AZ, 1997), pp 283–303; Paul Avis, *Anglicanism and the Christian church: theological resources in historical perspective* (Edinburgh, 1989), pp 23–4, 32–3, 42–4; Egil Grislis, 'The role of consensus in Richard Hooker's method of theological inquiry' in *The heritage of Christian thought: essays in honour of Robert Lowry Calhoun*, ed. Robert E. Cushman and Egil Grislis (New York, 1965), pp 64–8; Gunnar Hillerdal, *Reason and revelation in Richard Hooker* (Lund, 1962), pp 53–5; Munz, *Place of Hooker*, pp 95–9.

> receive Gods promise so, as they are generally set forth to us in the
> Scriptures; and that for our actions and manners, for our life and
> conversation, we follow that will of God, which is expressly declared
> to us in his Word. (VII, 127)

What is noticeable is Donne's endorsement of a synod that refrained from
emulating Trent's rigid codification of Christian doctrine. The determinations
of Dort, in Donne's view, at any rate, allowed individual adherence to scripture
to take precedence over a commitment to the determinations of any human
council.

It is helpful, by way of recapitulation, to close this chapter by looking briefly
at Donne's sonnet 'Show me deare Christ, thy Spouse, so bright and clear'. One
of the relatively few poems written by Donne after he had entered orders, this
sonnet, in its treatment of the church, answers, across the years of Donne's
career, the ideas of Satyre III.[18] It shares a number of the Satyre's key elements:
the identification of the church as a woman, the explicit figuring of this female
figure as the object of a quest, the identification of painted Rome and the
despoiled churches of reformed Europe as opposing ecclesiological positions,
and a refusal to be complacent about the status of the English church. Key to
understanding the unique contribution of this sonnet is the fact that Donne, by
imploring that he be granted a view of Christ's spouse, is looking for an eschatological revelation – Biblically it is only at the end of time that the church is
unveiled as Christ's spouse, that he presents her to himself 'a glorious church,
not having spot, or wrinkle, or any such thing; but that it should be holy and
without blemish' (Ephesians 5:27). In this context, his examination of earthly,
visible churches, whether in Rome, Germany or in England, seems calculated to
reveal how little any national and temporal church corresponds to the international and eternal Catholic body of believers. But there is also a polemical edge
to this sonnet: Donne invokes and entirely subverts a crucial image of
Presbyterian ecclesiology. 'For inscribed at the heart of the Presbyterian project
lay a moment of transcendence when the division between the internal and the
external government of the church was dissolved and Christ's spiritual body
became visible, embodied in the community of the godly which had been called
together and sustained by the purely scriptural ordinances and offices of the
discipline'.[19] Donne is seeking a moment of transcendence that sounds similar,
but is, in fact, fundamentally opposed to such expectations. His closing appeal to
Christ to

---

18 See, on Donne's post-ordination poetry, David Novarr, *The disinterred muse: Donne's texts and
contexts* (Ithaca, NY, 1980).   19 Peter Lake, 'Presbyterianism, the idea of a national church and
the argument from divine right' in *Protestantism and the national church in sixteenth-century
England*, ed. Peter Lake and Maria Dowling (London, 1983), p. 200.

> Betray kind husband thy spouse to our sights,
> And let myne amorous soule court thy mild Dove,
> Who is most trew, and pleasing to thee, then
> When she is embrac'd and open to most men. (lines 11–14)

is deliberately shocking in its overt sexual implications, and forcefully expresses Donne's belief that a true church is an inclusive church. The articulation of the belief is unusually stark, but it remains an expression of the same basic ecclesiology that we have traced throughout Donne's career. For Donne, the church did not function as a select society of the godly, whose membership requirements were designed to exclude all but the very elect. Nor could he accept the Roman model, where inclusion was obtained only at the price of a confining and crippling over-definition of acceptable belief. Rather, Donne, with Hooker, saw the church as a supernatural society, the locus of orderly religious life, an expression of a national and international unity in the essentials of the Christian faith.

5

Defending the place of preaching

One of the most memorable scenes recorded in Izaak Walton's *Life of Donne* comes close to the end of his account, as Donne, the paragon of preachers, delivers his final sermon:

> Before that month ended, he was appointed to preach upon his old constant day, the first *Friday* in *Lent*; he had notice of it, and had in his sickness so prepared for that imployment, that as he had long thirsted for it: so he resolved his weakness should not hinder his journey; he came therefore to *London*, some few days before his appointed day of preaching. At his coming thither, many of his friends ... doubted his strength to perform that task; and did therefore disswade him from undertaking it, assuring him however, it was like to shorten his life; but he passionately denied their requests; saying, *he would not doubt that God who in so many weaknesses had assisted him with an unexpected strength, would now withdraw it in his last employment; professing an holy ambition to perform that sacred work.* And, when to the amazement of some beholders he appeared in the Pulpit, many of them thought he presented himself not to preach mortification by a living voice: but mortality by a decaying body and a dying face. ... Many that saw his tears, and heard his faint and hollow voice professing they thought the Text prophetically chosen, and that Dr Donne *had preach't his own Funeral Sermon.*[1]

The sermon, at least in Walton's account, was both the conclusion and the climax of Donne's preaching. His text, his exposition and his appearance join together – 'his form and cause conjoined' – to make his final sermon uniquely effective, uniquely memorable.

For Walton, the preaching of the sermon later published as *Death's Duel* was a unique occasion, but it was also the culmination of a remarkable preaching career: the power of Donne's final act of preaching had been foreshadowed throughout Donne's ecclesiastical career. Donne had consistently:

> preach[ed] the Word so, as shewed his own heart was possest with those very thoughts and joys that he laboured to distill into others: A

1 Walton, *Lives*, pp 55–6.

> Preacher in earnest; weeping sometimes for his Auditory, sometimes with them: always preaching to himself, like an Angel from a cloud, but in none: carrying some, as St Paul was, to Heaven in holy raptures, and inticing others by a sacred Art and Courtship to amend their lives; here picturing a vice so as to make it ugly to those that practised it; and a virtue so, as to make it beloved even by those that lov'd it not; and all this with a most particular grace and an inexpressible addition of comeliness.[2]

For Donne's first biographer, then, and for many of his contemporaries, it was as a preacher that Donne was to be remembered and celebrated. This is fitting: Donne himself found in preaching a work that gave shape and meaning to his life; a task that demanded the highest pitch of the oddly assorted talents with which his earlier life had furnished him. To understand Donne's view of the preacher's office is essential to our understanding of Donne's own self-image.

This understanding is of particular moment for our present study. For, if the authority of scripture and the church delineated truth for Donne, it was the office of the preacher to impart that truth to his congregation. The pulpit, then, became more than a stage for performance or a shop counter for the peddling of crowd-pleasing sermons. Rather, it was a point of contact between God and his people, and the preacher, in his preaching of the Word of God became a conduit of divine grace. And, while there was, clearly, a dignity about this function, it was a dignity that came with an alarming burden of responsibility – to God, to the church to the congregation. It is this sense of obligation that that Donne repeatedly expresses by his appropriation of the Pauline *væ si non* ... – 'Woe be unto me if I preach not the gospel ...'.

Donne's understanding of the preacher's role illuminates more than the details of his biography. That insight is, unquestionably, both useful and necessary. Of equal importance, in our present study, is the pertinence of this understanding to our effort to locate Donne in relation to the intellectual and theological currents of the reformed church in which he ministered. Our endeavour to do so is a particularly notable instance of the advantages of reading Donne in the context of his time. As we shall see, the place of preaching in the economy of the English church was being renegotiated throughout Donne's career. When this is borne in mind, two remarkable facts emerge – firstly that Donne interacts vigorously and with some clarity with the changes proposed by the avant-garde conformists; secondly, this interaction never explicitly invokes contemporary controversy. Donne is engaged less in a defence of orthodoxy than a defensive orthodoxy and he responds to the challenge of the avant-garde by consistently restating the established doctrine of the English church.[3]

2 Ibid., p. 31. 3 A point that is much emphasised, in the service of a clear evangelical adgenda, by Peter Adam, *'To bring men to heaven by preaching': John Donne's evangelistic sermons* (London,

While the role of preaching became an increasingly contested issue during Donne's career, the role of the preacher had been a complex and often contested issue since the beginning of the Reformation.[4] The English church quickly adopted the logocentric orientation espoused by the magisterial reformers, but episodes like Elizabeth's clashes with Edmund Grindal and his defence of both 'prophesyings' and of preaching more generally are a useful reminder that homiletic enthusiasm was neither universal nor unequivocal.[5] For the most part, however, the primacy of the word preached was a hallmark of the English church. And this importance was constantly restated throughout the Elizabethan and Jacobean periods, inflected in sermons and apologetics, and endorsed by those from across the spectrum of the English church.[6] It was only towards the close of James' reign that this consensus on the importance of preaching became an issue of contention. Though those who set about this demolition proclaimed their continuity with historical Christianity, they represented a new development in the English church.

Commencing during the reign of James, the re-evaluation of the place of the sermon culminated, under Laud and Charles I, in a radical reorientation of the piety of the English church. As historians have sought to account for the emergence of the allied and overlapping forces of Laudianism and Arminianism, they have highlighted the origins of this new piety in the works of Richard Hooker and Lancelot Andrewes, and its popularisation by John Buckeridge and by Laud himself.[7] These men form the core of the avant-garde conformity of

2006).   4 Preaching had, of course, been a mainstay of the continental reformation. See, for a discussion of its importance, Pettegree, *Culture of persuasion*, pp 10–39. We should also note that preaching was not by any means exclusive to the Reformed Church. Indeed, Susan Wabuda, *Preaching during the English reformation* (Cambridge, 2002) traces developments in late medieval preaching that, in her compelling thesis, laid the homiletic basis for the diffusion of Reformed teaching.   5 For an account of this episode, see *Archbishop Grindal*, pp 233–52. Prophesyings were rather different from the sort of sermons that we find Donne engaged in. Nonetheless, we should note that Grindal's fateful letter to Elizabeth I is as much a defence of preaching in general as it is of the specific form of 'prophesying': see Edmund Grindal, *The remains of Edmund Grindal, successively bishop of London and archbishop of York and Canterbury*, ed. William Nicholson (Cambridge, 1843), pp 376–90. On the nature of prophesying, see Peter Iver Kaufman, 'Prophesying again', *Church History* 68:2 (1999), 337–58. Collinson also draws our attention to the importance attached by preaching by Ridley, Grindal's mentor (pp 57–65, passim), and to the centrality given to preaching in Grindal's approach to the ignorance prevailing in his new diocese of York (pp 205–10, 226).   6 Eric Josef Carlson, 'Good pastors or careless shepherds? parish ministers and the English Reformation', *History* 88 (2003), 423–36 surveys the evidence for the centrality of preaching in a range of polemical, apologetic and homiletic writing. Kenneth Fincham, *Prelate as pastor: the episcopate of James I* (Oxford, 1990), esp. pp 9–34 suggests that the preaching of the gospel was one end of the Episcopal dipole, and marshals impressive evidence for the importance of preaching in the perception of the bishop's office.   7 See, inter alia, Lake, *Anglicans and Puritans?*; Lake, 'Avant-garde conformity at the court of James I'; Lake, 'The Laudians and the argument from authority'; Fincham and Lake, 'The ecclesiastical policy of King James I'; Fincham and Lake, 'The ecclesiastical policies of James I and Charles I'; Fincham, *The early Stuart church, 1603–1642*; Fincham, *Prelate as pastor,* the Jacobean church. The place of preaching was a central point of dissension between these avant-garde conformists the mainstream of the English church.[8] Peter McCullough, in his study of sermons at the Elizabethan and Jacobean court, recognises the development of a very similar agenda of change, and, as befits the scope of his study, concentrates especially on its implications for preaching. He recounts James' demand that, on his arrival in his closet to hear the sermon, the liturgical portion of the service be cut short: the minister was obliged to segue, with what grace he could muster, into the sermon. In the light of this, he argues that it was 'James' brusque elevation of sermon over service [that] focused and fuelled a debate over the efficacy of preaching versus prayer that has simmered in England since the Reformation'.[9]

McCullough's characterisation of the debate should be noted with care: it was indeed concerned with the 'efficacy of preaching versus prayer'. None of the avant-garde argued that it was either possible or desirable to dispense with preaching. On the contrary, these divines had a very high estimation of the sermon. Hooker, indeed, made this explicit when he stated:

> So worthie a part of divine service we should greatlie wronge, if we did not esteeme preaching as the blessed ordinance of God, sermons as keyes to the kingdom of heaven, as winges to the soule, as spurres to the good affections of man, unto the sound and healthie as foode, as phisicke unto diseased mindes. Wherefore how highlie soever it may please them with wordes of truth to extol sermons, they shall not herein offend us.[10]

In spite of this view of preaching, Hooker's suggestion that the reading of the scriptures might, at times, be both more beneficial, and (being unmediated) less

---

esp. pp 231–47, 277–88; Tyacke, *Anti-Calvinists: the rise of English Arminianism, c.1590–1640* (Oxford, 1987); Milton, *Catholic and reformed*. Julian Davies, *The Caroline captivity of the church: Charles I and the remoulding of Anglicanism, 1625–1641* (Oxford, 1992) provides a useful marshalling of relevant evidence, but his interpretation of that evidence is open to challenge, especially in relation to the roots of the avant-garde movement in the Jacobean reign. Tyacke, 'Anglican attitudes', provides an instructive survey of the 'Anglican' historiography embodied in a number of studies, and provides a helpful examination Davies' work (pp 156–67). 8 Helpful discussions of the debate over preaching are found in Lake, 'Avant-garde conformity', esp. pp 123–6; Fincham, *Prelate as pastor*, pp 233–47, Mary Morrissey, 'Scripture, style and persuasion in seventeenth-century English theories of preaching', *Journal of Ecclesiastical History* 53:4 (2002), 686–706; Peter E. McCullough, 'Making dead men speak: Laudianism, print and the works of Lancelot Andrewes, 1626–1642', *Historical Journal* 41:2 (1998), 401–24; Peter E. McCullough, *Sermons at court: politics and religion in Elizabethan and Jacobean preaching* (Cambridge, 1998), pp 121–2, 158–66. Lori Anne Ferrell, *Government by polemic: James I, the king's preachers and the rhetorics of conformity, 1603–1625* (Stanford, CA, 1998) covers many of these issues in her discussion of James' 'tuning of the pulpits'. 9 McCullough, *Sermons at court*, p. 156. 10 Richard Hooker, *The Folger Library edition of the works of Richard Hooker, 3: Of the laws of ecclesiastical polity*, ed. Paul G. Stanwood (Cambridge, MA, 1981), p. 87.

susceptible to misinterpretation than preaching, was of crucial importance to the development of the avant-garde reappraisal of preaching. Also of vital importance was Hooker's understanding of the efficacy of scripture, as the Word of God, and of preaching, as the medium to convey that word:

> He also seems to suggest that the salvific function of Scripture, read or preached, stems from the information that it imparts, rather than from the operation of grace on those present. Scripture 'serveth than onlie in the nature of a doctrinall instrument. It saveth because it maketh *wise unto salvation*'. ... [I]f sermons are 'doctrinall instruments' (in Hooker's phrase) then they are means of salvation only insofar as they teach the hearers what is required to be saved. The event of the sermon is not itself an opportunity for the receipt of grace.[11]

We find Hooker's ideas developed in the sermons of Lancelot Andrewes, 'the most famous preacher against preaching'.[12] Like Hooker, Andrewes insisted on the importance of preaching, in its place. This he expressed characteristically in a sermon preached before the King in 1607, on James 1:22: 'But be ye doers of the word, and not hearers only, deceiving your own selves'.

> [I]n dealing with Scriptures that consist of *Negatives* by comparison (not *hearers*, but *doers*; and such like) we had need to walk warily: ... lest we cast out one Devil with another, as the manner of some is: the devil of *hearing* only, with the devil of *not hearing at all:* ... *We must take heed we preserve both, both* hearing and doing, each in their severall right: and so doe the former, that the latter *we leave not undone.* ... The reason of which our continuall being *hearers,* is the continuall necessitie of *hearing of the Word of God.*[13]

11 Morrissey, 'Scripture, style and persuasion', 697.   12 Ibid. On Andrewes, see Peter E. McCullough, 'Andrewes, Lancelot (1555–1626)', *Oxford dictionary of national biography* (2004). www.oxforddnb.com/view/article/520 (accessed 18 Feb. 2013); McCullough (ed.), *Andrewes' sermons*; Nicholas Tyacke, 'Lancelot Andrewes and the myth of Anglicanism' in *Conformity and orthodoxy in the English church, c.1560–1660,* ed. Peter Lake and Michael C. Questier (Woodbridge, 2000), pp 5–33. For Andrew's influence on Laud, see Hugh Trevor-Roper, *Archbishop Laud, 1573–1645* (3rd ed., Basingstoke, 1988); Kevin Sharpe, *The personal rule of Charles I* (New Haven, CT, 1996); Tyacke, *Anti-Calvinists,* pp 113–14; Nicholas Tyacke, 'Archbishop Laud' in *The early Stuart church, 1603–42,* ed. Kenneth Fincham (Basingstoke, 1993), pp 51–70; Lake, 'Avant-garde conformity', p. 114. Peter E. McCullough, 'Donne and Andrewes', *John Donne Journal* 22 (2003), 165–201 provides an excellent study of the contrasts between two preachers who are sometimes simplistically compared. McCullough's article identifies as important a number of the central issues discussed in this chapter.   13 Lancelot Andrewes, *XCVI. Sermons by the Right Honorable and Reverend Father in God, Lancelot Andrewes, late Lord Bishop of Winchester,* ed. William Laud and John Buckeridge (London, 1629), p. 132

So, while Andrewes insisted on the importance of the sermon he was concerned to identify it as just one of the means of grace, and to locate, or to re-locate, preaching in a hierarchy of those means, to reverse what he saw as the entirely reprehensible tendency in the Church of England to privilege preaching above prayer and sacraments. And he made this point, even as he insisted upon the place of preaching, in his Whitsun sermon for 1606:

> Howsoever it be, if these three[1] *Prayer*,[2] *The Word*,[3] *The Sacraments* be every one of them as an *arterie*, to conveigh the *Spirit* into us; well may we hope, if we use them all three, we shall be in a good way to speede of our desires. For, many time we misse, when we use this one, or that one alone; where it may well be, God hath appointed to give it us by neither, but by the third.[14]

For the Christian to restrict him or her self to any one artery, then, was dangerous: God's blessings might well rush past unseen in other, neglected, conduits. And, in Andrewes' view, it was in just such dangerous folly that his age was engaged:

> In, at our *eares*, there goes, I know not how many *Sermons*: and every day more and more, if we might have our wills. *Infers auribus*, into the *eares* they goe; the *eare* and all *filled*, and even *farced* with them: but there, the *eare* is all. It puts me in mind of the great absurdity, as *Saint Paul* reckons it. What, *is all hearing?* (saith he; *All hearing?* Yes: *all is hearing with us*. But, that all should be *hearing* is as much as if all one's *body* should be *noting but an eare*, and that were a strange body. But, that absurdity are we fallen into. The *corps*, the whole body of some mens profession; all *godlinesse* with some, what is it, but *hearing a sermon?* ... They were wont to talke much of *Auricular Confeßion*: I cannot tell, but now all is turned to an *auricular Profeßion*.[15]

And, we must qualify his treatment of the importance of preaching, in the sermon on James 1:22, quoted above, by noting his opening jeremiad:

> And this (to speake with *Salamon*) is and *evill disease under the Sunne*, which hath possessed the world; or (with S. *Iames*) *a strong illusion* of our ghostly enemy, Who when he cannot draw us *wholly* from the *Service* of God, maketh us single out some *one part* of it from the rest, and to be superstitiously conceited of that part; to make much of it, and to magnifie it *highly*, nay *onely*; with neglect, and (even as it were) with some disgrace to all besides it.[16]

(2nd pagination). 14 Ibid., p. 607. 15 Ibid., p. 240. 16 Ibid., p. 130 (2nd pagination).

   Andrewes' most acute problems arose, then, when preaching was valued more
highly than the sacraments and liturgy:

> Thus *serve* we *Him*, in His *holy worship:* how *serve* we *Him*, in his holy
> things? How *serve* we *Him*, in our *holineße* there? I will begin, and take
> up the same complaint that the Prophet *Malachi* doth. First, *Mensa
> Domini despecta est: The Table of the Lord is not regarded.* That
> Sacrament, that ever hath beene compted, of all Holies the most holy,
> the highest and most solemne *service* of God; (Where are delivered to
> us, the holy Symbols, the precious memorials of our greatest *Delivery*
> of all;) why, of all others they speed worst. How are they in many
> places, denied any reverence at all, even that which Prayer, which
> other parts have. ... Shall we now come to the service *indeed?* ... It is
> no new thing, for one *species* to carie away the name of the *genus* from
> the rest, as in this: For, though there be other parts of Gods *service*:
> yet Prayer hath borne away the name of *service*, from them all. ... As
> indeed, when all is done, devotion is the proper, and most kindly work
> of *Holineße;* and in that *serve* we God, if ever we *serve* Him.
>   *Thou hast magnified thy Name, and thy Word above all things*; saith
> the Psalme. After invocation then of His Name, let us see how we
> *serve* His Word; that part of his *service*, which in this Age (I might say,
> in the error of this Age) caries away all. For, what is it to *serve* God *in
> holineße?* Why, to go to a Sermon: All our holiday *holineße*, yea, and
> our working-day too, both are come to this, to heare (nay, I dare not
> say that, I cannot prove it) but, to be at a Sermon.[17]

In this extract, Andrewes' ire is directed in equal measure against those who too
lightly esteem sacrament and liturgy. In his Whitsun sermon for 1618, however,
his especial target was the suggestion that prayer was superfluous in the salvific
economy:

> I dare not end with *Prophetabunt*, or with this; I dare not omit, but
> joyne *invocaverit* to them, For what? From *Prophetabunt*, come we to
> Salvabitur straight, without any *medium* betweene? No, we must take
> *Invocaverit* in our way; no passing to *salvation*, but by and through it.
> For what? Is the *powring of the Spirit*, to end in *preaching*, and
> *preaching* to end in it self (as it doth with us; a *circle of preaching* & in
> effect nothing els) but *poure in prophesying enough*, and then all is safe?
> No: there is another yet, as needful, nay more needful to be called on
> (as the current of our Age runs) and that is *Calling on the name of the*

17 Ibid., pp 991–2.

> *Lord.* This, it grieveth me to see, how *light* it is sett; nay, to see, how
> busy the devil hath beene, to *power contempt* on it, to bring it to
> disgrace with disgraceful termes: to make nothing of *Divine Service*,
> as if it might well be spared, and *invocaverit* (heer) be stricken out.[18]

The fact that this sermon was preached before King James adds emphasis to this
section when we recall what we have already remarked in relation to James'
tendency to dispense with the liturgy that the sermon might commence.

Andrewes was not the only avant-garde conformist to minister during the
reign of James. Richard Meredeth, indeed, had begun the charge, and his two
surviving sermons, in both their content and their presentation, represent a clear
elevation of prayer over preaching.[19] John Buckeridge, who, as Lake and
McCullough both point out, is a key figure in the development of the new
conformity, endorsed a ceremonialism and a sacramentalism that went beyond
what Andrewes had contemplated. He also provides us with a clear link between
Andrewes and Laud.[20] Few of these men, however, were as influential as
Andrewes, and the publication, under the editorship of Buckeridge and Laud, of
the *XCVI Sermons* in 1629 helped to perpetuate that influence after his death. It
is, therefore, in his reappraisal of the place of preaching that we find the context
of Donne's implicit defence of his role, his function, his art.

In the context of this avant-garde reappraisal of the value of the word
preached, it is helpful to commence our consideration of Donne's views of the
authority of the preacher by observing his insistence on the importance of the
sermon. This insistence is marked by the moderation that, by now, we should
recognise as a hallmark of Donne's approach to the contentious or the controversial. In spite of this moderation, the importance that Donne attaches to
preaching is emphasised by the the consistency with which he stressed it, and the
significance of the homiletical contexts in which he chose to articulate it. The
sermon, for Donne, took its place alongside the sacraments as a conduit of divine
grace.[21] Thus, while he distinguishes between sermon and sacrament, and
between sermon and liturgy, he does so in order to argue for a relationship of
equality and not of hierarchy. And Donne contends for this equality not just

18 Ibid., p. 719. **19** See McCullough, *Sermons at court*, pp 156–9; Tyacke, *Anti-Calvinists*, pp
112–13. McCullough draws our attention to the typographical eccentricity of Meredeth's printed
sermons: 'The printed version of these sermons was set in the black-letter gothic that looked, by
the date of their printing, in 1606, noticeably, even deliberately, antiquated'. He accounts for this
eccentric typographical choice by pointing out the status of black-letter 'as the standard typeface
for official government and church documents including *The Book of Common Prayer*'. Thus, the
typeface of *Two Sermons* visually linked Meredith's book with the printed liturgical texts of the
English Church, a connection made explicit in the text of the second sermon, where the preacher
made unprecedented use of passages from the prayer book as exempla and proof texts.
20 Lake, 'Avant-garde conformity at the court of James I'; McCullough, 'Laudianism, print and
Andrewes'. **21** See McCullough, 'Donne and Andrewes'; Lori Anne Ferrell, 'Donne and His
Master's Voice, 1615–1625', *John Donne Journal* 11 (1992), 59–72.

during the reign and in the presence of the remarkably homilophilic James, but also when preaching before the more liturgically preoccupied Charles.

SERMON AND SACRAMENT

This relationship and the sort of balance with which it was expressed are both exemplified in Donne's Easter sermon for 1622. Taking his perennial Easter theme of resurrection, Donne spoke from 1 Thessalonians 4:16 and 17: 'For the Lord himself shall descend from heaven with a shout, with the voice of the archangel, and with the trump of God: and the dead in Christ shall rise first: Then we which are alive and remain shall be caught up together with them in the clouds, to meet the Lord in the air: and so shall we ever be with the Lord'. In this context, Donne gave warning that the minister – the angel – must speak the word of God, or be accursed. And, for the individual Christian, the preaching and praxis of the church provide the vital assurance of divinely originating authenticity:

> Yet thou must heare this voice of the Archangell in the Trumpet of God. The Trumpet of God is his loudest Instrument; and his loudest instrument is his publique Ordinance in the Church; Prayer, Preaching, and Sacraments; Heare him in these; In all these; come not to heare him in the Sermon alone, but come to him in Prayer, and in the Sacrament too. (IV, 71)

This is a paradigmatic account of the place of the sermon in Donne's theology – not an option to be chosen *a la carte*, but a vital and integral part of Christian life. Or, as Donne expresses it a little later in the same sermon,

> [T]his we say to you, by the Word of the Lord (by harmony of all the Scriptures) thus, and no other way, By the pure word of God, delivered and applied by his publique Ordinance, by Hearing, and believing, and Practising, under the Seales of the Church, the Sacraments, is your first resurrection from sin, by grace, accomplished. (IV, 72)

The following day, Donne was preaching at the Spittle, with similar thoughts on his mind. His text on this occasion was II Corinthians 4:6: 'For God, who commanded the light to shine out of darkness, hath shined in our hearts, to give the light of the knowledge of the glory of God in the face of Jesus Christ'. The obvious connection with Pauline biography and the description of the gospel in the verse are more than sufficient stimuli for a further meditation on the role of the preacher and of preaching. In this sermon, indeed, Donne engages in a more extensive discussion of the correlation between sermon and sacrament, drawing upon both Paul's experience on the Damascus road and the 'infusion of the Holy Ghost into the Apostles at Pentecost'. In both of these instances, Donne points out, the work of God was expressed in

> an effectual, a powerful shining. And in both those cases, there were tongues too. The Apostles first, was fiery tongues, and *S. Pauls* light, was accompanied with a voice; for then does God truly shine to us, when he appears to our eyes and to our ears, when by visible and audible means, by Sacraments which we see, and by the Word which we heare, he conveys himself unto us. In *Pauls* case, there were some that saw the light, but heard not the voice: God hath joyn'd, separate them not: Upon him that will come to hear, and will not come to see; will come to the *Sermon*, but not to the *Sacrament;* or that will come to see, but will not come to hear; will keep his solemn, and festival, and Anniversary times of receiving the *Sacrament*, but never care for being instructed in the duties appertaining to that high Mystery, God hath not shin'd. They are a powerful thunder, and lightning, that go together: Preaching is the thunder that clears the air, disperses all clouds of ignorance; and then the *Sacrament* is the lightning, the glorious light, and presence of Christ Jesus himself. And in the having and loving of these, the *Word* and the *Sacraments*, the outward means of salvation, ordained by God in his Church, consists this Irradiation, this Coruscation, this shining. (IV, 105)

Six years later, Donne expressed the same understanding of the role of the sermon, not, on this occasion, to a large Easter congregation, but to the elite of Whitehall as he preached before King Charles, then backing the early stages of the Laudian transformation of the English church. In this more charged context, Donne's exposition was terse but no less unequivocal:

> God hath put nothing else into his Churches hands to save men by, but Christ delivered in his Scripture, applied in the preaching of the Gospel, and sealed in the Sacraments. (VIII, 248)

Notably, the physical reality of the meteorological figure used in the 1622 sermon would reverse the order in which Donne glosses them, complicating any straightforward sense of hierarchical ordering. Before the king, however, the order seems clearly to privilege to place of the sermon above the sacrament and to place it in a more immediate relationship to Christ himself.

It is as much the liturgical as the historical context that lends force to Donne's treatment of the sermon. His allusion to the subject at Easter, for instance, gains force when we remember that Easter Sunday was one of the three occasions during the church's liturgical year when the taking of communion was mandatory for all. Indeed, notwithstanding the requirements of the 1559 *Book of Common Prayer* and the canons of 1603, Easter was 'the one occasion during the year when all adults were expected to receive communion'.[22] Furthermore, the significance of Lent as a time of preparation for the climactic reception of communion added to the sacramental focus of the season. At Easter, then, the sacrament enjoyed a peculiar prominence and Donne's efforts to balance that prominence are the more noticeable in this liturgical context. Nor was this limited to the sermons preached in 1622; in 1624 he returned to the same topic and the same arrangement:

> Christs first tongue was a tongue that might be heard, He spoke to the Shepherds by Angels; His second tongue was a Star, a tongue which might be seene; He spoke to the Wisemen of the East by that. Hearken after him these two waies; As he speakes to thine eare (and to thy soul, by it) in the preaching of his Word, as he speaks to thine eye (and so to thy soule by that) in the exhibiting of his Sacraments. (VI, 79)

Once more, the topic was resurrection. Donne was concerned to instruct his auditory how they might attain to the resurrection 'from the fearfull death of heinous sin' (78). To this end, the means provided in the sermon and sacrament were alone effectual. Donne contrasted these effective means with worldly delights, with good works with 'a relation to God himselfe, but not as God hath manifested himselfe to thee, not in Christ Jesus'. Above all these, the sermon stands as a central and vital element in God's salvific programme.

Equally noticeable in this context are sermons preached by Donne at christenings. Again, these occasions had a primary sacramental purpose and the treatment of the significance of the sacraments generally, and of baptism in particular, was only to be expected. Less expected is Donne's consistent treatment of the relationship of preaching to the sacraments. The fact that few of the christening sermons are dated prevents us from attempting to integrate them into a particular historical context, and this, in turn, complicates an effort to map a development in Donne's understanding of the sermon. This notwithstanding, these sermons, taken along with the preoccupation of the Easter sermons are indicative of the importance that Donne attaches to preaching. This is exemplified in the christening sermon preached on 1 John 5:7 and 8: 'For there are three that bear record in heaven, the Father, the Word, and the Holy Ghost: and these

---

22 Arnold Hunt, 'The Lord's Supper in early modern England', *Past and Present* 161 (1998), 41.

three are one. And there are three that bear witness in earth, the Spirit, and the water, and the blood: and these three agree in one'. Congruent with the occasion, Donne glosses the witness of the water as referring to baptismal water. He discusses alternative interpretations – the actual natural water employed in 'the *ablutions* of the old law' (V, 146), an alternative allegorical reading of the waters as '*affliction*, and tribulation' (147), or as 'waters of *Contrition*, and repentant *teares*' – and, while allowing them some usefulness for edification, ultimately dismisses them, because such non-sacramental waters are unworthy of equality with preaching:

> That water which is made equall with the *preaching* of the Word, so farre as to be a fellow-witnesse with the Spirit) that is onely the *Sacrament of baptisme*, without which (in the ordinary dispensation of God) no soule can be surer that Jesus is come to him, then if he had never heard the Word preached. (V, 147)

Donne goes on to interpret the witness of the blood as a reference to the Eucharist, with the reluctance to be explicit about the operation of divine presence that we have already noted in an earlier chapter:

> I am not ashamed to confesse, that I know not *how*, but the bloud of Christ is a *witnesse upon earth*, in the Sacrament, and therefore, upon the earth it is. Now this witnesse being made equall with the other two, with *preaching*, and with *baptisme*, it is as necessary, that he will have an assurance, that *Jesus* is come to him doe receive this *Sacrament*, as that he doe heare *Sermons*, and that he be *baptized*. (V, 148)

In keeping with this imbricated importance of sermon and sacrament, Donne goes on to outline the appropriate trajectory of the Christian life, of which baptism is only the beginning. All three witnesses will be necessary at the other end and will be vital in an eschatological context:

> ... *woe unto you Hypocrites, that make cleane onely the outside of your Cuppes and Platters*. That baptize, and wash your owne, and your childrens bodies, but not their mindes with instructions. When we shall come to say ... *we have heard thee preach in our streets*, we have continued our hearing of thy Word, when we say ... we have eate in thy presence, at thy table, yea ... we have eaten thy selfe, yet for all this outward show of these three witnesses, of *Spirit*, and *Water*, and *bloud*, *Preaching*, and *Baptisme* and *Communion*, we shall heare that fearfull disclaiming from Christ Jesus, *Nescio vos*, I know not whence

you are. But these witnesses, he will always heare, if they testifie for us, that Jesus is come unto us; for the *Gospell*, and the *preaching* thereof, is as the deed that conveys *Jesus* unto us; the *water*, the *baptisme*, is as the *Seale*, that assures it; and the *bloud*, the *Sacrament*, is the delivery of Christ into us; and this is *Integritas Jesu*, the entire, and full possession of him. (V, 148–9)

In another undated christening sermon, this time on Ephesians 5:25–7, Donne developed these themes in greater detail, based on his treatment of the divine intention to 'present ... himself a glorious Church', and the means by which this was to be accomplished: 'That he might sanctify and cleanse it with the washing of water by the word'. The water and the word provide Donne with the opportunity to present the expected balance:

> He therefore stays not so long, for our *Santification*, but that we have meanes of being sanctified here; Christ stays not so long for his glory, but that he hath here a *glorious Gospell*, his *Word*, and *mysterious Sacraments* here. Here then is the *writing*, and the *Seale*, the *Word*, and the *Sacraments;* and he hath given power, and commandement to his Ministers to deliver both writing, and Seale, the *Word* and *Baptisme* to his children. This Sacrament of Baptisme is the first; It is the Sacrament of *inchoation*, of *Initiation;* The Sacrament of the *Supper*, is not given but to them, who are instructed and presum'd to understand all Christian duties; and therefore the *Word* (if we understand the Word, for the *Preaching* of the Word) may seeme more necessary at the administration of this Sacrament, than at the other. Some such thing seems to be intimated in the institution of the Sacraments. In this institution of the Supper, it is onely said, *Take, and eate and drinke*, and doe that in *remembrance of me*; and it is onely said that they *sang a Psalme, and so departed.* In the institution of *Baptisme* there is more solemnity, more circumstance; for first, it was instituted after Christs *Resurrection*, and then Christ proceeds to it, with that majesticall preamble, *All power is given unto me in heaven, and in earth*; and therefore, upon that title he gives power to his Apostles, to joine heaven and earth by *preaching*, and by *baptisme*: but there is more then *singing of a Psalme*; for Christ commands them first to *teach*, and then to *baptize*, and then after the commandement of Baptisme, he refreshes that commandement againe of *teaching* them, whom they baptized, to observe all things, that he had commanded them. (V, 127)

Donne, to an even greater extent than usual, is engaged in a balancing act in this sermon. For conformists, even for those who resisted the increasing sacramentalism of the Laudian programme, one of the most inexcusable puritan excesses was the refusal of some parents to allow their children to be baptised without an accompanying sermon. By the same token, however, Donne dismisses the contentions of those who evacuated the 'word' of its homiletic significance and who limited it to the formula of words spoken in the administration of the sacrament:

> I speake not this, as though *Baptisme* were uneffectuall without a *Sermon; S. Augustines* words, *Accedat verbum, & fiat Sacramentum,* when the Word is joined to the element, or to the action, then there is a true Sacrament, are ill understood by two sorts of Men; first by them, that say that it is not ... the word of *Prayer,* nor the word of *preaching,* but ... that very phrase, and forme of words, by which the water is sanctified, and enabled of it selfe to cleanse our Soules; and secondly, these words are ill understood by them, who had rather their children dyed unbaptized, then have them baptized without a *Sermon.* ... A *Sermon* is usefull for the congregation, not necessary for the *child,* and the accomplishment of the Sacrament.
>
> From hence then arises a convenience, little lesse, then necessary (in a kind) that this administration of the Sacrament be accompanied with *preaching;* but yet they that would evict out of it an *absolute necessity* of it, out of these words, force them too much. (V, 128–9)

Donne is consciously and explicitly steering a balanced course between two extreme views, yet his belief in the necessity (though less than absolute) of the preaching of the word is clear and, as we have seen, gains impact in the sacramental context of the sermon. Its impact is further increased by Donne's location of this discussion at the end of his sermon, immediately before his peroration.

In these sermons, and on these sacramentally significant occasions, therefore, Donne consistently insisted on the necessity of preaching, along with prayer and sacrament, in the conveyance of salvation. In a number of other sermons, Donne goes beyond this and argues that the sermon has, in itself, an incarnational and a sacramental function. So, in a sermon in which he identifies preaching as an ordinary means of 'manifesting Christ', he goes on to say '*caro in verbo,* he that is made flesh comes in the word, that is, Christ comes in the preaching thereof' (II, 251). Similarly, in a sermon preached at Whitehall during Lent of 1625, Donne's discussion of the ritual value of fasting leads him on to a discussion of preaching and sacrament in the sort of terms that we have already remarked. He goes on from this to collapse any too-stable distinction between sermon and sacrament:

> This fasting then, enjoyned by God, for the generall, in his Word, and thus limited to this Time, for the particular, in his Church, is indeed

but a continuation of a great Feast: Where, the first course (that which we begin to serve in now) is Manna, food of Angels, plentifull, frequent preaching; but the second course, is the very body and blood of Christ Jesus, shed for us, and given to us, in that blessed Sacrament, of which himselfe makes us worthy receivers at that time. Now, as the end of all bodily eating, is Assimilation, that after all other concoctions, that meat may be made *Idem corpus*, the same body that I am; so the end of all spirituall eating, is Assimilation too, That after all Hearing, and all Receiving, I may be made *Idem spiritus cum Domino*, the same spirit, that my God is: for, though it be good to Heare, good to Receive, good to Meditate, yet (if we speake effectually, and consummatively) why call we these good? There is nothing good but One, that is, Assimilation to God. (II, 223–4)

A similar dynamic is at work in an undated Whitsunday sermon, assigned by Potter and Simpson to 1618, 1620 or 1621. Donne took as his passage Acts 10:44: 'While Peter yet spake these words, the Holy Ghost fell on all them which heard the word'. He treats Peter's preaching as a paradigm of the preparation, delivery and results of preaching. This meditation on the means and end of preaching includes one of Donne's most far-reaching declarations of the power of the word preached, a declaration rendered the more noticeable for the cautious qualification with which Donne voices it:

> *He hath commanded us to preach*; that is, he hath established a Church, and therein, visible means of salvation; And, then, this is our generall text, the subject of all our Sermons, *That through his name, whosoever beleeveth in him shall have remission of sins.* So that this is all that we dare avow concerning salvation, that howsoever God may afford salvation to some in all nations, yet he hath manifested to us no way of conveying salvation to them, but by the manifestation of Christ Jesus in his Ordinance of preaching.

Very much of a piece with these Easter and christening sermons are those sermons preached by Donne at churchings. The churching sermon itself is an interesting phenomenon, indicative of distinctive stresses in the reformed church. The service of churching, adapted by the Roman church from the Jewish ritual purification following childbirth, was far from having the deep and hotly contested theological significance that was ascribed to the sacraments. Nonetheless, its retention in the English church was controversial: it was felt by more rigidly Protestant reformers to be at best of questionable value, at worst thoroughly disreputable.[23] Thus, while Richard Hooker designated it an

23 The significance of churching in late medieval England has been most influentially surveyed in Keith Thomas, *Religion and the decline of magic: studies in the popular belief of sixteenth- and*

adiaphoron, he also felt the need to defend it, as a duty of thanksgiving.[24] In this context, the insertion of a sermon into the service of churching was of considerable symbolical importance in the 'protestantising' of the rite, adding to its ritual function an opportunity for some profitable preaching the possibility of using the sermon to define and contain the meaning of the rite enacted. Thus, it can persuasively be argued, the churching sermon had as much to do with the inoculation of a dubious ceremony against the threat of popery as it did with the instruction of the newly purified mother and her friends.

Donne's churching sermons clearly partake in this project. More notable than their existence, however, is their content, for Donne makes use of the opportunity provided to speak clearly about the responsibility of the preacher and the function of the sermon. Potter and Simpson's edition contains three churching sermons. The first of these was preached at Essex House on the occasion of the churching of Lady Doncaster. The remaining two printed sermons are an expansion of one sermon preached at the churching of the countess of Bridgewater. Donne's 'digesting' of the one preached sermon into two – fairly substantial – printed sermons is a salutary reminder of the gulf between the sermon as an oral and a printed artefact. For the purposes of the present argument, however, this gulf matters less than it might in other contexts. What is significant, from our point of view, is Donne's recognition that a churching sermon provided a *mise en scène* amenable to the discussion of the preacher and preaching. Whether he introduced it, or simply retained it, its presence in the printed version is testament to the fact that he thought the point worth making.

Donne's sermon at the churching of Lady Doncaster took as its text the second clause of Canticles 5:8: 'I have washed my feet; how shall I defile them?' Donne draws on patristic interpretation and exegesis to apply the cleansing mentioned to the cleansing of the life from sin, specifically an initial washing in baptism, and the ongoing examination and purification of the life by the individual believer. The redefinition of the churching ceremony already remarked can be seen at work here, for Donne's references to the specifics of childbirth and the sort of defilement that it entailed are slight:

> It is a degree of uncleannesse, to fix our thoughts too earnestly upon the unncleannesse of our conception, and of our birth: when wee call that a testimony of a right coming, if we come into the world *with our head forward*, in a head-long precipitation; and when we take no other

seventeenth-century England (London, 1971). A significant recent study that draws explicitly upon Thomas' account is provided in William Coster, 'Purity, profanity and puritanism: the churching of women, 1500–1700' in *Women in the church*, ed. W.J. Sheils and Diana Wood (Oxford, 1990), pp 377–87. For a more valuable account, privileging historical data above theory, see David Cressy, 'Purification, thanksgiving and the churching of women in post-reformation England', *Past and Present* 141 (1993), 106–46. **24** Hooker, *Works*, III, 406–9.

> testimony of our being *alive*, but that we were heard to *cry*; and that
> for an earnest, and a Prophecy, that we shall be ... bloudy, and deceit-
> full Men, false and treacherous, to the murdering of our owne soules
> we come into this world, as the Egyptians went out of it, swallowed,
> and smothered in a red sea ... weake, and bloudy infants at our births.
> (V, 171–2)

Not one to gloss over the earthier facts of life, Donne is, nonetheless, quick to
carry his thoughts 'from *materiall* to *spirituall* uncleannesses', and the remainder
of the sermon is occupied with spiritual exhortation. Donne, by drawing his
audience's attention to the personal possessive pronoun in the text insists on the
individual's responsibility for personal spiritual cleanliness, and to this precept
he lends force by applying it to his own condition as a preacher:

> This washing of the feet, is the spirit of *discerning*, and censuring
> particular particular actions: but it is *pedes meos*, a discerning, and
> censuring of *my actions*, not onely, or not principally the actions of
> *other Men;* ... *how beautifull are the feet of them, that preach peace*, says
> Saint *Paul*, out of the mouth of two witnesses, two Prophets, that had
> said so before. If we will *preach peace*, that is, relieve the consciences
> of *others*, by presenting them their sinnes, we must have *speciosos
> pedes*, cleane ways, and a cleane life of our owne; so it is with us, and
> our profession; But *Gens sancta, regale Sacerdotium*, as the Apostle
> joines them, If ye be a *holy people*, you are also a *royall priesthood;* If
> you be all *Gods Saints*, you are all *Gods Priests*; and if you be his
> priests, it is your office to preach too; as we by our words, you by your
> holy works; as we by contemplation, you by conversation; as we by our
> doctrine, so you by your lives, are appointed by God to preach to one
> another: and therefore every particular Man, must wash his owne feet,
> look that he have *speciosos pedes*, that his example may preach to
> others, for this is truly *Regale Sacerdotium*, a regall priesthood, not to
> work upon others by words, but by actions. ... There is a priestly duty
> lies upon every Man, brotherly to reprehend a brother, whom he sees
> trampling in foule ways, wallowing in foule sinnes, but I may *preach to
> others and be my selfe a reprobate* (as Saint *Paul* speakes with terror to
> Men of our coate) in his own person, I may bring others to heaven,
> and bee shut out my selfe. (V, 180)

There is a great deal worthy of note in this extract: we should note, in passing,
that Donne identifies preaching as a key responsibility of priesthood, that the
imperative to preach is the result of a divine appointment and the concept that
it is holiness of life, above all else, that gives the preacher his authority. These are

significant markers, to which we will return. For the present, it is sufficient that we consider Donne's decision to include, at the climax of this section, and close to the end of the sermon, an exhortation that relies so heavily upon an appreciation, shared by preacher and congregation, of the role and responsibility of the preacher.

The sermons preached to the Countess of Bridgewater reveal a similar understanding of the authority of the preacher and his sermon. Both sermons deal with Micah 2:10: 'Arise ye, and depart; for this is not your rest: because it is polluted, it shall destroy you, even with a sore destruction'. Of the two, it is the second that seems most closely connected with the occasion. The first, consisting of a detailed discussion of the relevance of the text to the history of Israel, and its application, by way of spiritualisation, to the church, and the individual Christian, contains no direct reference to the churching, although there is, doubtless a significance in Donne's choice of the language of Ezekiel 16:4 ('And as for thy nativity, in the day thou wast born thy navel was not cut, neither wast thou washed in water to supple thee; thou wast not salted at all, nor swaddled at all') to summarise the sinfulness of Israel. By contrast, the second sermon opens with a direct reference to the occasion of its preaching:

> [T]he words admit a just accommodation to this present occasion,
> God having rais'd his honourable servant, and hand-maid here
> present, to the sense of the *Curse*, that lyes upon *women*, for the trans-
> gression of the first woman, which is painfull, and dangerous
> *Childbirth*; and given her also, a sense of the last glorious resurrection,
> in having rais'd her, from that Bed of weaknesse, to the ability of
> coming into his presence, here in his house. (V, 198)

Indeed, there is a far clearer sense of audience in this second sermon, and this, taken with the fact that it could easily stand on its own as a sermon, makes it likely that it is this sermon, rather than the preceding one, that most accurately reflects Donne's performance at the churching.

Be that as it may, this churching sermon provides one of Donne's most clearly self-reflexive commentaries on preaching, on the mechanics of effective rebuke of sin. He draws upon the very current discussions of freedom of speech, and in particular on debates about the most effective way of counseling the monarch.[25] In keeping with the substance of these debates, he outlines both classical precedent and the practice of the Jacobean age:

> There was such a tendernesse, among the orators, which were used to
> speake in the presence of the people, to the Roman Emperours (which

---

25 See David Colclough, *Freedom of speech in early Stuart England* (Cambridge, 2005).

was a way of *Civill preaching*) that they durst not tell them then their duties, nor instruct them, what thet should doe, any other way then by saying, that they had done so before; They had no way to make the Prince wise, and just, and temperate, but by a false praising him, for his former acts of wisedom, and justice, and temperance, which he had never done; and that served to make the people believe, that the Princes were so; and it served to teach the Prince, that he ought to be so. And so, though this were an expresse, and a direct flattery, yet it was a collaterall increpation too; And on the other side, our later times have seen another art, another invention, another workmanship, that when a great person hath so abused the favour of his Prince, that he hath growne subject to great, and weighty increpations, his owne friends have made *Libells* against him, thereby to lay some light asper-sions upon him, that the Prince might thinke, that this coming with the malice of a *Libell*, was the worst that could be said of him: and so, as the first way to the Emperours, though it were a direct flattery, yet it was a *collaterall Increpation* too, so this way, though it were a direct increpation, yet it was a *collaterall flattery* too. (V, 200)

These two examples have their relevance for the preacher and for his preaching, and Donne outlines the two corresponding avenues open to him in his sphere, and on the homiletic dilemmas associated with each:

If I should say of such a congregation as this, with acclamations and shows of much joy, Blessed company, holy congregation, in which there is no pride at all, no vanity at all, no prevarication at all, I could be thought in that, but to convey an increpation, and a rebuke mannerly, in a wish that it were so altogether. If I should say of such a congregation as this, with exclamations and show of much bitter-nesse, that they were sometimes somewhat too worldly in their owne businesse, sometimes somewhat too remise, in the businesse of the next world, and adde no more to it, this were but as a plot, and a *faint libelling*, a punishing of small sinnes to keep greater from being talk'd of: slight increpations are but as *whisperings*, and work no farther, but to bring men to say, Tush, no body hears it, no body heeds it, we are never the worse, nor never the worse thought of for all that he says. And loud and bitter increpations, are as a *trumpet*, and work no other-wise, but to bring them to say, Since he hath published all to the world already, since all the world knowes of it, the shame is past, and we may goe forward in our ways againe. (V, 200–1)

Such a meditation upon the difficulties of faithful preaching, the machinations of the human heart and the general slipperiness of language would attract our attention at any locus in Donne's canon. Its inclusion here, in the intimate pastoral context of a churching, adds to its intrinsic significance a great deal of importance. This is equally true of Donne's succeeding remarks; his attempt to answer his own question, 'Is there then no way to convey an increpation profitably?':

> God hath provided a way here, to convey, to imprint this increpation, this rebuke, sweetly and successfully; that is, by way of counsaile: by bidding them *arise*, he chides them for falling, by presenting the exaltation and exultation of a peacefull conscience, he brings them to a foresight, to what miserable distractions, and distortions of the soule a habite of sinne will bring them to. If you will take knowledge of Gods fearfull judgements no other way, but by hearing his mercies preached, his *Mercie is new every morning*, and his dew falls every evening, and morning, and evening we will preach his mercies unto you. If you will believe a *hell* no other way, but by hearing the joyes of heaven presented to you, you shall heare enough of that; we will receive you in the morning, and dismisse you in the evening, in a religious assurance, in a present inchoation of the joyes of heaven. It is Gods way, and we are willing to pursue it; to shew you that are Enemies to Christ, *we pray you in Christs stead, that you would be reconciled to him*; to shew you, that you are faln, we pray you to *arise*, and *si audieritis*, if you hear us so, if any way, any means, convey this rebuke, this sense into you . . . *If you hear, we have gain'd a brother*; and that's the richest gain, that we can get, if you may get salvation by us. (V, 201)

Even shorn of its context, this analysis would demand our consideration. Its reflexivity provides us with one of our most intimate insights into Donne's understanding of the role of his own preaching. Especially notable is Donne's disavowal of the rhetorical tropes of free speech, in favour of 'God's way', with the objective of his audience's salvation. This is not an eschewal of stylish preaching, rather a subordination of method to ends. Once more, the context in which these words were preached multiplies their significance and, even as they explicitly shape our understanding of Donne's view of the intrinsic importance of the word preached, they implicitly reveal his grasp of its relative place in the life of the Christian and of the church.

Donne's sermons on churching have been singled out for consideration by a number of critics. Jeffrey Johnson's consideration, while set in a different context to the present study, is worthy of note. Johnson argues that both sermons 'reveal Donne's desire to move his auditors beyond a strictly liturgical or a culturally delimiting understanding of the churching service'.[26] More specifically he argues that

26 Johnson, *Theology*, xi.

the churching sermons ... reveal Donne's theological and ministerial integrity in the midst of a cultural view of churching as merely ceremonial. The purification Donne prescribes in the sermons for these two aristocratic women, while associated with the bodily cleansing outlined in Leviticus, derives fundamentally from his own sense of calling to preach the gospel that is repentance. In these sermons, he enlarges the need for purification to include all of fallen humanity; the churching of Francis Egerton and of Lucy Percy were for him particular occasions that touched the more universal condition of human sinfulness. Because of original sin, as well as the inevitability of actual sins, birth brings forth death, and as Donne makes clear in these churching sermons, the only way to seal one's repentance, is through a communal participation in the Word and Sacraments.[27]

Johnson's account, which reads the sermons in the context of the importance that Donne attached to repentance and to the communal expression of that repentance meshes with this reading when we appreciate that, for Donne, it was preaching that produced repentance. Thus, his realignment of a slightly dubious ceremonial occasion by stressing the primacy of preaching sanctifies and makes useful the ritual of churching.

PREACHING AND PRAYER

If the conflict between a word-based and a sacramental piety is of central consequence to our understanding of Donne's estimation of the importance of the sermon, and a key marker that qualifies and problematises any simple identification of Donne with the Hookerian avant-garde, we ought also to consider Donne's less extensive engagement with another aspect of the realignment of the English church: the programme begun by Andrewes and Richard Meredith, and vigorously promoted by Laud, to privilege prayer – the liturgy – above the preaching of the word. We have already noted instances in which Donne triangulates the benefits of sacrament, sermon and prayer. For more explicit engagements with the value of public, liturgical prayer, we must turn to sermons that seek to address the primary function of the church or chapel. McCullough summarises this question in the words of Richard Meredith – were the nation's churches to be *oratoria* or *auditoria*?[28] That this question was of relevance to Donne is clear from his engagement with it in two sermons. One of these was

27 Ibid., 104–5. 28 McCullough, *Sermons at court*, p. 156. See Lake, 'The Laudians and the argument from authority' for an extensive discussion of the Laudian re-evaluation of the nature and use of consecrated space.

preached at the dedication of the new chapel in Lincoln's Inn. Donne had been heavily involved in this project, and his sermon of dedication preached in 1623 saw him discuss the purpose of the new building. The second relevant sermon is an undated Candlemas day sermon, dated by Potter and Simpson to either 1617 or 1623, with 1623 as overwhelmingly the most likely.

One way or another, the undated sermon is probably Donne's earliest detailed discussion of the primary function of church buildings. The wider context in the sermon is an account of the Christian's debts to God – praise and prayer. In his discussion of praise, Donne had already touched upon the pulpit, to deplore its use as 'the shop, and the theatre of praise upon present men, and God left out', and sermons that speak 'more of Great men, then of our Great God' (IV, 307). As he turns to prayer, he invokes the classic proof-text of Isaiah 56:7 – 'mine house shall be called an house of prayer for all people' – and bases his discussion upon the identification of the Judaic temple with the Christian church:

> [M]y house, saies God, is a house of prayer; for this use, and purpose, he built himselfe a house upon earth; He had praise and glory in heaven before, but for Prayer he erected a house here, his Church. All the world is his Exchequer, he gives in all; from every creature, from Heaven, and Sea, and Land, and all the inhabitants of them, we receive benefits; But the Church is his Court of Requests, there he receives our petitions, there we receive his answers. It is true that neither is that house onely for prayer, nor prayer onely for that house: Christ in his person, consecrated that place by Preaching too: And for prayer elsewhere, Christ did much accustome himselfe to private prayer ... But when we meet in Gods house, though, by occasion, there be no Sermon, yet if we meet to pray, we pay our debt, we doe our duty; so doe we not, if we meet at a Sermon without a prayer. The Church is the house of prayer, so, as that upon occasion, preaching may be left out, but never a house of preaching so, as that Prayer may be left out. (IV, 309)

This extract is typical of Donne's insistence on the centrality of preaching. He instances the proof-text, but, picking up on its quotation by Christ in the cleansing of the temple, stresses the relevance of the passage to preaching as well as to prayer.[29] Further, his acknowledgment that preaching might be omitted 'upon occasion' clearly implies that, for Donne, at least, the sermon was to be a normal part of the service of God.

29 Lake, 'The Laudians and the argument from authority', pp 151–2 outlines the use made by Laudians of those scriptures that referred to the Jewish Tabernacle and Temple. By comparison, Donne's insistence on the place of preaching is the more noticeable.

The sermon preached at the dedication of the Lincoln's Inn chapel deals with the subject in a similar fashion.[30] This similarity extends to Donne's choice of John 10:22–3 as his text: 'And it was at Jerusalem the feast of the dedication, and it was winter. And Jesus walked in the temple in Solomon's porch'. Donne, then, is extending his use of the Jewish temple as a paradigm for the Christian church. The sermon is an important one, and sees Donne interacting with a number of subjects that were emerging, or would emerge, as the shibboleths of the Laudian project. Chief among these is the place of preaching and prayer, and Donne's response to it would surely have found acceptance with his somewhat puritanically inclined auditors, who were unlikely to have been so puritan as to be offended by Donne's defence of the practice of consecrating church buildings, which immediately precedes this section.[31] Donne's prose is not at its clearest in this extract, but we must follow its flow carefully if we are fully to understand the significance of this negotiation of the question:

> In *Nature*, in the *Law*, in the *Gospell*, in *Precept*, in Practise, these Consecrations are established. This they did. But to what use did they consecrate them? not to one use only; and therfore it is a frivolous contention, whether *Churches* be for *preaching*, or for *praying*. But if *Consecration* be a kind of *Christning* of the *Church*, and that at the *Christning* it have a name, wee know what name *God* hath appointed for his House, Domus mea, Domus orationis vocabitur. My House shall bee called the House of Prayer. And how impudent and inexcusable a falsehood is that in *Bellarmine*, That the *Lutherans* and *Calvinists* doe admit *Churches* for *Sermons* and *Sacraments*, *Sed reprehendunt quod fiant ad orandum*, They dislike that they should be for *Prayer*: when, as *Calvin* himselfe (who may seeme to bee more subject to this reprehension then *Luther*) (for there is no such *Liturgie* in the *Calvinists Churches*, as in the *Lutherean*) yet in that very place which *Bellarmine* cites, says *Conceptæ preces in Ecclesia Deo gratæ* ... Still

---

30 The attendant circumstances of this consecration, and the liturgical context in which Donne preached this sermon have been discussed by Jeffrey Johnson, 'Consecrating Lincoln's Inn Chapel', *John Donne Journal* 23 (2004), 139–60.   31 The precise extent of the puritan influence in the Inns of Court generally, and Lincoln's Inn specifically, is somewhat problematic. Doerksen, *Conforming to the Word: Herbert, Donne and the English church before Laud*, passim buttresses his case for a conformist Donne by drawing attention to the Calvinist credentials of his predecessors in the ministry. Wilfred R. Prest, *The inns of court under Elizabeth I and the early Stuarts, 1590–1640* (Harlow, 1972), pp 187–219 presents a considerably more nuanced account, which still concludes that there existed a definite interest in puritan ideals among the benchers of the Inn. See also Ian D. Aikenhead, 'Students of the common law, 1590–1615: lives and ideas at the Inns of Court', *University of Toronto Law Journal* 27:3 (1977), esp 253; Alan Harding, *A social history of English law* (London, 1966), pp 175–90; R.M. Fisher, 'The reformation of clergy at the Inns of Court, 1530–1580', *Sixteenth Century Journal* 12:1 (1981), 69–91; Emma Rhatigan, 'John Donne's Lincoln's Inn Sermons' (PhD, Oxford, 2006), pp 11–68.

> consider Consecration to be a *Christning* of the place; and though we
> find them often called *Templa propter Sacrificia*, for our sacrifices of
> praier, and of praise, and the merits of *Christ*, and often called *Ecclesia
> ad conciones*, Churches, in respect of congregations, for preaching,
> and often call'd *Martyria*, for preserving with respect, and honor the
> bodies of *Martyrs*... and often, by other names, *Dominica*, *Basilica*,
> and the like, yet the name that *God* gave to his house, is not
> *Concionatorium*, nor *Sacramentarium*, but *Oratorium*, the House of
> Prayer. (IV, 373)

The dynamics of this quotation are most interesting. Donne's admission that the
church is properly called oratorium is, as we have seen, fully consonant with
avant-garde terminology, but the cautious, even grudging nature of the admission is anything but. Notable is Donne's appeal to tradition, which did not
consecrate churches to one exclusive use. Further, his defence of the reformed
churches of the Continent against Bellarmine's unmerited slur pre-empts
controversy, by collapsing any 'us and them' binary, and thus preventing
attempts too closely to identify a word-centred piety with an anti-liturgical bias.

And the priorities that underlie Donne's approach become clearer when we
find him immediately following the extract quoted above with these words:

> And therefore without prejudice to the other functions too (for as
> there is a *væ* upon me, *Si non Euangelizavero*, If I preach not my selfe,
> so may that *væ* be multiplied upon any, who would draw that holy
> ordinance of God into a dis-estimation, or into a slacknesse,) let us
> never intermit that dutie, to present ourselves to *God* in these places,
> though in these places there bee then, no other Service, but Common
> prayer. For then doth the House answere to that name, which *God*
> hath given it, if it be a house of prayer. (IV, 374)

This is an unmistakably clear claim for the importance of preaching, and Donne
refers, as he so often does, to the words of the Apostle Paul, which, as we shall
see, formed a vital element in Donne's understanding of the responsibility of his
ministry. Because the imperative to preach is divinely ordained, nothing must
allow preaching to be hindered, or even to be 'dis-estimated'. Thus, even while
concurring with the concept of prayer as the *raison d'être* of the Christian
church, Donne appeals to primitive precedent, Protestant practice and personal
pastoral responsibility to insist on the central importance of the sermon in the
life of the Christian.

A careful reading of Donne's work, then, makes it clear that preaching
occupied a central part in his understanding of how a reformed church should
function. He was deeply conscious of the environment in which he ministered

and acutely aware of the trend away from the primacy of the pulpit. However, he chose not to overtly resist these trends. Rather, time and again, he articulated his view that preaching cannot be displaced by liturgy. From the moment he took orders, Donne was determinedly about the business of preaching his preoccupation with homiletic activity portrayed his ideal for the reformed English church.

6

The office and authority of the preacher

At this stage, the primary importance attached to the sermon by Donne is clear. In the light of this status, an enormous stress falls upon the role of the preacher his authority, in the mediation of the truth of scripture and the traditions of the church. Donne is very conscious of the authority of this role and, in a number of sermons, explicitly adumbrates his understanding of the privileges and responsibilities of his office. It is worthy of note that these treatments arise in sermons with specific and immediate pastoral contexts – at moments that underline the relationship of the preacher to his congregation. Thus, a crucial discussion occurs in the second sermon preached by Donne after his arrival at St Dunstan's, where it forms part of his discussion of the respective responsibilities of preacher and hearers. Along with this sermon of introduction, we have one of valediction: preached by Donne as he departed for Germany, and resonant of his uncertainty about a safe return. Both these sermons emphasise the pastoral imperative that underlies all of Donne's preaching.

APOSTLE OR PROPHET

The first of these sermons was preached by Donne in April of 1624: the second at St Dunstans. Donne took for his text the words of Psalm 34:11: 'Come, ye children, hearken unto me: I will teach you the fear of the Lord'. The two clauses of the verse provide Donne with the framework to examine the reciprocal responsibilities that interest him most. The main substance of the discussion of preaching is contained at the heart of this, fairly lengthy, sermon, but it opens in a way that clearly sets Donne's remarks in a homiletic context:

> The Text does not call *children* simply, literally, but such men, and women, as are willing to come in the *simplicity* of children; such children, as *Christ* spoke of, *Except ye become as little children, ye shall not enter into the Kingdome of heaven; Come ye children*; come *such* children. Nor does the Text call such as come, and would fain be gone again; it is *Come* and *Hearken;* not such as wish *themselves away*, nor such as wish *another man here*; but such as value Gods ordinance of *Preaching*, though it be, as the Apostle says, but the *foolishnesse of Preaching*, and such, as consider the *office*, and not the person, how

> meane soever; *Come ye children*; And, when ye are come, *Hearken*,
> And, though it be but *I*, *Hearken unto me; And, I will teach you the
> feare of the Lord*; the most noble, the most courageous, the most
> magnanimous, not *affection*, but *virtue*, in the world; *Come ye children,
> Hearken unto me, and I will teach you the feare of the Lord*. To every
> Minister and Dispenser of the word of God, and to every
> Congregation belong these words; And therefore we divide the Text
> between us; To you one, to us appertains the other part. (VI, 95)

Notably, Donne conceptualises his relationship with his new congregation as
primarily that of a preacher; he is, above all else, a 'dispenser of the word of
God'. This dispensing is his chief responsibility, and must be carried out with
an objective that is both clearly defined, and clearly pastoral:

> In our Part there is first a *Teaching*; for, else, why should you *come*, or
> *hearken unto me*, or *any?* It is a *Teaching*, it is not onely a *Praying*; And
> then, there is a *Catholique* doctrine, a *circular* doctrine, that walks the
> round, and goes the *compasse* of our whole lives, from our first, to our
> *last childhood*, when *age* hath made us children again, and it is the *Art
> of Arts*, the root, and fruit of all true wisdome, *The true feare of the
> Lord. Come ye children, hearken unto mee, and I will teach you the feare
> of the Lord*. (VI, 96)

The significance of Donne's statement that his responsibility is teaching, and
not only praying, is patent. Equally obvious is his conviction that, for all in his
congregation, for all, indeed, in his new cure, his preaching is an essential
resource for their development as Christians.

  Donne is very clear in his belief that, if profitable preaching is his responsibility, diligent hearing is his congregation's:

> *Faith comes by hearing*, saith the Apostle; but it is by that hearing of
> the soul, *Hearkning, Considering*. And then, as the soul is infused by
> God, but diffused over the whole body, and so there is a *Man*, so *Faith*
> is infused from God, but diffused into our *works*, and so there is a
> *Saint*. Practise is the *Incarnation of Faith*, Faith is incorporated and
> manifested in a body, by works; and the way to both, is that *Hearing*,
> which amounts to this *Hearkning*, to a diligent, to a considerate, to a
> profitable *Hearing*. In which, one essentiall circumstance is, that we be
> not over affectionately transported with an opinion of any *one person*,
> but apply our selves to the *Ordinance*, *Come*, and *hearken* unto *me*, To
> *any* whom God sends with the Seale and *Character* of his Minister.
> (VI, 102)

Donne, therefore, desires that his preaching issue in faith and accompanying probative works. He is also anxious to disavow any intention to portray himself as a superstar of the pulpit, or to claim any exclusive right of audience from his parishioners. His right to expect the diligent hearkening of his congregation has rather to do with his position than with his person, as he turns from the responsibilities of the congregation to those of the minister, he outlines his understanding of the source and the nature of the authority that he assumes over the parishioners of St Dunstan's.

That authority is seated firmly in the call of the minister – a call affirmed, to be sure, by a suitability of life and the possession of ability, but ultimately transcending these considerations:

> *David* doth not determine this in his own person, that you should
> hearken to *him*, and *none but him*, but that you should hearken to him
> in that capacity and qualification, which is common to *him* with
> others, as we are sent by God upon that Ministery; that you say to all
> such, *Blessed art thou that comest in the Name of the Lord.* ... He is a
> perverse servant, that will receive no commandment, except he have
> it immediately from his Masters mouth; so *is he too*, that pretendeth
> to rest so wholly in the *Word of God*, the *Scriptures*, as that he seeks *no*
> *interpretation, no exposition, no preaching* ... He is also a perverse
> servant, that wil receive no commandment by any *Officier* of his
> Masters, except he like the *man*, or, if his Master might, in his
> opinion, have chosen a *fitter man*, to serve in that place. And such a
> perversnesse is in those hearers who more respect the *man*, then the
> *Ministery*, and his *manner* of delivering it, then the *message* that he
> delivers. (VI, 102–3)

Such perversity in responding to a preacher is based, Donne contends, upon a fundamental misunderstanding of the role of the preacher of the nature and source of the authority with which he speaks:

> *Let a man so account of us, as of the Ministers of Christ, and Stewards of*
> *the mysteries of God.* That is our *Classis*, our rank, our station, what
> names soever we brought into the world by our extraction from this or
> that family, what name soever we took in our *baptisme*, and contract
> between God and us, that name, in which we come to you, is *that, The*
> *Ministers of Christ, The stewards of the Mysteries of God, And so let men*
> *account of us*, says the Apostle. *Invention*, and *Disposition*, and *Art*, and
> *Eloquence*, and *Expression*, and *Elocution*, and *reading*, and *writing*, and
> *printing*, are secondary things, accessory things, auxiliary, subsidiary
> things; men may account us, and make account of us, as of *Orators* in

> the pulpit, and of *Authors*, in the shop; but if they account of us as *of Ministers and Stewards*, they give us our due; that's our name to you. (VI, 103)

Donne, then, is defined by his position as a preacher and, he goes on to explain, occupies that position primarily by virtue of his calling. And, in elucidation of that calling, Donne points his audience to Biblical prototype, echoing Tyndale's commentary on John the Baptist:

> All the Evangelists mention *John Baptist* and his *preaching;* but two of the foure say never a word of his *austerity of life*, his *Locusts*, nor his *Camels haire*; and those two that do, *Matthew* and *Marke*, they insist, *first*, upon his *calling*, and *then* upon his *actuall preaching*, how he pursued that Calling, And *then* upon the *Doctrine* that he preached, *Repentance*, and *Sanctification*, and *after that*, they come to these secondary and subsidiary things, which added to his estimation, and assisted the passage of his Doctrine, His good life. Learning, and other good parts, and an exemplar life fall into second places; They have a first place, in *their* consideration who are to call them, but in *you*, to whom they are sent, but a second; fixe you, in the first place, upon that *Calling*. This Calling circumcised *Moses* uncircumcised lips; This made *Jeremy* able to speak, though he called himself a childe; this is *Esays coale from the Altar, which takes away even his sinne, and his iniquity.* Be therefore content to passe over some infirmities, and rest yourselves upon the *Calling.* (VI, 103)

By calling the preacher, then, the church gives recognition to his suitability for the work of a preacher, and the primary responsibility of the congregation is to accept that endorsement. The calling does not place the preacher above all reproach, nor, as we shall see, does it allow for an unbecoming life. The imprimatur of the calling does, however, give Donne, and his fellow ministers, the authority to command their audience's respect their audience's ear.

But, if the calling lays responsibility upon the congregation, it has its concomitant obligations for the preacher. Called to preach, he must preach, and the singular imperative of this duty must govern him in his life and in his performance in the pulpit:

> [W]e are bound to *teach*, and that this *teaching* is to *preach*; And *Væ si non*, *Wo be unto us*, if we do *not preach*. Wo to *them*, who out of *ease*, or state, *silence themselves*; And woe to *them* too, who by their *distemper*, and *Schismaticall* and seditious *manner* of preaching, occasion and force *others to silence them*; and think (and think it out of a profitable,

and manifold experience) That as forbidden books sell best, so silenced Ministers thrive best. It is a Duty, *Docendum*, we must teach, *Preach*; but a duty that excludes not *Catechizing*; for catechizing seems especially to be intended here, where he calls upon *them* who are to be taught, by that name, *Children*. It is a duty that excludes not *Praying*; but Praying excludes not *it* neither. Prayer and Preaching may consist, nay they must meet in the Church of God. Now, he that will teach, must have *learnt* before, many yeers before; And he that will preach, must have *thought* of it before. *Extemporall Ministers*, that resolve in a day what they will *be*, *Extemporall Preachers*, that resolve in a minute, what they will *say*, out-go Gods Spirit, and make too much hast. It was Christs way; He took first Disciples to learne, and then, out of them, the tooke *Apostles* to teach; and those Apostles made more Disciples. Though *your* first consideration be upon the *Calling*, yet *our* consideration must be for our *fitnesse* to that Calling.[1] (VI, 104)

There is much in this extract that is familiar: Donne's balancing of preaching with catechising and prayer echoes precisely the approach that we have already noted as an enduring theme of Donne's belief, and his quotation of Paul's exclamation – 'woe be unto me if I preach not the gospel' – is likewise something that occurs on almost every occasion that Donne speaks about preaching. To what we have already seen, the extract adds Donne's focus on the importance of the preacher's fitness – to be evaluated personally, if not by his congregation. Donne's inveterate balance emerges once again: the preacher must guard against being indolent in the pursuit of his calling, on the one hand, and against excessive zeal, and deliberate provocation on the other. The preacher can allow neither to compromise his calling.

Thus it was that Donne laid out the parameters of his approach to the souls in his cure at the commencement of his ministry in St Dunstan's. In Donne's sermon of valediction to his Lincoln's Inn congregation at his going into Germany, preached in 1619, we get a view of his more mature relationship with this congregation, one which had reason to occupy a special place in Donne's affections. This statement of his feeling for those who have sat regularly under his preaching has a heightened sense of poignancy in the light of Donne's grave misgivings about the prospect of his safe return. Thus, he uses his sermon of valediction to summarise his relationship with his first congregation, a group that occupies a warm place in his affection. Even as he does so, Donne emphasises the sort of reciprocity of affection and of duty that we have already observed:

1 For an instructively similar criticism of ministers who preached or conducted themselves so as to cause their 'mouths to be stopped', see Holland 'Archbishop Abbott', 25 .

As we remember God, so for his sake, let us remember one another. In my long absence, and far distance from hence, remember me, as I shall do you in the ears of that God, to whom the farthest East, and the farthest West are but as the right and left ear in one of us; we hear with both at once, and he hears in both at once; remember me, not my abilities; for when I consider my Apostleship that I was sent to you, I am in St *Pauls quorum, quorum ego sum minimus*, the least of them that have been sent; and when I consider my infirmities, I am in his *quorum*, in another commission, another man, *Quorum ego maximus*; the greatest of them; but remember my labours, and endeavors, at least my desire, to make sure your salvation. And I shall remember your religious cheerfulness in hearing the word, and your christianly respect towards all them that bring that word unto you, and towards myself in particular far [a]bove my merit. And so as your eyes that stay here, and mine that must be far of, for all that distance shall meet every morning, in looking upon that same Sun, and meet every night, in looking upon that same Moon; so our hearts may meet morning and evening in that God, which sees and answers every where; that you may come thither to him with your prayers, that I (if I may be of use for his glory, and your edification in this place) may be restored to you again; and may come to him with my prayer that what *Paul* soever plant amongst you, or what *Apollos* soever water, God himself will give the increase: That if I never meet you again till we have all passed the gate of death, yet in the gates of heaven, I may meet you all, and there say to my Saviour, that which he said to his Father and our Father, *Of those whom thou hast given me, have I lost none.* (II, 248)

Donne's affection for, and keen sense of duty towards, his congregation are patent. What is also clear is the extent to which the relationship with his congregation is contained in the act of preaching. Donne presents preaching as his chief discharge of his overarching function – to 'make sure your salvation' – and the reverent response of his hearers as the chief expression of their Christianity. It is notable that attention to the word of God comes first – respect for the minister has also its place, but is secondary to attentive listening to the voice of God.

Donne's characterisation of his ministry to his Lincoln's Inn congregation in this sermon introduces us to another important theme in Donne's understanding of the preacher's office. His depiction of his ministry as an apostleship is significant, and alerts us to the importance of the contemporary debate over the nature of the minister's authority. The issue of apostolic succession was, increasingly, a vexed one in the English church. There is a tendency, in the wake of the Oxford Movement, to think of apostolic succession primarily in terms of the tracing back of episcopal ordination through the centuries, to Apostolic times. Such an interpretation of succession did exist among Donne's contemporaries, and can be seen especially in the work of Francis Godwin (1562–1633). Godwin's *Catalogue of the bishops of England*, published in a two of editions in 1601 and 1615, attempted just this sort of tracing. A later edition of this book was published in 1625 as *The succession of the bishops of England*, a change of title that Anthony Milton suggests offers a telling index of the increased concern with apostolic succession.[2]

For others, however, apostolic succession was less a matter of tracing the orderly progression of bishops from the apostles to the present – schism had made it problematic for even the Roman church to make any very sweeping claims in that regard. Indeed, the doctrine of succession, as officially formulated for the first time by the Council of Trent, was concerned with the authority of the bishop rather than his historical pedigree:

> [I]f any one affirm, that all Christians indiscrimately are priests of the New Testament, or that they are all mutually endowed with an equal spiritual power, he clearly does nothing but confound the ecclesiastical hierarchy, which is as an army set in array; as if, contrary to the doctrine of blessed Paul, all were apostles, all prophets, all evangelists, all pastors, all doctors. Wherefore, the holy Synod declares that, besides the other ecclesiastical degrees, bishops, who have succeeded to the place of the apostles, principally belong to this hierarchial order; that they are placed, as the same apostle says, by the Holy Ghost, to rule the Church of God; that they are superior to priests; administer the sacrament of Confirmation; ordain the ministers of the Church; and that they can perform very many other things; over which functions others of an inferior order have no power.[3]

This understanding of apostolic succession only slowly penetrated the English church. Bishop John Jewel 'refused to endorse apostolic succession, rejecting it in favour of doctrinal succession. He believed apostolic succession undemonstrable and rationally unsupportable. During his long controversy with the puritans, John Whitgift expressly denied the doctrine as an infringement of monarchical power'.[4] Richard Hooker appeared to approach this understanding more closely:

> The ruling superiority of one Bishop over many Presbyters in each church, is an order descended from Christ to the Apostles, who were themselves Bishops at large, and from the Apostles to those whom

2 Milton, *Catholic and reformed*, p. 284.   3 J. Waterworth (ed.), *The canons and decrees of the sacred and oecumenical Council of Trent* (London, 1848), pp 172–3.   4 Stanley Archer, 'Hooker on apostolic succession: the two voices', *Sixteenth Century Journal* 24:1 (1993), 68.

> they in their steads appointed Bishops over particular Countries and
> Cities; and even from those antient times, universally established, thus
> many years it hath continued throughout the World; for which cause
> Presbyters must not grudge to continue subject unto their Bishops,
> unless they will proudly oppose themselves against that which God
> himself ordained by his Apostles, and the whole Church of Christ
> approveth and judgeth most convenient.[5]

Yet, this notwithstanding, Hooker qualified this endorsement of apostolic
succession:

> On the other side Bishops albeit they may avouch with conformity of
> truth, that their Authority hath thus descended even from the very
> Apostles themselves, yet the absolute and everlasting continuance of
> it, they cannot say that any commandment of the Lord doth injoyn.[6]

More complete, but still guarded, endorsements of this understanding of
apostolic succession were to be found in a Paul's Cross sermon preached by
Richard Bancroft, in which he excoriated puritan and Presbyterian innovators,
and defended the episcopacy on the basis that 'ever since Saint *Marks* time the
care of church government hath been committed. They had authoritie over the
rest of the ministry'.[7] For some avant-garde conformists, at least, the concept of
apostolic succession was crucial to the authority and the authenticity of the
ministry of the reformed Church of England. Such a succession guaranteed that
apostolic authority continued to be vested in the hierarchy of that church. This
model of ministerial authority stressed the importance of calling and of ecclesiastical sanction. The message, in some senses, became subservient to the man.

For those on the more puritan end of England's ecclesiastical continuum, this
emphasis on the apostolic succession was objectionable, little more than popery
dressed up, or, perhaps more accurately, dressed down. For these Protestants, the
message was primary, and the authority of the preacher was vested in their
proclamation of God's word rather than any ecclesiastical ceremony. Those who
adopted this position found a congenial paradigm in the lives of the Old
Testament prophets and tended to theorise the authority of the preacher using
prophetic, rather than apostolic, terminology. Such terminology was common to
a broad swathe of the ecclesiastical spectrum. Conformists, like Edmund
Grindal, who emphasised the role of preaching, had no difficulty with

5 Hooker, *Works*, III, pp 167–8. It should be noted that Book VII of the *Lawes* was not published
during Hooker's lifetime, although it did circulate in MS. See C.J. Sisson, *The judicious marriage
of Mr Hooker and the birth of The laws of ecclesiastical polity* (Cambridge, 1940). 6 Hooker,
Works, III, p. 168. 7 Richard Bancroft, *A sermon preached at Paules Crosse the 9 of Februarie,
being the first Sunday in the parleameant, Anno 1588* (London, 1588), pp 14–15.

describing gatherings for the preaching of the word as prophesyings; Donne's own 'godly' contemporary, William Perkins, entitled his book of advice for preachers *The arte of prophesying*, and, in his two treatises on the duty and calling of the minister, defined that duty in prophetic terms. More radical puritans, however, went beyond the mere use of terminology and saw in the lives of Biblical prophets a pattern of God-granted authority that transcended political structures and authority. For those who opposed the religious policies of the Tudor and Stuart monarchs, such prototypes offered a pattern of an authority based in a God-given mandate and message – an authority that was not weakened, and which could be validated, by ecclesiastical or secular disapprobation. And such disapprobation was generally forthcoming; the prophetic paradigm was perceived as one more occasion for puritan rebelliousness. Donne's sermons demonstrate his familiarity with both views of the minister's authority, and, in typical fashion, he generally maintains a position of equipoise less by rejecting both than by adopting elements from both views, to serve his immediate rhetorical purpose. But, as in other matters, this equipoise should not be understood as indifference: Donne has left us an explicit and very clear discussion of the claims of the opposing paradigms of preaching.

This discussion takes place in a very interesting context: it forms part of the second of the two sermons into which Donne digested the one preached at The Hague.[8] The peculiarly reformed nature of Donne's audience may have provided him with an impetus for his discussion, and it is probably true that his remarks would have been palatable to those who listened. There seems, however, no need to dismiss Donne's remarks as the mere *ad hominem* posturing of a crowd-pleasing preacher. If nothing else, his own preparation of the sermon for publication suggests that he regarded it as an accurate statement of his views. And while Donne was sensitive to the rhetorical possibilities of presenting his ministry as apostolic, on the one hand, or prophetic on the other, the view of his ministerial authority embodied in this sermon is endorsed by his sermons as a whole.

Donne's choice of text for the sermon was an interesting one, and one that gave particular point to the discussion of calling. He spoke from Matthew 4:18–20: 'And Jesus, walking by the sea of Galilee, saw two brethren, Simon called Peter, and Andrew his brother, casting a net into the sea: for they were fishers. And he saith unto them, Follow me, and I will make you fishers of men. And they straightway left their nets, and followed him'. This is the primeval calling of the first apostles. Donne applies the calling practically and pastorally,

8 On Donne's time in Europe with Doncaster, see Sellin, *Donne and diplomatic contexts*; R.C. Bald, *John Donne: a life* (Oxford, 1970), pp 338–65. Dudley Carleton recorded the event in his letters but, while he mentioned Donne's sermon, he was more occupied with practical details. See Jr Lee, Maurice (ed.), *Dudley Carleton to John Chamberlain, 1603–1624: Jacobean letters* (New Brunswick, NJ, 1972), pp 273–6.

and exhorts his audience to the following of Christ 'as well in doctrinall things as in practicall' (II, 302). Having dealt with the responsibilities that lay upon the two brothers as a result of their calling, he turns to consider 'what they shall get by this' – their gain because of Christ's calling. It is typical of Donne, and consonant with what we have already seen, that he sees the gain rather in terms of a particular duty than the dignity of a position:

> They shall be *fishers*; and what shall they catch? *men*. They shall be fishers of men. And then, for that world must be their Sea, and their net must be the Gospel. And here in so vast a sea, and with so small a net, there was no great appearance of much gaine. And in this function, whatsoever they should catch, they should catch little for themselves. (II, 302)

Above all else, then, the apostles were preachers. Donne has little to say about any sacramental privilege or ecclesiastical authority: the apostles, in his account, are primarily proclaimers of the gospel. As such, their calling is a burden, at least as much as it is a privilege and, Donne goes on to stress, it was an extraordinary calling that left no room for ideas of succession:

> The Apostleship, as it was the fruitfullest, so it was the barrennest vocation; They were to catch all the world; there is their fecundity; but the Apostles were to have no Successors, as Apostles; there is their barrennesse. The Apostleship was not intended for a function to raise houses and families; The function ended in their persons; after the first, there were no more Apostles. (II, 302)

The statement is certainly unequivocal, as is Donne's reiteration that 'the Apostleship was an extraordinary office instituted by Christ, for a certaine time, and to certaine purposes, and not to continue in ordinary use' (II, 303). Between these two statements, Donne had given a polemical edge to his argument, and had directed it against the apostolic pretensions of the Pope, against his claim to 'Apostolicall authority, ... Apostolicall dignity and Apostolicall jurisdiction' (II, 302). This in no way evacuates his words of their relevance to the present discussion, for to deny the possibility of apostolic succession was to deny it to Canterbury as well as to Rome, to the pulpit of St Paul's as well as to the altar of St Peter's. Furthermore, Donne's immediate progression to a discussion of the extraordinary nature of the prophet's office and his denial of the idea that its functions have transferred to the Christian minister clearly indicate his belief that apostolic barrenness has implications for the contemporary understanding of the authority of the preacher and indicate too, his expectation, indeed his intention, that his words be understood to have just such an import.

Donne is, perhaps, more explicit in his statement that 'the office of the Prophet was in the Old Testament an extraordinary office, and was not transferred then, nor does not remaine now in the ordinary office of the Minister' (II, 303). The lack of justification for the treatment of the prophetic office in his text is indicative of the degree to which claims of apostolic and prophetic calling were, for Donne, the Scylla and Charybdis of the preacher's authority and role. And, it quickly emerges, it is the political import of claims to prophetic office that most disquiets Donne:

> [T]hey argue impertinently, and collect and infer sometimes seditiously that say, The prophet proceeded thus and thus, therefore the Minister may and must proceed so too; The Prophets would chide Kings openly, and threaten the Kings publiquely, and proclaime the fault of the Kings in the eares of the people confidently, authoritatively, therefore the Minister may and must do so. God sent that particular Prophet *Ieremy* with that extraordinary Commission, *Behold I have this day set thee over Nations, and over the Kingdomes, to roote out, and to pull down, to destroy and throw downe, and then to build, and to plant againe*; But God hath given none of us his Ministers, in our ordinary function, any such Commission over nations, and over Kingdomes. Even in *Ieremies* Commission there seemes to be a limitation of time; *Behold this day I have set thee over them*, where that addition (*this day*) is not onely the the date of the Commission … but … is the terme, the duration of the Commission, that it was to last but that day. (II, 303)

Ultimately, for Donne, both the apostolic and the prophetic views of the office and authority of the Christian minister are anachronistic and equally to be reprehended. They both stem from a failure correctly to apprehend the nature of God's purposes in the past and at the present moment:

> And therefore, as they argue perversely, forwardly, dangerously that say, The Minister does not his duty that speakes not as boldly, and as publiquely too, and of Kings, and great persons, as the Prophets did, because theirs was an Extraordinary, ours an Ordinary office (and no man will thinke that the Justices in their Sessions, or the Judges in their Circuits may proceed to executions, without due tryall by a course of Law, because Marshals, in time of rebellion and other necessities, may doe so, because one hath but an ordinary, the other an extraordinary Commission) So doe they deceive themselves and others, that pretend in the Bishop of Rome an Apostolicall jurisdiction over all the world, whereas howsoever he may be S. *Peters*

successor, as Bishop of Rome, yet he is no Successor to S. *Peter* as an
Apostle; upon which onely the universall power can be grounded, and
without which that universall power fals to the ground: The
Apostolicall faith remaines spread over all the world, but the
Apostolicall jurisdiction is expired in their persons. (II, 303–4)

Thus far, Donne's discussion of the ministry has been a negative one: he has
denied the applicability of the two models most often used in describing ministerial function. Donne clearly appreciates this, for, having eliminated these
models, he sets about to provide a new model, in their place, one that acknowledges some common ground with prophetic and apostolic prototypes, but that
ultimately insists upon the radically different and essentially innovative nature of
the preacher's authority.

In adumbrating this model, Donne insists that essence is of more importance
than presentation, that an appreciation of the responsibilities of ministerial
office is more appropriate than glorification in the status of such an office. Thus,
it is the humility of the calling to be fishers of men that, for Donne, defines the
calling to preach the gospel:

> These twelve Christ cals *Fishers:* why fishers? Because it is a name of
> labour, of service, and of humiliation; and names that tast of humili-
> ation, and labour, and service, are most properly ours; (fishers we may
> be) names of dignity, and authority, and command are not so properly
> ours (Apostles wee are not in any such sense as they were). Nothing
> inflames, nor swells, nor puffes us up, more then that leaven of the
> soule, that empty, aery, frothy love of Names and Titles. (II, 304)

Thus it is that, in defining the nature of the preacher's duty, Donne still appeals
to the disciples as exemplars, but to their example as evangelists, not as apostles.
His text, therefore, allows him to insist that the office of the preacher is linked
to a calling; or, rather, is linked with two callings, an internal and an external
validation of ministry:

> [God] does not call them from their calling, but he mends them in it.
> It is not an Innovation ... but it is a Renovation ... and Renovations
> are always acceptable to God; that is, the renewing of a mans selfe, in
> a consideration of his first estate, what he was made for, and wherein
> he might be most serviceable to God. Such a renewing it is, as could
> not be done without God; no man can renewe himselfe, regenerate
> himselfe; no man can prepare that work, no man can begin it, no man
> can proceed in it of himselfe. The desire and the actuall beginning is
> from the preventing grace of God, and the constant proceeding is

from the concomitant, and subsequent, and continuall succeeding grace of God; for there is no conclusive, no consummative grace in this life; no such measure of grace given to any man, as that a man needs no more, or can lose or frustrate none of that. The renewing of these men in our text, Christ takes to himself; *Faciam vos, I will make yee fishers of men*; no worldly respects must make us such fishers; it must be a calling from God; And yet (as the other Euangelist in the same history expresses it) it is *Faciam fieri vos, I will cause yee to be made fishers of men*, that is I will provide an outward calling for you too. Our calling to this Man-fishing is not good, *Nisi Dominus faciat, & fieri faciat*, except God make us fishers by an internall, and make his Church to make us so too, by an external calling. Then we are fishers of men, and then we are successors to the Apostles, though not in their Apostleship, yet in this fishing. And then, for this fishing, the world is the Sea, and our net is the Gospel. (II, 305–6)

Donne's use of the terminology of grace in this extract is striking. He is, in effect, taking the Calvinist aetiology of conversion, and applying it to a calling to the ministry. This identification of conversion with the call to the ministry is fascinating, especially given the context of Donne's life. The same biographical context may seem to render ironical the insistence on the importance of an internal calling. Yet, the insistence that the call to the ministry of the church must come, in the first instance, from God is consistent throughout Donne's sermons, and there is at least a suggestion here that this passage provides us with fresh light on Donne's often-remarked reluctance to respond to James' urgings that he be ordained. Certainly, his insistence, in soteriological terminology, on the need for God's grace, lends support to Walton's contention that his delay was occasioned by a sense of unworthiness of the position to which he was called. Also notable is Donne's conceptualisation of the external calling by the church. Such a calling was essential, given Donne's understanding of ecclesiastical authority, but, by linking it with an inward calling, he makes it something more than the mechanical recruitment of candidates for ecclesiastical positions.

As well as outlining the sort of callings associated with this distinctly new form of divine service, Donne comments on the scope of his ministry and the methods to be employed in its pursuit. The world, he remarks, is the sea, in which the divinely mandated fishing is to take place and, like the sea, 'is subject to stormes, and tempests, and presents a danger of drowning 'in a calme, as in a storme', as well in prosperity, as in adversity. This world offers immense and unrestricted possibilities for fishing, and the faithful preacher is not to limit this scope by any personal predilection or ambition:

And in this Sea, are we made fishers of men; Of men in generall; not of rich men, to profit by them, nor of poore men, to pierce the more

> sharply, because affliction hath opened a way into them; Not of
> learned men, to affect them with an astonishment, or admiration of
> our gifts: But we are fishers of men, of all men, of that which makes
> them men, their soules. And for this fishing in this Sea, this Gospel is
> our net. (II, 307)

Twice over, by this time, Donne has identified the Gospel as the net by which
the divinely ordained fishing is to be carried out. He goes on to develop this
point, defining the Gospel by opposition:

> Eloquence is not our net; Traditions of men are not our nets; onely
> the Gospel is. The Devill angles with hooks and bayts; he deceives and
> he wounds in the catching; for every sin hath his sting. The Gospel of
> Christ Jesus is a net; It hath leads and corks; It hath leads, that is, the
> denouncing of Gods judgements, and a power to sink down, and to lay
> flat any stibborne and rebellious heart, And it hath corks, that is, the
> power of absolution, and the application of the mercies of God, that
> swimme above all his works, means to erect an humble and contrite
> spirit, above all the waters of tribulation, and affliction. (II, 307–8)

Significantly, Donne immediately follows this extract with a section which
begins 'A net is . . . a knotty thing, and so is the Scriptures' that we have considered in some detail in a previous chapter. Thus he collapses any distinction
between the gospel that he is called to preach, and the scriptures that proclaim it
– the gospel prescribes both matter and method. That it is the word preached
that Donne has in view at this point is evident in his closing, appealingly
personal, expression of faith in God's ability and intention to bless the word
preached:

> And that is truly the comfort that refreshes us in all our Lucubrations,
> and night-studies, through the course of our lives, that that God that
> sets us to Sea, will prosper our voyage, that whether he fix us upon
> our owne, or send us to other Congregations, he will open the hearts
> of those Congregations to us, and blesse our labours to them. For as
> S. *Pauls Væ si non*, lies upon us wheresoever we are (Wo be unto us if
> wee doe not preach) so (as S. *Paul* sayes too) we were of all men most
> miserable, if wee preached without hope of doing good. (II, 309)

Donne returned to the relevance of the prophetic ministry as a paradigm for
the ministerial in his Christmas sermon for 1628.[9] He took as his text the

9 Donne's Christmas sermons have been examined in detail in Dayton Haskin, 'John Donne and
the cultural contradicitons of Christmas', *John Donne Journal* 11 (1992), 133–57.

question 'Lord, who hath believed our report?', and drew the attention of his congregation to the three Biblical occurrences of the words: Isaiah 53:1, John 12:38 and Romans 10:16. Donne made these three passages the three sections of his sermon and discussed the question as raised by a prophet, an evangelist and an Apostle and pertaining to the 'prophetic Christ', as foretold by Isaiah, the 'historical Christ', recorded by John and Christ as applied 'to every soule, in the settling of a Church, in that concatenation of meanes for the infusion of faith expressed in that Chapter, *sending*, and *preaching*, and *hearing*' (VIII, 294). We have considered this very important discussion of the church's role in a previous chapter, and the treatment, as part of that discussion, of the place of preaching in bringing salvation fits very closely with the recurrence of the theme in Easter sermons, given that communion was also, at least theoretically, obligatory at Christmas. For our present purposes, though, Donne's remarks on the office of the prophet are where our interest lies, and here, as in the sermon preached in The Hague, his chief interest was to distinguish between the prophet's office and Donne's own function:

> The office and function of a Prophet, in the time of the Law, was not so evident, nor so ordinary an office, as the office of the Priest and Minister in the Gospel now is; There was not a constant, an ordinary, a visible calling in the Church, to the office of a Prophet. Neither the high-priest, nor the Ecclesiastical Consistory, the *Synedrium*, did by any imposition of hands, or other Collation, or Declaration, give Orders to any man so, as that thereby that man was made a Prophet. I know some men, of much industry, and perspicacy too, in searching into those Scriptures, the sense whereof is not obvious to every man, have thought that the Prophets had an outward and a constant declaration of their Calling. And they think it proved, by that which is said to *Eliah*, when God commands him to anoint *Hazael* King of Syria, and to anoint *Iehu* King of Israel, and to anoint *Elisha* Prophet in his own room: Therefore, say they, the Prophet had as much evidence of his Calling, as the Minister hath, for that unction was as evident a thing, as our Imposition of hands is. And it is true, it was so, where it was actually, and really executed. ... But howsoever it may have been for their Kings, there seemes to be a plaine distinction betweene them and the Prophets in the Psalme, for this evidence of unction; *Touch not mine Anointed*, sayes God there: They, they that were Anointed, constitute one rank, one classis; and then followes, *And doe my Prophets no harme*: They, they who were not Anointed, the Prophets, constitute another classis, another rank. So that then an internall, a spirituall unction the Prophets had, that is an application, an appropriation to that office from God, but a constant, an evident calling to

that function, by any externall act of the Church, they had not, but it
was an extraordinary office, and imposed immediately by God. (VII,
296–8)

In this fairly lengthy section, Donne is concerned less with the contrast between
the duties of prophet and minister than he is with the difference in their calling.
Once again, he is keen to stress the extraordinary nature of the prophet's calling
and clearly distinguishes it from the ordinary and evident calling of the minister.
Significantly, the role of the church in this ministerial calling is repeatedly
stressed. The precise importance of ecclesiastical recognition becomes clear
when we consider the broader context of the sermon. The lack of any external
ritual connected with the calling of the prophet, Donne argues, might excuse the
Israelite polity 'if they did not believe a Prophet presently' (VII, 298). Thus, it
was essential that their extraordinary divine mandate be confirmed by extraordinary means:

> Therefore when God does any extraordinary worke, he accompanies
> that work with an extraordinary light, by which, he, for whose
> instruction God does that work, may know that work to be his. (VII,
> 298)

The minister of the gospel required a similar validation: and, as an ordinary
office, finds it in the recognition, the ordination of the church, established, by
God, as 'a visible and constant, and permanent meanes of salvation' (VII, 307).
And, it is worth noting that Donne insists not only on the importance of
preaching to the mission of the church – commanded to '*goe, and preach the
Gospell to every creature*' – but also to its very existence, as he echoes the Thirty-
Nine Articles in declaring that 'the true Church is that, where the word is truly
preached, and the Sacraments duly administered'. Preaching, then, is at the very
core of the nature and the mission of the reformed church, and thus central to
the role of the 'Priest and Minister in the Gospel'.

In a frustratingly undated sermon, preached at St Paul's, on the key homiletic
text in II Corinthians 5:20: 'Now then we are ambassadors for Christ, as though
God did beseech you by us: we pray you in Christ's stead, be ye reconciled to
God', Donne marked off the function of the priest from that of the prophet with
even greater clarity:

> Though God sent Jeremy with that large Commission, Behold this
> day I have set thee over the Nations, and over the Kingdomes, to
> pluck up, and to rout out, to destroy and to throw down; and though
> many of the Prophets had their Commissions drawn by that prece-
> dent, we claime not that, we distinguish between the extraordinary

> Commission of the Prophet, and the ordinary Commission of the Priest, we admit a great difference between them, and are farre from taking upon us, all that the Prophet might have done; which is an errour, of which the Church of Rome, and some other over-zealous Congregations have been equally guility, and equally opposed Monarchy and Sovereignty, by assuming to themselves, in an ordinary power, whatsoever God, upon extraordinary occasions, was pleased to give for the present, to his extraordinary Instruments the Prophets. (X, 121)

The preacher is not a prophet, and Donne marks off his position from that of Rome and of 'other over-zealous Congregations'. In doing so, he raises the odds of the discussion considerably, making a proper understanding of the prophet's role a vital marker of ecclesiological propriety.

PREACHER OR PRIEST

Both of these sermons refer to the ministers of the Church of England as priests and thus call our attention to a term that has, thus far, been conspicuous by its absence from this chapter. We have delayed discussion of it to this point because the evidence available suggests that the concept of priesthood was of far less importance to Donne than those ideas that clustered around the office of the preacher. This relative lack of importance is evident on a crudely quantitative basis – examination of Troy Reeves' index to topics in the Sermons reveals approximately thirty references to priests, as against a combined total well in excess of 250 for 'Preacher' and 'Preaching'.[10] In itself, there is nothing exceptional about this lack of references to priesthood. That term carried with it enough pre-Reformation baggage to make it uncomfortable ground for any minister of the English church. What is more significant, however, is the fact that Donne does not provide us with any systematic treatment of the sacramental or sacredotal role of the minister. By contrast, the sermons feature discussions, both extensive and intensive, of the minister's role as a preacher of the gospel. This silence would be arresting in any case, but it is highly significant given the burgeoning tensions between alternative understandings of ministerial responsibility in the period.[11]

The sermon on II Corinthians 5:20, quoted above, is the most detailed treat-

---

10 Troy D. Reeves, *Index to the sermons of John Donne, 2: index to proper names*, ed. James Hogg (Salzburg, 1981), pp 153–6. 'Minister' and 'Ministry', admittedly more 'catch-all' terms, net a combined total of some two hundred mentions.   11 Fincham, *Prelate as pastor*, esp. pp 212–94 and Daniel W. Doerksen, 'Preaching pastor versus custodian of order: Donne, Andrewes and the Jacobean church', *Philological Quarterly* 73:4 (1994), 417–30.

ment that we have, in the sermons, of the topic of priesthood. Donne is very explicit about his interest in priesthood: in his division of the text, he draws the attention of his hearers to the 'two kinds of *persons, we* and *you*' (X, 120). The first part of the sermon, then, addresses 'our office towards you, and our stipulation and contract with you, *We pray you*; we come not as Lords or Commanders over you, but in humble, in submissive manner, *We pray you*'. And, far from making any exalted claims about the office of the priest, Donne is anxious, as he develops his subject, to disavow any claim to any mastery over the heritage of God, and, as we have seen him do repeatedly, stresses rather his duty to his congregation:

> First, then, for *our office* towards you, because you may be apt to say, *You take too much upon you, you sonnes of Levi*; *We* the sonnes of *Levi*, open to you our Commission, and we pursue but that we professe, that we are sent but to pray, but to intreat you; and we accompany it with an outward declaration, we stand bare, and you sit covered. When greater power seems to be given us, of treading upon *Dragons* and *Scorpians*, of *binding* and *loosing*, of *casting out Devills*, and the like, we confesse these are powers over *sinnes*, over *Devills* that doe, or endeavour to posess you, *not over you*, for *to you* we are sent to pray and intreat you. (X, 121)

This extract is remarkable for the way in which Donne mentions the more spectacular aspects of priesthood, only to dismiss them as of no real importance to the relationship between himself and his congregation. Indeed, even as he raises them, he acknowledges doubt as to their existence. Priesthood, for Donne, is not a thaumaturgic office. Rather, it is bound up in preaching, and preaching is a business best carried out in the absence of pride:

> [A]s Christ being the light of the world, called his Apostles the light of the world too; so, . . . the Saviour of the world communicates to us the name of Saviours of the world too, yet howsoever instrumentally and ministerially that glorious name of *Saviour* may be afforded to *us*, though to a high hill, though that Mount Sion, we are lead by a low way, by the example of our blessed Saviour himself. (X, 122)

And the protestations of humility do not end there. Donne is not only happy to pray his audience, but to 'throw down', to 'deject' himself, to 'admit any undervalue, any exination, any evacuation of our selves, so we may advance this great work' (X, 123). Later, he recalls that the Holy Ghost 'suffered his Apostles to be thought drunk', and gives a contemporary application: 'a dramme of zeal more than ordinary, against a *Patron*, or against a great Parishioner, makes us presently

scandalous Ministers'. Later, again, he calls to mind the occasions when both
Christ and Paul were accused of madness and of foolishness. While he stresses
that he speaks 'of the ministration of our office, for, for the office itself, nothing
can be more glorious, then the ministration of the Gospel' (X, 124) and, while
he later does spend some time on the dignity of speaking for God, it is his
conception of the lowliness of the priestly office and its basis in preaching that
is the overwhelming impression of this sermon. Equally noteworthy is Donne's
limitation of his priestly role to the proclamation rather than the enforcement of
truth:

> [W]e present to you our tears, and our prayers, his tears, and his
> prayers that sent us, and if you will not be reduced with these, our
> Commission is at an end. I bring not a *Star-chamber* with me up into
> the Pulpit, to punish a *forgery*, if you counterfeit a zeale in coming
> hither now; nor an *Exchequer*, to punish usurious contracts, though
> made in the Church; nor a high *Commission*, to punish incontinencies,
> if they be promoted by wanton interchange of looks in this place.
> Onely by my prayers, which he hath promised to accompany and
> prosper in his service, I can diffuse his overshadowing Spirit over all
> the corners of this Congregation, and pray that *Publican*, that stands
> below afar off, and dares not lift up his eyes to heaven, to receive a
> chearfull confidence, that his sinnes are forgiven him; and pray that
> *Pharisee*, that stands above, and onely thanks God, that he is not like
> other men, to believe himself to be, if not a rebellious, yet an unprof-
> itable servant. I can onely tell them, that neither of them is in the right
> way of reconciliation to God. (X, 122)

This attitude to priesthood is echoed in Donne's poetry. The late poem 'To
Mr Tilman after he had taken orders' is addressed to a newly ordained priest,
and outlines the consequences of the step that he has taken. These consequences
reiterate a good deal of what we have already seen. The link between calling and
conversion that Donne describes in his own experience is repeated in this poem.
Ordination should give rise, it is suggested, to 'new thoughts and stirrings', to
'new motions': it occasions a paradigm shift in existence. Yet, Donne is as clear,
and more emphatic, in his disavowal of any mystical change of Mr Tilman's
'substance':

> Thou art the same materials, as before,
> Onely the stampe is changed; but no more.
> And as new crowned Kings alter the face,
> But not the monies substance; so hath grace
> Chang'd onely Gods old Image by creation,
> To Christs new stampe, at this thy Coronation. (lines 13–18)

This 'coronation', like the impress on a coin, is something public and external and Donne is insisting, once again, upon the necessity of external calling. Nor does this external calling stand by itself – Tilman is responding to the promptings of his 'diviner soul' in taking orders and the external calling is confirming and validating those initial and inward promptings.

It is this double calling, then, that makes Tilman a minister, and the rewards of that calling that outweigh the social disadvantages of assuming a profession that is scorned by 'the foolish world'. And, this calling does have a mediatorial, a priestly aspect:

> If then th' Astronomers, whereas they spie
> A new-found Starre, their Opticks magnifie,
> How brave are those, who with their Engine, can
> Bring man to heaven, and heaven againe to man?
> These are thy titles and preheminences,
> In whom must meet Gods graces, mens offences,
> And so the heavens which beget all things here,
> And the earth our mother, which these things doth beare,
> Both these in thee, are in thy Calling knit,
> And make thee now a blest Hermaphrodite. (lines 45–54)

The poem, then, does describe a priesthood that represents God to man, and man to God. Donne, however, pays little attention to the sacerdotal elements of Mr Tilman's new status, according more space to a discussion of the problematic social standing of the ministry than he does to any mystical or hieratic elements. Further, Donne still strongly indicates on the importance of preaching, and, in the central section of the poem, suggests that it is the preaching of the Gospel, above all else that brings 'man to heaven, and heaven again to man':

> What function is so noble, as to bee
> Embassadour to God, and destinie?
> To open life? to give kingdomes to more
> Than Kings give dignities; to keep heavens doore?
> *Maries* prerogative was to beare Christ, so
> 'Tis preachers to convey him, for they doe
> As Angels out of clouds, from Pulpits speake;
> And blesse the poore beneath, the lame, the weake. (lines 37–44)

The weightiest claims of power and privilege, then, are made not for the minister *qua* priest, but *qua* preacher. The preaching of the word, as we have already seen, reincarnates Christ, transforms lives and takes souls to Heaven. This, for Donne, is the real dignity and authority of his calling.

Conclusion

The pulpit may her plain
And sober Christian precepts still retain;
Doctrines it may, and wholesome uses, frame,
Grave homilies and lectures; but the flame
Of thy brave soul, that shot such heat and light,
As burn'd our earth, and made our darkness bright,
Committed holy rapes upon the will,
Did through the eye the melting heart distil,
And the deep knowledge of dark truths so teach,
As sense might judge what fancy could not reach,
Must be desired for ever. . . .
Here lies a king that ruled, as he thought fit,
The universal monarchy of wit;
Here lies two flamens, and both those the best:
Apollo's first, at last the true God's priest. (lines 11–21, 95–8)[1]

Like all of the poets who contributed to the 'Elegies upon the Author' appended to the first edition of Donne's poems in 1633, Carew was conscious that he was commemorating two Donnes – the preacher and the poet. Carew's solution to the dilemma was elegant, and eminently suited to the requirements of elegy. Unfortunately, if inevitably, it was also a misrepresentation of his subject. For, while his description of the soul-melting fervour of Donne's preaching is easy enough to credit, the corresponding disestimation of plain pastoral preaching writes off the greater part of Donne's ministry. Donne was not reluctant to display, from time to time, such pyrotechnics of learning and delivery as he had at his command, but, throughout his career, pastoral priorities and a desire to impart simple and wholesome doctrines, exercised no inconsiderable control over his ministry. In a similar way, Carew's neat device of presenting Donne's life in two priesthoods suggests an understanding of Donne's preacherly vocation

---

1 Thomas Carew's 'An elegie upon the death of the dean of Pauls, Dr John Donne' is reproduced in John Donne, *The complete English poems of John Donne*, ed. C.A. Patrides (London, 1985), pp 496–8. Carew's elegy is discussed in John Lyon, 'Jonson and Carew on Donne: censure into praise', *Studies in English Literature, 1500-1900* 37:1 (1997), 97–118 and Scott Nixon, 'Carew's response to Jonson and Donne', *Studies in English Literature, 1500–1900* 39:1 (1999), 89–109.

that he did not himself share: a sacramental and mystical understanding of a primarily homiletic office that Donne summed up in his reiterated echo of Paul's '*vae si non …*'.

These two forces – the desire to give unity to Donne's life and a willingness to tamper with the facts of that life in order to create the illusion of unity – have dogged attempts to understand Donne: from Walton to Gosse to Carey and beyond, we can trace a genealogy of misrepresentation. This study has participated in the search for a unified Donne. In doing so, I have endeavoured, as much as possible, to allow Donne's own work to dictate the terms of enquiry. Taking the hints that his writings offer, this study has traced a consistency of thought that has always been striking and occasionally surprising. Essential to the uncovering of these career-spanning consistencies has been a willingness to allocate to religious topics and concerns something like the intrinsic importance that they had for Donne. For too long, these issues have attracted scholarly attention only as the referents of Donne's political, poetic, philosophical or even erotic ideology, but as early modern studies more generally exhibit a most encouraging trend towards methodologies that are sensitive to religious concerns, this study is a demonstration of the value of such methodologies when applied to Donne.

One of the chief effects of the application of these methodologies in this study is a fundamental challenge to the idea of an apostate Donne who became as Protestant as necessary while remaining as Catholic as possible. Rather, our consideration of the importance of the authority of scripture, the church and the preacher in Donne's thought reveals an estimation of the value of intellectual independence and of orderly community that is eloquent of the fundamental tendency of Donne's thought towards Protestantism. Donne found in the conformist mainstream of the Church of England a congenial ecclesiastical environment that enabled him to arrive at his own negotiation – often idiosyncratic, but always orthodox – of Christian life.

Scripture was essential to this negotiation and we have noted the importance that Donne accords to the individual engagement with scripture and his faith in the power of a new philology to assist in that engagement. The excoriation of blind and unquestioning obedience that so often marks Donne's pastoral concern for his flock is the concomitant of this estimation of the value of scripture. In line with this emphasis, Donne rejects any programmatically allegorical interpretation of scripture in favour of a literal approach to interpretation, which has room for both the church and the individual as interpretative authorities. Donne saw in the church an interpretative aid, which could guide and test interpretation, but which ought never tyrannically to control it. This commitment to the individual engagement with scripture is not negotiable with Donne: we have noted the increased place that he gave to the private reading of scripture, even as avant-garde conformity increasingly marginalised the importance of private lay reading. That he should, in such a context, so insist upon this right is further confirmation that Donne's theology is best understood be reference to the long context of reformation thought.

A similar picture emerges from our consideration of the role of ecclesiastical authority in Donne's thought. We have seen how Donne's loyalty to the English church was based, in part, upon his belief that its polity offered a model for this sort of inclusivity. Donne did not claim perfection for his church, nor did he ever suggest that she modelled the only form of church government and ceremony acceptable to God. But as a work in progress, as an approach to religious community, the English church had much to offer. Thus, Donne is unswerving in his loyalty and unrelenting in his denouncement of those who would disturb the peace of this Catholic and reformed church. Donne's commitment to accommodation and irenicism within the Church of England is also exemplified in his pursuit of what we have termed his essentialist ecumenism: his delineation of a set of core beliefs that could not, at any price, be compromised, and his relegation of other matters – both doctrinal and ceremonial – to the realm of things indifferent. Donne resisted the urge towards increased emphasis on ceremonialism, on one side, and a scrupulous Biblicism, on the other. Wherever a paralysing precisianism raises its head – be it in the deliberations of the Council of Trent, in the scripturalism of the puritans, or in the rigours of an emerging Laudian programme – Donne positions himself as its opponent.

Finally, we have considered Donne's understanding of what, as a preacher, his authority and duties were. The Christian ministry is, for Donne, deeply logocentric: the preaching of the Word of God is both its heaviest duty and its greatest dignity. Because the traditional place of preaching was identified as such a site of contest by the emerging avant-garde tendency, and because this reorientation of the English church away from preaching and around a dipole of sacrament and liturgy was so radical a reshaping of the status quo, Donne's orthodoxy is the more evident. This defensive orthodoxy is seldom explicit: Donne is slow to give a direct public airing to the divisions within the English church. Notwithstanding this, his opposition to the downgrading of the sermon's importance emerges clearly enough when his sermons are read in their religious and historical context. And the place given to preaching had direct implications for Donne's conceptualisation of his ministerial role. Donne is resistant to any definition of ministry that makes secondary the importance of preaching. The minister, in his understanding, is remarkable not for the sacerdotal importance of his role but because he speaks, as a preacher, for God. A crudely quantitative analysis of the sermons is enough to suggest what more detailed study confirms: Donne sees himself as preacher first, and as priest hardly at all. But this is no diminution of dignity. He is God's ambassador, and speaks with a consciousness of the burden of that great charisma. Thus, while the importance of the office demands that great care and skill be employed in finding out words to speak, the power of the preacher does not reside in his rhetorical accomplishment, but in the unction of the spirit.

This, then, is the picture of Donne that emerges from our study of his understanding of these fundamental loci of religious authority. Donne has suffered more than most from labelling, and it has been an important aim of this study to avoid imposing any such totalising terms upon his beliefs. That notwithstanding, we can, by this time, readily identify the key priorities of his theology. It is Protestant, not in its rigid adherence to any one system of theology, but in its basic assumptions, in its vital stress upon the responsibility of the individual correctly to respond to divine revelation, and in its continuity with the reformed tradition of the English church. It is pastoral in its emphasis: whether Donne is interpreting scripture, delineating the role of the church or speaking as a preacher to one of his congregations, his words are marked by a lively awareness of the needs and concerns of his listeners. Finally, it is principled. It is a pity to allow some of the less sympathetic readings of Donne too rigidly to set the terms of our inquiry. Nonetheless, it is difficult not to take some satisfaction in the way in which the contextualised study of Donne's entire *oeuvre* vindicates a man so abused by those who see in his life little that cannot be accounted for by the cocktail of apostasy and ambition that supposedly intoxicated the poet and the preacher. The consistency of Donne's views, his moderate but determined defence of the established church and his concern to protect his congregations from the pastorally disastrous effects of schism and fractious doctrinal debate remind us that his commitment to a church that was, increasingly, understanding itself as a compromise need not itself be a compromise.

'When thou hast done' the 'Hymne to God the Father' reiterates 'thou hast not done, / For, I have more'. Donne's appropriation of the congregational hymn for such an individual and personal purpose is typical. It is also somehow typical that his words of confession addressed to God, acknowledging Donne's inadequacy, re-echo to Donne's critics as a reminder of their own inability fully to embrace or understand the variegated tapestry and changeful trajectory of Donne's life. That remains a challenge as daunting for us as for Carew and his fellow elegists. This work is no exception: it is a beginning, and not an end. A careful and contextualised reading of the Donneian *oeuvre* has enormous potential to illuminate our understanding of the man and his context. Where this study has broken new ground is in its focus on the religious elements of Donne's thought, and its willingness to take those issues seriously in their own right, rather than as the referents of political or ideological positions. Studies predicated upon this assumption have a great deal of scope. The issue of authority alone is far from exhausted by this study, and there are a great many other theological issues that are of concern to Donne, and which ought to be important to Donne scholars. And, as early Stuart historiography moves away from its established focus on predestinarian theology, we are likely to realise the importance of a far wider range of religious and theological concerns.

But if this study suggests useful steps to be taken in increasing our understanding of Donne, it may also be of value in indicating an avenue to a greater understanding of the experience of the Jacobean and Caroline convert and Christian. Literary studies of the early modern period have suffered, to date, because the theorised general has been imposed upon the particular. If this flow is reversed, if the detailed study of specific cases is allowed to illuminate the general context, if we permit the antinomy of the individual to problematise and nuance our conveniently simplistic views of this most religiously complex of periods, the gains we stand to make are considerable indeed. And, it may be that Donne is an outstanding example of the value of this process. Certainly, it is difficult not to concur with Shami's contention that

> though no historians (in the purely disciplinary sense) have treated Donne seriously as an important figure in the construction of the English church, their insights about the tensions fracturing and shaping the English church are nowhere better examined than in this man – a compendium of conflicts, controversies, and harmonies, who epitomizes the efforts of the Church to remain whole, and whose daring experiments in interpretation and rhetoric predicted its highest achievements. His writings expose the fault lines and tensions in the early Stuart church, and his resistance to labelling makes all too clear the more extreme, less sophisticated, versions of the conflicts he embodied.[2]

That being the case, the study in which we have been engaged has the potential to benefit more than Donne scholars. But its chief contribution is the insight that it gives on the complex and compendious character of John Donne.

---

2 Shami, 'Trying to walk on logs', 87–8.

Bibliography

WORKS BY JOHN DONNE

Biathanatos. Ed. Ernest W. Sullivan (Newark, DE, 1984).

The complete English poems of John Donne. Ed. C.A. Patrides (London, 1985).

The courtier's library; or, Catalogus librorum aulicorum incomparabilium et non vendibilium. Ed. Evelyn Mary Simpson ([London], 1930).

Devotions upon emergent occasions. Ed. John Hanbury Angus Sparrow and Geoffrey Keynes (Cambridge, 1923).

Essayes in divinity: being several disquisitions interwoven with meditations and prayers. Ed. Anthony Raspa (Montreal, 2001).

Essays in divinity. Ed. Evelyn M. Simpson (Oxford, 1952).

Ignatius, his conclave. Ed. Timothy S. Healy (Oxford, 1969).

John Donne's sermons on the Psalms and Gospels: with a selection of prayers and meditations. Ed. Evelyn Mary Simpson (Berkeley, CA, 2003).

Letters to severall persons of honour (London, 1651).

Letters to severall persons of honour (1651). Ed. M. Thomas Hester (Delmar, NY, 1977).

Pseudo-martyr: wherein out of certaine propositions and gradations, this conclusion is evicted, that those which are of the Romane religion in this, may and ought to take the Oath of allegiance. Ed. Anthony Raspa (Montreal, 1993).

Selected prose. Ed. Neil Rhodes (London, 1987).

'John Donne's Sermons'. Brigham Young University, 2007. http://lib.byu.edu/digital/donne/.

The sermons of John Donne. Ed. G.R. Potter and Evelyn Mary Simpson (Berkley, CA, 1953).

OTHER PRIMARY SOURCES

Andrewes, Lancelot. XCVI. *Sermons by the Right Honorable and Reverend Father in God, Lancelot Andrewes, late lord bishop of Winchester.* Ed. William Laud and John Buckeridge (London, 1629).

Anon. *The institution of a christen man* (London, 1537).

—— *A most godly and learned discourse of the woorthynesse, authoritie, and sufficiencie of the holy scripture also of the cleerenesse, and plainnesse of the same, and of the true vse thereof. Wherin is discussed this famous question: whether the canonical scriptures haue authoritie from the church, or rather the church receiue authoritie from the scriptures. By occasion wherof are touched the dignities and duties of the church, touching traditions, with aunswere to all obiections.* Trans. John Tomkys (London, 1579).

—— *The preaching BISHOP reproving unpreaching PRELATES. Being a brief but faith-full collection of observable passages, in several sermons preached by the reverend father in God, Mr Hugh Latimer, bish. of Worcester* . . . (London, 1661).

Bacon, Francis. *The advancement of learning; and, New Atlantis.* Ed. Arthur Johnston (Oxford, 1974).

Bale, John. *Image of the both churches* (1545).

Bancroft, Richard. *A sermon Preached at Paules Crosse the 9 of Februarie, being the first Sunday in the parleameant, Anno 1588* (London, 1588).

Calvin, John. *Institutes of the Christian religion.* Trans. Henry Beveridge (Chicago, IL, 1990).

Cardwell, Edmund (ed.), *Documentary annals of the reformed Church of England: being a collection of injunctions, declarations, orders, articles of inquiry, &c. from the year 1546 to the year 1716* (Oxford, 1839).

Cranmer, Thomas. *Remains.* Ed. H. Jenkins (Oxford, 1833).

de Montaigne, Michel. *An apology for Raymond Sebond.* Trans. and ed. M.A. Screech (London, 1987).

Foxe, John. *Actes and monuments of the matters most special and memorable, happening in the church, with an universall historie of the same* (London, 1610).

—— *The first volume of the ecclesiastical history contayning the actes and monumentes of things passed in every kinges time, in this realme, especially in the Churche of England* (London, 1576).

Grindal, Edmund. *The remains of Edmund Grindal, successively bishop of London and archbishop of York and Canterbury.* Ed. William Nicholson (Cambridge, 1843).

Herbert, Edward. *De Veritate.* Trans. Meyrick H. Carré (London, 1992).

Herbert, George. *A priest to the temple; or, The country parson.* Ed. Ronald Blythe (Norwich, 2003).

—— *The Folger Library edition of the works of Richard Hooker, 1: Of the laws of ecclesi-astical polity,* ed. Georges Edelen (Cambridge, MA, 1977).

—— *The Folger Library edition of the works of Richard Hooker, 2: Of the laws of ecclesi-astical polity,* ed. William Speed Hill (Cambridge, MA, 1977).

—— *The Folger Library edition of the works of Richard Hooker, 4: Lawes: attack and response,* ed. John E. Booty (Cambridge, MA, 1982).

—— *The Folger Library edition of the works of Richard Hooker, 3: Of the laws of ecclesi-astical polity,* ed. Paul G. Stanwood (Cambridge, MA, 1981).

Jackson, Thomas. *A treatise of the holy catholike faith and church. Divided into three books. The first book* (London, 1627).

—— *The works of Thomas Jackson DD: sometime president of Corpus Christi College, Oxford, and Dean of Peterborough* (12 vols, Oxford, 1844).

James VI and I, king of Scotland and England. *King James VI and I political writings.* Ed. Johann P. Sommerville (Cambridge, 1994).

—— *The workes of the most high and mightie prince, Iames by the grace of God, king of Great Britaine, France and Ireland, defender of the faith &c.,* ed. James Montague (London, 1616).

Latimer, Hugh. *Fruitfull sermons preached by the reuerend father, and constant martyr of Iesus Christ, M. HUGH LATIMER, newly imprinted with others not heeretofore set forth in print, to the edefying of all which dispose themselues to the reading of the same* (London, 1607).

Laud, William. *A relation of the conference between William Lawd, then lord bishop of St Davids; now, lord archbishop of Canterbury: and Mr Fisher the Jesuit* (4th ed., London, 1639).

Luther, Martin. 'The Babylonian captivity of the church' in *Luther's Works, 36: Word and Sacrament II*, ed. Abel Ross Wentz (Philadelphia, PA, 1975).

—— *The Large Catechism*, trans. F. Bente and W.H.T. Dau (St Louis, MO, 1921).

—— *Luther's Works, 13: Selected Psalms*, ed. Jaroslav Pelikan (St Louis, MO, 1956).

—— *Luther's Works, 36: Word and Sacrament II*, ed. Abdel Ross Wentz (Philidelphia, PA, 1975).

—— *Luther's Works, 39: Church and ministry I*, ed. Eric W. Gritsch (Philadelphia, PA, 1970).

—— *Luther's Works, 40: Church and ministry II*, ed. Bergendoff (Philidelphia, PA, 1975).

Matthew, Tobie. *A collection of letters, made by Sr Tobie Mathews Kt. With a character of the most excellent lady, Lucy, countesse of Carleile: by the same author. To which are added many letters of his own, to severall persons of honour, who were contemporary with him* (London, 1660).

Mornay, lord of Plessie Marlie, Philip. *A woorke concerning the trewnesse of Christian religion, written in French, against atheists, Epicures, Paynims, Jewes, Mahumetists and other infidels*, trans. Sir Philip Sidney and Arthur Golding (London, 1587).

Perkins, William. *The arte of prophecying; or, A treatise concerning the sacred and onely true manner and methode of preaching first written in Latine by Master William Perkins; and now faithfully translated into English (for that it containeth many worthie things fit for the knowledge of men of all degrees) by Thomas Tuke* (London, 1607).

—— *Of the calling of the ministrie, two treatises describing the duties and dignities of that calling, delivered publikely in the Unviersity of Cambridge* (London, 1606).

—— *A reformed Catholike: a declaration shewing how neere we may come to the present Church of Rome in sundrie points of religion: and wherein we must for ever depart from them: with an advertisment to all favourers of the Roman religion, shewing that the said religion is against the Catholike principles and grounds of the catechisme* (Cambridge, 1558).

Robinson, Hastings (ed.), *The Zurich letters: comprising the correspondence of several English bishops and others with some of the Helvetian reformers, during the reign of Queen Elizabeth* (Cambridge, 1846).

Scott, W., and J. Bliss, eds. *The works of the most Reverend Father in God, William Laud DD* (7 vols, Oxford, 1847–60).

Strype, John. *The life and acts of John Whitgift DD* (Oxford, 1822).

Tyndale, William. *An answere unto Sir Thomas Mores dialogue made by William Tindale* (1531).

—— *The obedience of the Christian man*, ed. David Daniell (London, 2000).

—— *The parable of the wicked mammo[n] take[n] out of the. xvi. ca. of Luke with an*

exposicyon tervpon latley corrected [and] printed (Malborowe, in the lande of Hesse [London], 1528).
—— *The work of William Tyndale*, ed. G.E. Duffield (Appleford, 1964).
Whitgift, John. *The works of John Whitgift*, ed. J. Ayre (3 vols, Cambridge, 1851–3).

SECONDARY SOURCES

Adam, Peter. *'To bring men to heaven by preaching': John Donne's evangelistic sermons* (London, 2006).

Adlington, Hugh. 'The preacher's plea: juridical influence in John Donne's sermons, 1618–1623', *Prose Studies* 26:3 (2003), 344–56.

Aikenhead, Ian D. 'Students of the common law, 1590–1615: lives and ideas at the Inns of Court', *The University of Toronto Law Journal* 27:3 (1977), 243–56.

Allen, Don Cameron. 'Dean Donne sets his text', *ELH* 10:3 (1943), 208–29.

Archer, Stanley. 'Hooker on apostolic succession: the two voices', *Sixteenth Century Journal* 24:1 (1993), 67–74.

Atkinson, Nigel. *Richard Hooker and the authority of scripture, tradition and reason* (Carlisle, 1997).

Avis, Paul. *Anglicanism and the Christian church: theological resources in historical perspective* (Edinburgh, 1989).

Backus, Irena. *Reformation readings of the Apocalypse: Geneva, Zurich and Wittenberg* (Oxford, 2000).

Bacon, Francis. *The advancement of learning; and, New Atlantis*, ed. Arthur Johnston (Oxford, 1974).

Bainton, Roland H. 'The Bible in the Reformation' in *The Cambridge history of the Bible*, ed. S.L. Greenslade (Cambridge, 1963), iii, pp 1–37.

Bald, R.C. *John Donne: a life* (Oxford, 1970).

Bancroft, Richard. *A sermon preached at Paules Crosse the 9 of Februarie, being the first Sunday in the parleameant, Anno 1588* (London, 1588).

Battenhouse, Roy W. 'The grounds of religious toleration in the thought of John Donne', *Church History* 11:3 (1942), 217–28.

Bennett, R.E. 'Tracts from John Donne's library', *Review of English Studies* 13 (1937), 333–5.

Bentley, Jerry H. *Humanists and holy writ: New Testament scholarship in the Renaissance* (Princeton, NJ, 1983).

Born, Lester K. 'Ovid and allegory', *Speculum* 9:4 (1934), 362–79.

Bredvold, Louis I. 'The naturalism of Donne in relation to some renaissance traditions', *Journal of English and Germanic Philology* 22 (1923), 471–502.

Bredvold, Louis I. 'The religious thought of Donne in relation to medieval and later traditions' in *Studies in Shakespeare, Milton and Donne* (New York, 1925), pp 191–232.

Calvin, John. *Institutes of the Christian religion*, trans. Henry Beveridge (Chicago, IL, 1990).

Campbell, Gordon. *Bible: the story of the King James Version, 1611–2011* (Oxford, 2010).

Cargill Thompson, W.D.J. 'The philosopher of the "politic society"' in *Studies in Richard Hooker: essays preliminary to an edition of his works*, ed. William Speed Hill (Cleveland, OH, 1972).

Carlson, Eric Josef. 'Good pastors or careless shepherds? parish ministers and the English reformation', *History* 88 (2003), 423–36.

Clancy, Thomas H. 'Papist – protestant – puritan: English religious taxonomy, 1565–1665', *Recusant History* 13:4 (1976), 227–53.

Coffin, Charles Monroe. *John Donne and the new philosophy* (London, 1937).

Colclough, David. *Freedom of speech in early Stuart England* (Cambridge, 2005).

Collinson, Patrick. *Archbishop Grindal, 1519–1583: the struggle for a reformed church* (London, 1979).

Collinson, Patrick. *The religion of protestants: the church in English society, 1559–1625* (Oxford, 1979).

Comparetti, Domenico. *Vergil in the Middle Ages* (Princeton, NJ, 1997).

Considine, John. 'Golding, Arthur (1535/6–1606)', *Oxford dictionary of national biography* (2004). www.oxforddnb.com/view/article/10908 [accessed 24 May 2013].

Coster, William. 'Purity, profanity and puritanism: the churching of women, 1500–1700' in *Women in the church*, ed. W.J. Sheils and Diana Wood (Oxford, 1990), pp 377–87.

Cressy, David. 'Purification, thanksgiving and the churching of women in post-reformation England', *Past and Present* 141 (1993), 106–46.

Cummings, Brian. *The literary culture of the reformation: grammar and grace* (Oxford, 2002).

d'Entrèves, A.P. *Natural law: an introduction to legal philosophy* (2nd (revised) ed., London, 1970).

d'Entrèves, A.P. *The medieval contribution to political thought: Thomas Aquinas, Marsilius of Padua, Richard Hooker* (Oxford, 1939).

Davies, Julian. *The Caroline captivity of the church: Charles I and the remoulding of Anglicanism, 1625–1641* (Oxford, 1992).

De Hamel, Christopher. *The book: a history of the Bible* (London, 2001).

de Montaigne, Michel. *An apology for Raymond Sebond*, ed. M.A. Screech (London, 1987).

Doerksen, Daniel W. 'Preaching pastor versus custodian of order: Donne, Andrewes and the Jacobean church', *Philological Quarterly* 73:4 (1994), 417–30.

Doerksen, Daniel W. *Conforming to the Word: Herbert, Donne and the English church before Laud* (London, 1997).

Donne, John. *The complete English poems of John Donne*, ed. C.A. Patrides (London, 1985).

Edwards, David L. *John Donne: man of flesh and spirit* (Grand Rapids, MI, 2002).

Evans, G.R. *The language and logic of the Bible: the road to reformation* (Cambridge, 1985).

Faulkner, Robert K. 'Reason and revelation in Hooker's ethics', *American Political Science Review* 59:3 (1965), 680–90.

Faulkner, Robert K. *Richard Hooker and the politics of a Christian England* (Berkeley, CA, 1981).

Ferrell, Lori Anne. 'Donne and his master's voice, 1615–1625', *John Donne Journal* 11 (1992), 59–72.

Ferrell, Lori Anne. *Government by polemic: James I, the king's preachers and the rhetorics of conformity, 1603–1625* (Stanford, CA, 1998).

Field, George C. 'Donne and Hooker', *Anglican Theological Review* 48 (1966), 307–9.

Fincham, Kenneth, and Peter Lake. 'The ecclesiastical policies of James I and Charles I' in *The early Stuart church, 1603–1642*, ed. Kenneth Fincham (London, 1993), pp 23–49.

Fincham, Kenneth, and Peter Lake. 'The ecclesiastical policy of King James I', *Journal of British Studies* 24:2 (1985), 169–207.

Fincham, Kenneth. 'Clerical conformity from Whitgift to Laud' in *Conformity and orthodoxy in the English church, c.1560–1660*, ed. Peter Lake and Michael C. Questier (Woodbridge, 2000), pp 125–58.

Fincham, Kenneth. *Prelate as pastor: the episcopate of James I* (Oxford, 1990).

Fincham, Kenneth. *The early Stuart church, 1603–1642* (Basingstoke, 1993).

Fisher, R.M. 'The reformation of clergy at the Inns of Court, 1530–1580', *Sixteenth Century Journal* 12:1 (1981), 69–91.

Gilman, Ernest B. '"To adore, or scorne an image": Donne and the iconoclast controversy', *John Donne Journal* 5 (1986), 63–100.

Goodblatt, Christine. 'From "Tav" to the cross: John Donne's protestant exegesis and polemics' in *John Donne and the protestant reformation*, ed. Mary Arshagouni Papazian (Detroit, MI, 2003), pp 221–46.

Gordon, Bruce. 'Conciliarism in late mediæval Europe' in *The reformation world*, ed. Andrew Pettegree (London, 2000), pp 31–50.

Grace, Damien. 'Natural law in Hooker's *Of the laws of ecclesiastical polity*', *Journal of Religious History* 21:1 (1997), 10–22.

Greenblatt, Stephen, and Christine Gallagher. *Practising new historicism* (Chicago, IL, 2000).

Greenblatt, Stephen. *Hamlet in purgatory* (Princeton, NJ, 2001).

Grislis, Egil. 'The role of consensus in Richard Hooker's method of theological inquiry' in *The heritage of Christian thought: essays in Honour of Robert Lowry Calhoun*, ed. Robert E. Cushman and Egil Grislis (New York, 1965), pp 64–88.

Haigh, Christopher. 'The recent historiography of the English reformation' in *The English reformation revised*, ed. Christopher Haigh (Cambridge, 1987), pp 19–33.

Hall, Basil. 'Biblical scholarship: editions and commentaries' in *Cambridge History of the Bible*, ed. Stephen Greenslade (Cambridge, 1963), iii, pp 38–93.

Harding, Alan. *A social history of English law* (London, 1966).

Harland, Paul W. 'Donne and Virginia: the ideology of conquest', *John Donne Journal* 18 (1999), 127–52.

Haskin, Dayton. 'John Donne and the cultural contradicitons of Christmas', *John Donne Journal* 11 (1992), 133–57.

Haviland, J.B. 'The use of the Bible in the sermons of John Donne' (PhD, TCD, 1960).

Hester, M. Thomas. *Kinde pitty and brave scorn: John Donne's Satyres* (Durham, NC, 1982).

Hillerdal, Gunnar. *Reason and revelation in Richard Hooker* (Lund, 1962).

Holland, Susan. 'Archbishop Abbot and the problem of "puritanism"', *Historical Journal* 37:1 (1994), 23–43.

Hunt, Arnold. 'The Lord's Supper in early modern England', *Past and Present* 161 (1998), 39–83.

Jenkins, Gary. *John Jewel and the English national church: the dilemmas of an Erastian reformer* (Aldershot, 2006).

Johnson, Jeffrey. 'Consecrating Lincoln's Inn Chapel', *John Donne Journal* 23 (2004), 139–60.

Johnson, Jeffrey. 'John Donne and Paolo Sarpi: rendering the Council of Trent' in *John Donne and the protestant reformation*, ed. Mary Arshagouni Papazian (Detroit, MI, 2003), pp 90–112.

Johnson, Jeffrey. *The theology of John Donne* (Cambridge, 1999).

Johnson, Stanley. 'John Donne and the Virginia Company', *ELH* 14:2 (1947), 127–38.

Kaufman, Peter Iver. 'Prophesying again', *Church History* 68:2 (1999), 337–58.

Kenney, Anthony. *Medieval philosophy* (Oxford, 2005).

Kneidel, Gregory. *Rethinking the turn to religion in early modern English literature: the poetics of all believers* (London, 2008).

Lake, Peter, and Michael C. Questier. 'Introduction' in *Conformity and orthodoxy in the English church, c.1560–1660*, ed. Peter Lake and Michael C. Questier (Woodbridge, 2000), pp ix–xx.

Lake, Peter. 'Serving God and the times: the Calvinist conformity of Robert Sanderson', *Journal of British Studies* 27:2 (1988), 81–116.

Lake, Peter. 'Anti-popery: the structure of a prejudice' in *Conflict in early Stuart England: studies in religion and politics, 1603–1642*, ed. Richard Cust and Ann Hughes (London, 1989), pp 72–106.

Lake, Peter. 'Anti-Puritanism: the structure of a prejudice' in *Religious politics in post-reformation England: essays in Honour of Nicholas Tyacke*, ed. Kenneth Fincham and Peter Lake (Woodbridge, 2006), pp 80–97.

Lake, Peter. 'Business as usual? The immediate reception of Hooker's *Ecclesiastical polity*', *Journal of Ecclesiastical History* 52:3 (2001), 456–86.

Lake, Peter. 'Introduction: puritanism, arminianism and Nicholas Tyacke' in *Religious politics in post-reformation England: essays in honour of Nicholas Tyacke*, ed. Kenneth Fincham and Peter Lake (Woodbridge, 2006), pp 1–15.

Lake, Peter. 'Lancelot Andrewes, John Buckeridge and avant-garde conformity at the court of James I' in *The mental world of the Jacobean court*, ed. Linda Levy Peck (Cambridge, 1991), pp 113–33.

Lake, Peter. 'Matthew Hutton: a puritan bishop?' *History* 44 (1979), 182–204.

Lake, Peter. 'Presbyterianism, the idea of a national church and the argument from divine right' in *Protestantism and the national church in sixteenth-century England*, ed. Peter Lake and Maria Dowling (London, 1983), pp 193–224.

Lake, Peter. 'The Laudians and the argument from authority' in *Court, country and culture: essays on early modern British history in honor of Perez Zagorin*, ed. Bonnelyn Young Kunze and Dwight D. Brautigam (Rochester, NY, 1992), pp 149–76.

Lake, Peter. *Anglicans and puritans? Presbyterianism and English conformist thought from Whitgift to Hooker* (London, 1988).

Lee, Maurice Jr, ed. *Dudley Carleton to John Chamberlain, 1603–1624: Jacobean letters* (New Brunswick, NJ, 1972).

Leishman, J.B. *The monarch of wit: an analytical and comparative study of the poetry of John Donne* (5th ed., London, 1962).

Littell, Franklin Hamlin. *The origins of sectarian protestantism: a study of the Anabaptist view of the church* (New York, 1964).

Loretz, Oswald. *The truth of the Bible*, trans. David J. Bourke (London, 1968).

Lowe, Irving. 'John Donne: the middle way', *Journal of the History of Ideas* 22:3 (1961), 389–97.

Lunderberg, Marla Hoffman. 'John Donne's strategies for discreet preaching', *Studies in English Literature, 1500–1900* 44:1 (2004), 97–119.

Lyon, John. 'Jonson and Carew on Donne: censure into praise', *Studies in English Literature, 1500–1900* 37:1 (1997), 97–118.

MacCullough, Diarmuid. *Thomas Cranmer, a life* (New Haven, CT, 1996).

Maltby, Judith D. *Prayer Book and people in Elizabethan and early Stuart England* (Cambridge, 1998).

Marsden, George M. *Fundamentalism and American culture: the shaping of twentieth-century Evangelicalism, 1870–1925* (New York, 1980).

Marshall, John Sedberry. *Hooker and the Anglican tradition: an historical and theological study of Hooker's Ecclesiastical polity* (London, 1964).

McCullough, Peter E. 'Andrewes, Lancelot (1555–1626)', *Oxford dictionary of national biography* (2004). www.oxforddnb.com/view/article/520 [accessed 14 Mar. 2013].

McCullough, Peter E. 'Donne and Andrewes', *John Donne Journal* 22 (2003), 165–201.

McCullough, Peter E. 'Donne as preacher at court: precarious "inthronization"' in *John Donne's Professional lives*, ed. David Colclough (Cambridge, 2003), pp 179–204.

McCullough, Peter E. 'Donne as preacher' in *The Cambridge companion to John Donne*, ed. Achsah Guibbory (Cambridge, 2006), pp 167–82.

McCullough, Peter E. 'Making dead men speak: Laudianism, print and the works of Lancelot Andrewes, 1626–1642', *Historical Journal* 41:2 (1998), 401–24.

McCullough, Peter E. *Sermons at court: politics and religion in Elizabethan and Jacobean preaching* (Cambridge, 1998).

McCullough, Peter E., ed. *Lancelot Andrewes: selected sermons and lectures* (Oxford, 2005).

McDonald, Lee Martin, and James A. Sanders, eds. *The canon debate* (Peabody, MA, 2002).

McDonald, Lee Martin. 'Canon' in *The Oxford handbook of Biblical studies*, ed. J.W. Rogerson and Judith M. Lieu (Oxford, 2006), pp 777–809.

McGrath, Alister E. *In the beginning: the story of the King James Bible and how it changed a nation, a language and a culture* (London, 2002).

McGrath, Alister E. *Reformation thought: an introduction* (Oxford, 1999).

McGrath, Alister E. *The intellectual origins of the European reformation* (2nd ed., Oxford, 2004).

McNees, Eleanor. 'John Donne and the Anglican doctrine of the Eucharist', *Texas Studies in Literature and Language* 29:1 (1987), 94–114.

Milton, Anthony. 'The Church of England, Rome and the True Church: the demise of a Jacobean consensus' in *The early Stuart church, 1603–1642*, ed. Kenneth Fincham (Basingstoke, 1993), pp 187–210.

Milton, Anthony. *Catholic and reformed: the Roman and protestant churches in English protestant thought, 1600–1640* (Cambridge, 1995).

Mornay, Charlotte. *A Huguenot family in the XVI century: the memoirs of Philippe De Mornay, Sieur Du Plessis Marly*, trans. Lucy Cramp (London, n.d.).

Mornay, lord of Plessie Marlie, Philip. *A woorke concerning the trewnesse of Christian religion, written in French, against atheists, epicures, Paynims, Jewes, Mahumetists and other infidels*, trans. Sir Philip Sidney and Arthur Golding (London, 1587).

Morrissey, Mary. 'Interdisciplinarity and the study of early modern sermons', *Historical Journal* 42:4 (1999), 1111–23.

Morrissey, Mary. 'Scripture, style and persuasion in seventeenth-century English theories of preaching', *Journal of Ecclesiastical History* 53:4 (2002), 686–706.

Munz, Peter. *The place of Hooker in the history of thought* (London, 1952).

Nicholson, Adam. *Power and glory: Jacobean England and the making of the King James Bible* (London, 2003).

Nixon, Scott. 'Carew's response to Jonson and Donne', *Studies in English Literature, 1500–1900* 39:1 (1999), 89–109.

Novarr, David. *The disinterred muse: Donne's texts and contexts* (Ithaca, NY, 1980).

O'Sullivan, Orlaith (ed.), *The Bible as book: the reformation* (London, 2000).

Oakley, Francis. 'Natural law, the *Corpus Mysticum* and consent in conciliar thought from John of Paris to Matthew Ugonis', *Speculum* 56:4 (1981), 786–810.

Oberman, Heiko A. *The harvest of medieval theology: Gabriel Biel and late medieval Nominalism* (Oxford, 1963).

Ornstein, Richard. 'Donne, Montaigne and natural law' in *Essential articles for the study of John Donne's poetry*, ed. John R. Roberts (Hassocks, 1975), pp 129–41.

Pailin, David A. 'Should Herbert of Cherbury be regarded as a "Deist"?', *Journal of Theological Studies* ns, 51:1 (2000), 113–49.

Patterson, Annabel. *Censorship and interpretation: the conditions of writing and eeading in early modern England* (Madison, WI, 1984).

Patterson, W.B. 'Hooker on ecumenical relations: conciliarism in the English refomation' in *Richard Hooker and the construction of Christian community*, ed. A.S. McGrade (Tempe, AZ, 1997), pp 283–303.

Pelikan, Jaroslav. *The reformation of the Bible: the Bible of the reformation* (New Haven, CT, 1996).

Pettegree, Andrew. *Reformation and the culture of persuasion* (Cambridge, 2005).

Pollard, Alfred W., ed. *Records of the English Bible: the documents relating to the translation and publication of the Bible in English, 1525–1611* (Oxford, 1911).

Prest, Wilfred R. *The inns of court under Elizabeth I and the early Stuarts, 1590–1640* (Harlow, 1972).

Questier, Michael C. *Conversion, politics and religion in England, 1580–1625* (Cambridge, 1996).

Quinn, Dennis B. 'Donne and the wane of wonder', *ELH* 36:4 (1969), 626–47.

Quinn, Dennis B. 'Donne's Christian eloquence', *ELH* 27:4 (1960), 276–97.

Quinn, Dennis B. 'John Donne's principles of Biblical exegesis', *Journal of English and Germanic Philology* 61 (1962), 313–29.

Rand, E.K. *Ovid and his influence* (New York, 1963).

Raspa, Anthony, and Judith Scherer Herz. 'Response', *Renaissance and Reformation* 20 (1996), 97–8.

Redworth, Glyn. *The prince and the infanta: the cultural politics of the Spanish match* (New Haven, CT, 2003).

Reeves, Troy D. *Index to the sermons of John Donne, 2: index to proper names*, ed. James Hogg (Salzburg, 1981).

Rhatigan, Emma. 'John Donne's Lincoln's Inn sermons' (PhD, Oxford University, 2006).

Saenger, Paul, and Kimberly Van Kampen, eds. *The Bible as book: the first printed editions* (London, 1999).

Sandeen, Ernest R. *The roots of Fundamentalism: British and American millenarianism, 1800–1930* (Chicago, IL, 1970).

Schevill, Rudoph. *Ovid and the Renascence in Spain* (Berkeley, CA, 1913).

Schwarz, Werner. *Principles and problems of Biblical translation* (Cambridge, 1955).

Scodel, Joshua. 'John Donne and the religious politics of the mean' in *John Donne's religious imagination: essays in honor of John T. Shawcross*, ed. Raymond-Jean Frontain and Frances M. Malpezzi (Conway, AR, 1995), pp 45–80.

Scott, W., and J. Bliss, eds. *The works of the most reverend Father in God, William Laud DD* (Oxford, 1847–60).

Sellin, Paul R. 'The proper dating of John Donne's "Satyre III"', *Huntington Library Quarterly* 43:4 (1980), 275–312.

Sellin, Paul R. *So doth, so is religion: John Donne and diplomatic contexts in the Reformed Netherlands, 1619–1620* (Columbia, MO, 1988).

Serjeantson, R.W. 'Herbert of Cherbury before Deism: the early reception of the De Veritate', *Seventeenth Century* 16:2 (2001), 217–38.

Shagan, Ethan H. 'English Catholic history in context' in *Catholics and the 'protestant nation': religious politics and identity in early modern England* (Manchester, 2005), pp 1–21.

Shami, Jeanne M. '"Speaking openly and speaking first": John Donne, the Synod of Dort and the early Stuart church' in *John Donne and the protestant reformation*, ed. Mary Arshagouni Papazian (Detroit, MI, 2003), pp 35–65.

Shami, Jeanne M. 'Donne's sermons and the absolutist politics of quotation' in *John Donne's religious imagination: essays in honor of John T. Shawcross*, ed. Raymond-Jean Frontain and Frances M. Malpezzi (Conway, AR, 1995), pp 380–412.

Shami, Jeanne M. 'Labels, controversy and the language of inclusion in Donne's sermons' in *John Donne's Professional lives*, ed. David Colclough (Woodbridge, 2003), pp 135–57.

Shami, Jeanne M. *John Donne and conformity in crisis in the late Jacobean pulpit* (Cambridge, 2003).

Shami, Jeanne. '"Trying to Walk on Logs in Water": John Donne, religion and the critical tradition', *Renaissance and Reformation* 25:4 (2001), 81–99.

Shami, Jeanne. 'Reading Donne's sermons', *John Donne Journal* 11 (1992), 1–20.

Shami, Jeanne. 'Squint-eyed, left-handed, half-deaf: *imperfect senses* and John Donne's interpretative middle way' in *Centered on the Word: literature, scripture and the Tudor–Stuart middle way*, ed. Daniel W. Doerksen and Cristopher Hodgkins (Newark, DE, 2004), pp 173–92.

Sharpe, Kevin. *The personal rule of Charles I* (New Haven, CT, 1996).

Sheehan, Jonathan. *The Enlightenment Bible* (Princeton, NJ, 2005).

Sherwood, Terry G. 'Reason in Donne's sermons', *ELH* 39:3 (1972), 353–74.

Sherwood, Terry G. *Fulfilling the circle: a study of John Donne's thought* (Toronto, 1984).

Shuger, Debora Kuller. '"Societie supernaturall": the imagined community of Hooker's *Lawes*' in *Richard Hooker and the construction of christian community*, ed. A.S. McGrade (Tempe, AZ, 1997), pp 307–29.

Shuger, Debora Kuller. *Habits of thought in the English renaissance: religion, politics and the dominant culture* (Toronto, 1997).

Shuger, Debora Kuller. *The renaissance Bible: scholarship, sacrifice and subjectivity* (Berkeley, CA, 1994).

Sisson, C.J. *The judicious marriage of Mr Hooker and the birth of the laws of ecclesiastical polity* (Cambridge, 1940).

Smith, Logan Pearsall, ed. *Donne's sermons: selected passages* (Oxford, 1919).

Stafford, John K. 'Richard Hooker's doctrine of the Holy Spirit' (PhD, University of Manitoba, 2005).

Stanwood, P.G. 'Donne's earliest sermons and the penitential tradition' in *John Donne's religious imagination*, ed. Raymond-Jean Frontain and Frances M. Malpezzi (Conway, AR, 1995).

Strier, Richard. 'Radical Donne: "Satire III"', *ELH* 60:2 (1993), 283–322.

Strier, Richard. *Resistant structures: particularity, radicalism and renaissance texts* (Berkeley, CA, 1995).

Sweetnam, Mark S. 'Calvinism, counter-reformation and conversion: Alexander Montgomerie's religious poetry' in *Literature and the Scottish reformation*, ed. Crawford Gribben and David George Mullan (Farnham, 2009).

Sweetnam, Mark S. '*Hamlet* and the reformation of the Eucharist', *Literature and Theology* 21:1 (2007), 11–28.

Sweetnam, Mark. 'Foundational faults: heresy and religious toleration in the later thought of John Donne' in *Heresy and orthodoxy in early English literature*, ed. Eiléan Ní Chuilleanáin and John Flood (Dublin, 2010), pp 113–26.

Tebeaux, Elizabeth de Volin. 'John Donne and Anglicanism: the relationship of his theology to Richard Hooker's' (PhD, Texas A&M University, 1977).

Tebeaux, Elizabeth de Volin. 'John Donne and the problem of religious authority: "Wranglings That Tend Not to Edification"', *South Central Bulletin* 42:4 (1982), 137–43.

Thomas, Keith. 'Art and iconoclasm in early modern England' in *Religious politics in post-reformation England: essays in honour of Nicholas Tyacke*, ed. Kenneth Fincham and Peter Lake (Woodbridge, 2006), pp 16–40.

Thomas, Keith. *Religion and the decline of magic: studies in the popular belief of sixteenth- and seventeenth-century England* (London, 1971).

Torrance Kirby, W.J. (ed.), *Richard Hooker and the English reformation* (Dordrecht, 2003).

Trevor-Roper, Hugh. *Archbishop Laud, 1573–1645* (3rd ed., Basingstoke, 1988).

Tyacke, Nicholas. 'Anglican attitudes: some recent writings on English religious history, from the reformation to the Civil War', *Journal of British Studies* 35 (1996), 139–67.

Tyacke, Nicholas. 'Archbishop Laud' in *The early Stuart church, 1603–42*, ed. Kenneth Fincham (Basingstoke, 1993).

Tyacke, Nicholas. 'Lancelot Andrewes and the myth of Anglicanism' in *Conformity and orthodoxy in the English church, c.1560–1660*, ed. Peter Lake and Michael C. Questier (Woodbridge, 2000), pp 5–33.

Tyacke, Nicholas. *Anti-Calvinists: the rise of English Arminianism, c.1590–1640* (Oxford, 1987).

von Campenhausen, Hans. *The formation of the Christian Bible*, trans. John Austin Baker (London, 1972).

Wabuda, Susan. *Preaching during the English reformation* (Cambridge, 2002).

Walton, Izaak. *The lives of John Donne, Sir Henry Wotton, Richard Hooker, George Herbert and Robert Sanderson* (London, 1951).

Waterworth, J., ed. *The canons and decrees of the sacred and oecumenical Council of Trent* (London, 1848).

Whalen, Robert. 'Sacramentalizing the Word: Donne's 1626 Christmas sermon' in *Centered on the Word: literature, scripture and the Tudor–Stuart middle way*, ed. Daniel W. Doerksen and Cristopher Hodgkins (Newark, DE, 2004), pp 193–223.

Whalen, Robert. *The poetry of immanence: sacrament in Donne and Herbert* (Toronto, 2002).

Woudhuysen, H.R. 'Sidney, Sir Philip (1554–1586)', *Oxford dictionary of national biography* (2004; online ed., May 2005). www.oxforddnb.com/view/article/25522 [accessed 24 May 2013].

Yates, Frances A. 'Paolo Sarpi's "History of the Council of Trent"', *Journal of the Warburg and Courtauld Institutes* 7 (1944), 123–43.

Index